The UCAS Guide to getting into

SPORTS SCIENCE AND PHYSIOTHERAPY

For entry to university and college in 2013

378.41

Published by: UCAS Rosehill New Barn Lane Cheltenham GL52 3LZ

Produced in conjunction with GTI Media Ltd

© UCAS 2012

UCAS, a company limited by guarantee, is registered in England and Wales number: 2839815
Registered charity number: 1024741 (England and Wales) and SC038598 (Scotland)

UCAS reference number: PU040013
Publication reference: 12_050
ISBN: 978-1-908077-19-6
Price £15.99

Further copies available from UCAS (p&p charges apply):

Contact Publication Services PO Box 130 Cheltenham GL52 3ZF

email: publicationservices@ucas.ac.uk or fax: 01242 544 806

For further information about the UCAS application process go to www.ucas.com.

If you need to contact us, details can be found at www.ucas.com/about_us/contact_us.

UCAS QUALITY AWARDS

Contents

Foreword

THINKING ABOUT SPORTS SCIENCE AND PHYSIOTHERAPY?

Finding the course that's right for you at the right university or college can take time and it's important that you use all the resources available to you in making this key decision. We at UCAS have teamed up with **TARGETjobs.co.uk** to provide you with *UCAS Guide to getting into Sports Science and Physiotherapy* to show you how you can progress from being a student to careers in sports science and physiotherapy. You will find information on what the subject includes, entry routes and real-life case studies on how it worked out for others.

Once you know which subject area you might be interested in, you can use the listings of all the full-time higher education courses in sports science and physiotherapy to see where you can study your subject. The course entry requirements are listed so you can check if getting in would be achievable for you. There's also advice on applying through UCAS, telling you what you need to know at each stage of the application process in just six easy steps to starting university or college.

We hope you find this publication helps you to choose and make your application to a course and university or college that is right for you.

On behalf of UCAS and **TARGETjobs.co.uk**, I wish you every success in your research.

Mary Curnock Cook,
Chief Executive, UCAS

At TARGETjobs we champion paid work experience for UK university students. Find internships and placements across all sectors, plus take part in the TARGETjobs Undergraduate of the Year awards.

TARGETjobs.co.uk

the best possible start to your career

Introducing sports science and physiotherapy

It could be you...

... assessing a swimmer's movement to improve competition timings — biomechanist

... designing a campaign to encourage people to be more active — health promotion specialist

... training a football team to win the FA Cup — sports coach

... advising clients on adapting to normal life after illness or injury — occupational therapist

... supporting a client to become mobile again after surgery — physiotherapist

... helping an athlete prepare mentally for competition — sports psychologist

... and lots more besides. Working in the sports science and physiotherapy fields gives graduates a huge range of choice. From encouraging children from disadvantaged backgrounds to take part in sports to enabling a world-class athlete win the Olympics, you will be making a difference, no matter at what level you practise. Could a career in a sports science-related field be for you?

A CAREERS IN SPORTS SCIENCE AND PHYSIOTHERAPY

A sports coach supporting athletes at international level can earn more than £100,000 per year before tax – see **A career in sports science and physiotherapy**, starting on page 13.

As well as any commitment to sports and other physical activities, admissions tutors also look for academic ability, people skills, an analytical approach and a commitment to work hard – see **The career for you?** on page 37.

Getting onto a sports-related degree course isn't a doddle. To see what you need to succeed, read **Routes to qualification** on page 58.

SPORTS SCIENCE AND PHYSIOTHERAPY IN CONTEXT

The reason why sports science and physiotherapy are so popular is because they play a major role in helping a wide variety of people lead more active and successful lives. While this can at one end involve training an athlete to win an Olympic gold, it can also be just as rewarding helping an elderly person learn to walk again after a major stroke. Being active makes a huge difference to people's lives. Think about when you have been either injured or ill and confined to bed. The novelty probably wore off pretty quickly and you wished you were up and about, cycling with your friends or playing football after school, or just walking to the shops. Human beings were made to be mobile and when we're not our physical and mental health can suffer.

People employed within the sports science and physiotherapy fields use the knowledge and skills that they have gained from their studies and work experience to help people deal with a wide variety of problems. For example, in any one day individuals in this area might be involved in any of the following situations (and plenty more besides):

- enabling a depressed person to get out of the house to enjoy a hobby and meet new people
- coming up with the most effective way to convey a public health message about the negative side effects of unhealthy eating
- restoring a person's feet to a much better condition, thus enabling them to walk more comfortably
- filming and assessing the way in which a runner sprints to see how they can run even faster by adjusting their stride
- counselling an athlete on how to cope with stress in major competitions.

YOUR PART IN SPORTS SCIENCE AND PHYSIOTHERAPY

Are you good with people? Do you have well-honed observation skills and an analytical nature? Great! Because you will need a wide and varied skills set to work in these fields. Many people forget that sports science and physiotherapy are *scientific* in nature, involving the study of such subjects as anatomy, biology, physiology, biomechanics, physics, and even engineering. It's not just about being good at kicking a ball, it's about understanding how kicking it in a certain way might score the winning goal, or how positive thinking might just give someone the confidence to believe they can do it. This is what makes these areas so interesting to work in; they combine personal skills such as listening and observation with very scientific approaches to gathering information – giving you the whole picture of what's going on with an athlete, both mentally and physically.

If you're interested in a possible career in any of these areas, then this guide can help to point you in the right direction. Read on to discover:

- the main areas of work and roles on offer
- what it takes to work in sports science-related areas and physiotherapy
- how to get in and the paths to qualification
- advice from recent graduates on how they got to where they are today.

Why sports science and physiotherapy?

Choose a career that is...

VARIED

There are few careers that offer as much variety as those in sports science and physiotherapy, in terms of both the people you will deal with and the problems that they face. Leading a more active life is something that everyone needs to aspire to for their emotional and physical well-being, so being involved in ways that enable them to enjoy exercise to the best of their ability can be incredibly rewarding. You could be coaching school football teams, teaching dance or aerobics to the elderly, or helping a talented long-jumper to adapt their style to become more aerodynamic. Or you could be helping individuals recover from serious illnesses and injuries and giving them hope by assisting them in becoming more mobile. Whatever you do, the buzz you get from helping a person achieve their goals – no matter how big or small – can be amazing.

VITAL TO SOCIETY

While being healthy and active might not be absolutely essential for society to survive, it is certainly becoming such an issue that governments are always looking into new ways to make people more responsible for their lives.

This includes changing unhealthy and potentially dangerous eating habits and making the prospect of physical activity more fun. Professionals involved in sports science and physiotherapy are at the forefront of this agenda, advising the general public and other healthcare professionals on how to make small but significant changes that could really turn someone's life around.

TECHNICAL *AND* PEOPLE-FOCUSED

Some careers are particularly appealing because they offer the chance to use two different types of skills – the opportunity to use your technical or scientific expertise alongside the chance to work with people. In sports science-related areas and physiotherapy, you will definitely be required to do this and therefore you will need a balance and interest in both. You'll use the latest research and technology, but you'll also see how these affect real people – **your** clients.

BECOMING INCREASINGLY IMPORTANT
Thanks to the 2012 Olympics, government expenditure in sports science and related areas has increased and brought further career opportunities. As society becomes more aware of the importance of physical activity you could be in the driving seat, alerting people to possibilities, supporting them in becoming involved, looking at ways to make their performance better and helping them if injury strikes.

ALWAYS IN DEMAND
People of all ages and from all walks of life will always need rehabilitative help, so your skills, knowledge and expertise will never be out of demand. Additionally, sports are very popular both to watch and to participate in, so there will always be a need for professionals who can help sportsmen and women achieve their best and recover quickly from injuries. The growing concern over educating people to adopt healthier lifestyles and to teach them good eating habits means that the professionals working in sports science-related areas and physiotherapy will have skills that have never been so valuable as they are today.

EARNING POTENTIAL
Depending on what path you take, the financial rewards can be excellent. However, some careers will be pursued for love more than money! The NHS is a major employer of allied health professionals, which includes the following occupations covered in this book: health promotion specialists, occupational therapists, physiotherapists, podiatrists, prosthetists, orthotists, and sport and exercise psychologists. Trainee salaries begin at around £21,000-£27,000. Podiatrists, physiotherapists and occupational therapists with experience can earn over £40,000, while prosthetists and orthotists can command salaries of up to £67,134. There are also possibilities of working in the private sector and earning substantially more.

Sports coaches earn fairly modest salaries at the beginning of their careers, ranging from £17,000 to £28,000, progressing at a more senior level to between £30,000 and £40,000. At national level coaches can earn more than £60,000. If you are interested in a career in sports development, starting salaries are similarly low (£15,000 to £20,000) – progressing to up to £35,000 with experience. At managerial level it is possible to earn around £50,000. Sports and exercise scientist posts command between £20,000 and £40,000, depending on experience.

WHAT DO SPORTS SCIENCE AND PHYSIOTHERAPY GRADUATES AND STUDENTS SAY?

'Being around academics and research, I am constantly learning new things. I also love helping students produce better research and being part of projects that develop over time.'
Andrew Strong, biomechanics laboratory technician, page 46

'My biggest enjoyment is helping others to access and develop in their chosen sport – it's a real buzz. There is nothing better than helping someone else achieve their goals and knowing that they wouldn't have managed it without my help.'
Sarah Tilling, partnership officer, page 48

'I've always been interested in sport and had the academic background and interest in science so it seemed logical to pursue both (and I didn't want to give up either one!).'
Amy Dyer, science officer, page 50

'The lecturers are really friendly and willing to help. The content is interesting, engaging and relevant to sport rehabilitation and exercise in the community today.'
Kendal Barrett-Brown, third-year student, sports and exercise sciences, page 52

'It's fine to want to choose sport as a degree – especially if you want to make a career out of a hobby. This has been a great experience for me, and I can't wait to see what will happen over the next few years.'
Rebecca Taylor, account manager and senior academy assessor, page 54

Focus your career with the TARGETjobs Careers Report.

Using biographical data, information about your interests and insightful psychometric testing, the Careers Report gives you a clear picture of jobs that match your skills and personality.

TARGETjobs.co.uk

the best possible start to your career

A career in sports science and physiotherapy

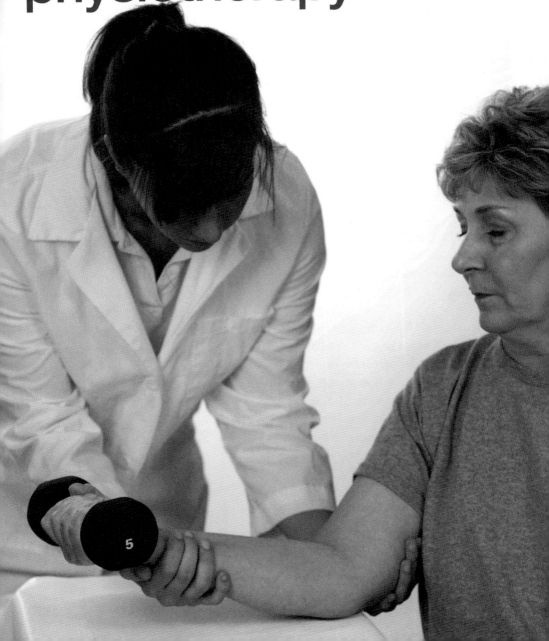

A career in sports science and physiotherapy

Areas of work

This section aims to give you an overview of the main career choices, specialisms and working conditions for those working in sports science and physiotherapy in the UK today.

If you have an interest in both sports and sciences, and a desire to work with people, then a career in sports science and physiotherapy could be for you. At this stage, you don't need to decide on a particular speciality, although you will normally need to make your mind up between a more general sports science degree and the more specific physiotherapy, psychology or podiatry courses. The training is different for all three of these courses, and it's not really possible to move from one to the other without starting again in the relevant undergraduate study.

Equally, if you think your interest lies in the very specialised field of sports and exercise psychology, your training route will probably be longer than that undertaken in other fields. This would involve either an undergraduate degree in psychology followed by further postgraduate specialised study in sports psychology, or you could study sports science (or another subject) and then take a psychology conversion course, followed by the relevant postgraduate training.

TIME WELL SPENT

It might seem bewildering to have to make such big decisions now. This is why we have compiled the next section for you, where we look at various job roles within sports science, podiatry, physiotherapy and sports and exercise psychology so you can gain a clearer picture about what's involved in each, including typical responsibilities, working hours and skills required. We also look at the pros and cons and where you can find more information should you choose to investigate further. It is worthwhile spending some time considering your options at this stage so that when you are making your university applications you will know, with confidence, that you have chosen your subject wisely.

Biomechanist

THE WORK

Biomechanics is a very scientific field, covering such diverse aspects as physics, mechanics, biology, mathematics, statistics and anatomy. While it is employed frequently in the sports arena, it is not, in itself, a sports discipline. Rather, biomechanists work with sportsmen and women in an analytical way, to help improve their performance through a scientific study of how certain forces affect the way in which they move. These forces can either be internal – ie inside the athlete's own body – or external – ie outside influences such as gravity and aerodynamics.

A biomechanist will use their knowledge of these disciplines to work out the various factors that affect individuals when performing certain physical movements or activities, such as how water might affect a swimmer's speed or how gravity and air can impact on a long-jumper's performance. Pushing, pulling, lifting, and moving are the sorts of movements that are examined. A detailed analysis of such factors can also help biomechanists advise sportsmen and women on suitable changes they can make to avoid the risk of injury.

Biomechanists carry out analysis by observing how a person moves in their physical activities. Additionally or alternatively, they will also ask them to participate in a series of special tests so that proper assessment can take place, normally with the help of technological equipment such as computer simulation. They will often record their sessions to examine more thoroughly what the individual is doing and to show them ways in which their movement is either slowing them down or causing injury (for example).

Biomechanists don't work just with athletes and sportspeople, however. They also work more generally with people to help identify and solve – or at least improve – problems that are causing pain and discomfort, such as physical disabilities or injuries. A growing area of development is in surgery, where biomechanics can help in the design of better artificial joints and tissue replacement, for instance.

THE CONDITIONS

Biomechanists work in a variety of locations, from the running track, tennis court and swimming pool, to a local hospital, a special clinic or independently on a self-employed basis. Some biomechanists lecture on university courses, and will therefore spend some of their time within an academic setting. Hours can range from a normal working day if spent in a hospital or clinic to long and demanding schedules if you're travelling with a sports team and, for example, attending international competitions.

THE ROUTE

Biomechanics is not a subject that you can specialise in at undergraduate level. While it is offered as part of a general sports science degree, you normally will have to do postgraduate study – at masters and/or PhD level – to concentrate solely on this area. Normally, you will need a good honours degree (minimum 2.1) in either sports science or a related area to be accepted on to a course.

THE UPSIDE

The chance to work and travel internationally with sportsmen and women at the top of their career, helping them to achieve their best and stay fit and well, is a big attraction. Helping individuals to live a more comfortable life by assessing their movement and suggesting small ways in which they can change this to relieve pain can be very satisfying and rewarding.

THE DOWNSIDE

The long and potentially unsociable hours if you do work with sports teams or individuals can be tiring and demanding.

FURTHER INFORMATION

- The British Association of Sport & Exercise Sciences **www.bases.org.uk**
- International Society of Biomechanics **www.isbweb.org**

Health promotion specialist

THE WORK

Healthy living is a phrase that's on the tip of everyone's tongue these days, it seems. From Jamie Oliver's school dinners campaign to supermarkets joining the Government's 'responsibility deal' aimed at improving public health, the nation is waking up to the importance of caring for our bodies. The Government and the National Health Service are also encouraging us to take control over our own physical and mental well-being, but sometimes people need help in knowing how to improve their lives, and this is where health promotions specialists (aka health education specialists or officers) come in.

Normally working in community settings such as schools, hospitals and workplaces, health promotion specialists try to inform people how important it is to take good care of their bodies and minds. This means talking and distributing information about key areas such as healthy diets and regular exercise, to reduce the risk of obesity and diseases related to it, and the risks of smoking, drinking and unprotected sex.

To get the message out, health promotion specialists also contribute towards marketing campaigns (for example, to flag up the importance of childhood immunisations), producing leaflets, posters and flyers to distribute in health centres, hospitals, libraries and other places easily accessed by the general public. They may even appear on television and radio to raise awareness of their latest campaign. They also work with other key health professionals to implement strategies to improve public health at local, regional and even national levels. Research plays an important role in this as they need to know first the sorts of problems that are emerging in their community and how much the population knows about them.

Working with people obviously is a major part of this job, whether it's running workshops for the local community or meeting with health service managers to discuss future ideas and projects. Liaising with doctors, nurses and other healthcare providers is an essential responsibility.

THE CONDITIONS

Most job vacancies arise within NHS and Primary Care Trusts, although some positions exist in local authorities and relevant charities. However, this is still not a huge field so you'll need to be flexible about location – you may have to move around to find suitable jobs.

Working hours tend to be standard, although you will sometimes need to work at weekends or in the evenings, for example when launching local health initiatives or attending community events. While you will be based in an office, you should be happy to be out and about most of your working day, visiting different people and organisations within your local community.

THE ROUTE

Health promotion specialists working in the NHS normally have a degree in biological, social or behavioural sciences. Alternatively, they might have studied for a masters degree in a related area. Experience can count for a lot in this field too, with nursing, social work, medicine, and teaching in a similar area all welcomed. Paid or voluntary work experience also shows that you understand what the work involves and are committed to the area as a whole. If you don't already offer a relevant postgraduate qualification when you apply for a job, you would normally be expected to study for one within a year or so of taking up a post.

THE UPSIDE

Seeing the benefits of a healthy eating campaign on the health of a local community and the individuals you advise.

THE DOWNSIDE

The scarcity of jobs means a steady career route is currently something of an unknown.

FURTHER INFORMATION

- NHS Careers
  www.nhscareers.nhs.uk

Occupational therapist

THE WORK

Occupational health is a term bandied about in offices a lot but not many people know exactly what it means. Put simply, occupational therapists try to enable their clients to return to a life of normality after physical or emotional problems, encouraging them to be independent and confident. This could be by looking at ways in which a severely depressed individual could reintegrate themselves into society, or coming up with plans so that an employer can adapt their office space to accommodate a member of staff who is permanently disabled.

Because the problems they deal with can be quite complex, occupational therapists mainly work with clients on an individual basis to ensure that what they recommend is the best strategy. After the initial assessment, occupational therapists will continue monitoring progress, making any changes as appropriate and liaising with the client's family, friends and employers to ensure everyone's needs are being met as closely as possible. Sometimes these goals can be achieved after a few meetings, but more often you will be involved for several months and occasionally longer.

With degenerative diseases such as multiple sclerosis, you will find that the client's problems will change over time. It can be difficult for them to stay positive in light of what is happening to them, but a key responsibility of an occupational therapist will be to help motivate them despite this, gently encouraging them to be as active as they can for as long as they can.

THE CONDITIONS

Occupational therapists have a pretty normal working week – around 9am to 5pm, Monday to Friday, although part-time work is also possible. They are based in a variety of places, from hospitals, health clinics and GP surgeries to homes, workplaces and schools. Therefore, an ability and willingness to travel, certainly within the local area, is essential.

You could choose to specialise in such areas as paediatrics, mental health, cardiac care, stroke rehabilitation or burns and plastic surgery. Occupational therapists tend to work in multidisciplinary teams, alongside other health professionals, including nurses, doctors, social workers and physiotherapists.

Currently, the future looks very bright for occupational therapists. NHS Careers states that demand is strong and growing for practitioners in this area, so you shouldn't encounter any problems getting a job after qualifying.

THE ROUTE

Most people who go into this area do so after undertaking a three-year BSc in occupational health. However, if you'd rather study something else to keep your options open, a two-year accelerated course is offered to graduates from other disciplines. This will lead to a recognised qualification and registration to work either in the NHS or with social services.

THE UPSIDE

Helping someone who has been physically and/or emotionally hurt by accident or illness lead a more fulfilling life.

THE DOWNSIDE

The relatively low pay, although occupational therapists can, with experience, move into managerial posts within the NHS, for example, which would command a higher salary.

FURTHER INFORMATION

- NHS Careers
  www.nhscareers.nhs.uk
- British Association of Occupational Therapists and College of Occupational Therapists
  www.cot.co.uk

Physiotherapist

THE WORK

A physiotherapist is someone trained to help people of all ages prevent or recover from all sorts of physical complaints. This could range from helping a person who has undergone extensive surgery become mobile again, to training women how to strengthen their core muscles after having a baby. They will look at such issues as a client's lifestyle, state of mind, physical surroundings and general health, to work out an appropriate prevention or treatment plan, before working closely alongside their clients to meet and maintain these goals successfully.

Much of the remedial work done with patients involves:

- manual therapy, eg helping patients with chest problems after surgery to breathe more comfortably and efficiently
- therapeutic exercises, in which the physiotherapist designs certain stretches or movements that will help a patient regain strength or mobility
- electro-physical methods of treatment, such as pain-management systems like TENS machines and ultrasound.

The work is very hands-on and a practical approach is essential. However, you'll also need to be sensitive to the various factors that might influence a person's health and well-being (eg social, emotional and cultural factors). Therefore, you will need a compassionate and empathetic nature, patience to deal with issues that might take a long time to resolve, and the ability to work well in a team alongside other health professionals.

THE CONDITIONS

Physiotherapists are important members of health teams and, as such, can be found working in virtually all hospital departments with doctors and nurses. Most hospitals also have special physiotherapy gyms, where patients can undergo therapeutic exercises and hydrotherapy as part of their rehabilitation. Outpatients are also treated in these areas, receiving ultrasound therapy and advice on posture and movement.

However, it is also becoming increasingly common for individuals to seek out a private physiotherapist to avoid long waiting lists, so employment in private clinics is growing, with physiotherapists working either as part of a team or on their own. Additionally, physiotherapists work in various places in which an accident or injury can occur, from workplaces to leisure centres and educational establishments.

An average working week within the NHS is around 37 hours, Monday to Friday, but if you choose to work in private practice you may find your hours more attuned to your clients' timetables than your own preferences.

With experience, physiotherapists can move on from more general practice to specialise in such areas as care of the elderly, looking after individuals with learning disabilities, or supporting terminally ill patients. Teaching and research are also popular areas. Some people move out of physiotherapy and into health service management.

THE ROUTE

In order to qualify as a physiotherapist, you will need to study for a three- or four-year BSc degree in the subject. Following successful completion of this, you are eligible for registration, which every physiotherapist must attain before being accepted to work in the NHS. Your clinical experience will commence (or continue) after graduation and, at a later date, you will be able to specialise in the area that most appeals to you.

THE UPSIDE

Helping people to live more active and pain-free lives than they might otherwise without your help, and enabling them to learn how to walk again or perform other activities.

THE DOWNSIDE

The work might be physically demanding and tiring at times.

FURTHER INFORMATION

- NHS Careers
  www.nhscareers.nhs.uk
- The Chartered Society of Physiotherapy
  www.csp.org.uk

Podiatrist

THE WORK

Here's a surprising fact for you. According to NHS Careers, around 75 to 80% of adults will, at some time in their life, have a problem with their feet, ankles or lower limbs. This means business for podiatrists (aka chiropodists), who specialise in assessing, diagnosing and treating problems in these areas.

This might sound more serious than it is, but don't worry! Problems can range from chronic arthritis – in which a podiatrist will play a palliative role, helping to relieve and manage pain – to a pesky ingrown toenail, which might require a little local anaesthetic while the podiatrist alleviates or removes it. Sometimes, podiatrists just help a person maintain healthy feet, cutting toenails and removing hard skin when their client can't reach these areas. Although many clients are elderly, problems can affect anyone, from a toddler or baby requiring an artificial limb to allay pain or injury, to a person who has become a victim of fashion through wearing impractical heels!

Biomechanics (see page 16) plays a role in podiatry, with practitioners using its principles to work out why a person is having problem with their feet or lower legs. Podiatrists can therefore deal with sports injuries, and there is great demand for qualified practitioners in this area to help with recovering athletes' rehabilitation.

THE CONDITIONS

According to the Society of Chiropodists and Podiatrists, there are increasing demands for podiatrists because of our ageing population and 'the fact that foot and lower limb problems are so widespread'. Podiatrists work in a variety of settings, such as NHS clinics and hospitals, GP surgeries and patients' homes, private centres and also on a freelance basis. Some podiatrists work in leisure centres and in shops specialising in footwear. More specialised fields include research, academia and the relatively new field of forensic podiatry. Normally podiatrists start off undertaking more general work for a while before moving on to specialise in one of the many areas where their services are in demand. However, it is possible to remain more general if this would suit your interests more.

The nature of the work lends itself well to flexible hours, such as part time and flexitime, although you might have to work outside the normal 9am to 5pm routine, (particularly if you are self-employed), to fit in with your clients' busy schedules.

THE ROUTE

To qualify as a podiatrist you will need to undertake a three- or four-year full-time (or four-and-a-half-year part-time) degree course at an approved university. Around half of the course is theoretical, with the other half involving clinical experience. On graduating, you will normally start off in general practice before moving on to a specialism such as diabetes, paediatrics, biomechanics, rheumatology and dermatology – if you choose to do so.

THE UPSIDE

The excellent job prospects, the range of people you deal with and the flexibility this area offers are all attractive reasons to enter this profession.

THE DOWNSIDE

If you want a job with very regular hours this might not be for you, especially if you want to run your own practice. Also, some people hate the idea of working with feet!

FURTHER INFORMATION

- The Society of Chiropodists and Podiatrists
  www.feetforlife.org
- NHS Careers
  www.nhscareers.nhs.uk

Prosthetist/Orthotist

THE WORK

Apart from both having names which are difficult words to pronounce, prosthetists and orthotists have other similarities. They work with similar clients, in similar settings, and use similar skills and knowledge. However, there is one important distinction between the two.

A prosthetist is responsible for designing and fitting artificial limbs (called 'prostheses') for people who have lost their own limbs through illness or injury, or were born without the limbs in place. An orthotist, on the other hand, specialises in designing and fitting support items such as braces, collars and splints – which are normally used to help people during the recovery period after injuries and surgery. These 'orthoses' will either be needed on a temporary or permanent basis and will help the client move in a better and less painful way.

Prosthetists and orthotists work with a variety of people with different problems, such as arthritis, cerebral palsy, diabetes and strokes. In order to provide the best possible care, they will need to make a full and careful assessment of the client and their problem, (including relevant measurements), before fitting a limb or an orthosis. To do this accurately, a sound knowledge of physiology, anatomy, biomechanics and technology is essential – normally gained at degree level or higher.

Once the measurements have been taken, the prosthetist/orthotist will liaise with a technician to explain their designs and ideas before he or she begins to make them. Once the limb or orthosis is ready, a fitting will take place, and the prosthetist/orthotist will conduct regular check-ups to ensure that everything is going well and that the client is managing. Sometimes adjustments or minor repairs will need to be made.

As well as working with patients, prosthetists and orthotists also liaise with physiotherapists and occupational therapists to give the client suitable exercise regimes and to adapt to life with their new prosthesis or orthosis.

THE CONDITIONS

Professionals working in these fields are normally based in hospitals or in special physical rehabilitation centres. A standard working week will be around 37 to 40 hours long, from Monday to Friday. Many can and do work part time.

Graduates looking for a career in this area will not be disappointed. According to the British Association of Prosthetists and Orthotists, there is an international shortage in these areas so prospects are fantastic, whether you want to work in the UK or abroad. Jobs for newly qualified orthotists and prosthetists are normally found in the public sector, (in the NHS), or in the private sector, (in manufacturing companies). International work is also possible, especially with charities that help people injured in wars and other crises. At higher levels, prosthetists and orthotists can take on teaching roles or managerial positions, and there may also be opportunities to work in research and development.

THE ROUTE

The normal route to a career in this area is to complete a four-year degree course that has been approved by the Health Professionals Council (HPC). This will enable you to be eligible for registration, an essential requirement to practise in this field. The degree will combine a mixture of practical hands-on experience at local hospitals and academic/theoretical learning (encompassing areas such as life sciences, biomechanics, engineering and material sciences and prosthetic and orthotic sciences, as well as mathematics and IT).

THE UPSIDE

The variety – these jobs are fascinating because they combine both technical and analytical skills with regular client contact.

THE DOWNSIDE .

There aren't many prosthetics/orthotics courses out there so competition to get on one could be fierce.

FURTHER INFORMATION

- NHS Careers
  www.nhscareers.nhs.uk
- British Association of Prosthetists and Orthotists
  www.bapo.com

Sports and exercise psychologist

THE WORK

Imagine being faced with a stadium full of people and feeling the pressure to become the fastest sprinter in the world. How would you cope under that pressure? Would you use it to your advantage, using that adrenaline to make you run faster? Or would nerves get the better of you, possibly making you stumble or leave the block before the gun has been fired?

The mind can have a profound effect on the body. Sports and exercise psychologists study this relationship and apply it in a practical way to help sportspeople perform to the best of their ability. They help sportspeople prepare psychologically for competition in the following ways:

- teaching relaxation techniques so that energy is not wasted in an unhelpful way

- practising visualisation exercises – if you see yourself winning a race, your confidence levels should rise
- increasing levels of confidence – if you don't think you can score a winning goal, you probably won't
- instilling a positive attitude that won't flag when the going gets tough.

Sports and exercise psychologists can also share their insights and knowledge with coaches so they can help to motivate, not discourage, their athletes.

A growing field is looking at how the mind-body relationship works the other way around. It is generally accepted these days that exercise releases feel-good endorphins so physical activity can be incredibly beneficial in helping people to overcome mental illnesses such as depression.

Sports psychologists work with a wide range of people too – from amateurs to professionals, individuals to teams, coaches to referees, and ordinary people who aren't very sports focused but for whom activity would prove beneficial, including both adults and children.

THE CONDITIONS

Sports and exercise psychologists may work from an office or clinic but they are just as likely to be found travelling locally, nationally and internationally – wherever the need for their services is felt, often in sporting venues. Some find employment with a national sport governing body, while others lecture in universities. Most sports psychologists do a combination of consultancy and teaching because, while their services are in increasing demand, there still aren't enough vacancies for the number of applicants. Therefore, you'll probably find yourself working in a bizarre variety of settings, from a comfortable office or clinic to a freezing, wet rugby pitch!

THE ROUTE

It takes quite a while to qualify as a sports psychologist. Normally you will need to have completed either an undergraduate degree in psychology or a postgraduate conversion course, both of which should allow you to be eligible for the Graduate Basis for Registration (GBR). After this, you will need to undertake a further three years of postgraduate training, with supervision and clinical placements.

THE UPSIDE

Working with a wide variety of people in a range of settings, helping them to achieve their best mentally and/or physically.

THE DOWNSIDE

The training can be quite demanding, mentally and financially, especially when there are fewer jobs than there are graduates.

FURTHER INFORMATION

- The British Association of Sport & Exercise Sciences
  www.bases.org.uk
- The British Psychological Society
  www.bps.org.uk

Sports and exercise scientist

THE WORK

It might seem strange to combine science with sports but this is exactly what this career and study area does. So how are the two linked?

Sports and exercise scientists help both athletes and members of the general public improve their abilities and overall health through physical activity. They do this by applying principles from such diverse disciplines as physiology and psychology to positively influence the way in which a person can move, think or behave – helping them to recover from injuries, preventing illnesses and achieving the best of their ability no matter what their standard of fitness.

As such, working with people plays a major role in this career. You could be dealing with a wide variety of individuals, from other sports experts such as coaches and therapists, to doctors and other health professionals, individual athletes and teams. Your remit might be quite broad too – for example, liaising with Primary Care Trusts to come up with rehabilitative exercise programmes. There may also be work on research projects and invitations from sports goods companies to help design sports equipment.

THE CONDITIONS

Sports, health and well-being are high on the social and political agendas at the moment so, in theory, opportunities in this area should be good. However, while it can't be denied that this field is on the up, there are still not many vacancies around and competition for the few that are there is fierce. These can normally be found in places such as universities, health services, and private and public sporting organisations: or perhaps you'd rather work on a freelance basis, running your own business and working with athletes and teams. A degree and experience in this area could also help you become involved in related fields such as sports development and performance testing.

Working hours are normal, at around 38 per week. However, you might find some of these falling at weekends and evenings, to work around your clients' commitments, so antisocial hours are fairly common. Most sports scientists work from consultation rooms but some outdoor work is also possible, depending on the work you are undertaking with your clients.

THE ROUTE

Most people who work in this field come into it with a sports science degree, although it's also acceptable to have a qualification in a related field and then do a postgraduate course. Since competition is tough in this area, it's a good idea to get some experience in sports coaching or perhaps working as a fitness instructor, both of which could provide a valuable foot in the door.

THE UPSIDE

Imagine seeing an athlete win a race because of your advice!

THE DOWNSIDE

The opportunities are still few and far between and the ones that do exist don't command a mind-boggling pay packet.

FURTHER INFORMATION

- The British Association of Sports and Exercise Sciences (BASES)
  www.bases.org.uk
- Skills Active
  www.skillsactive.com

Sports coach

THE WORK

Sports coaches have been represented in a variety of ways on television and films – not normally in a very complimentary light! Often shown as being loud, aggressive, dictatorial and cruel, this portrayal is far from the truth. Their main job is to help individuals and teams of various standards, from the local under-tens football team to an Olympic 100-metre sprinter, to perform to the best of their ability.

Individuals all respond differently to motivation, so a sports coach must be able to decide what method would best suit their client(s), using their extensive knowledge to advise on how to win a game or improve a time. Most of this takes place in training sessions before major events, but a coach will be there on the day to offer support. Understanding how people think and interact with one another is a very important part of the job, as is identifying when a particular approach is not bringing about the desired results.

To make sure they are providing the very best for their athletes, coaches also seek assistance from outside their own area of expertise. For example, they may liaise with nutritionists to come up with suitable diets, or with physiotherapists to discuss training options after injury. And, with money being increasingly important in the world of sport, coaches may find themselves trying to negotiate sponsorship details with local, national or even international companies to help fund the training and travelling their sportsmen and women undertake.

THE CONDITIONS

Sporting events take place at all times of the day and night, at weekends and during public holidays, so say goodbye to a 'normal' working week if you want to specialise in this area! That said, some coaches are able to work part time, while others just work seasonally – eg in the summer at special sports camps for children and teenagers.

You won't be sitting in a comfortable office either. Your working locations may vary between schools and universities to local or national sports centres – wherever your athletes are training. This could be a swimming pool, a running track, a football pitch or in a sweaty gym. While you won't be competing yourself, you will still need to have a good standard of physical health and strength in order to cope with long training times and demonstrating techniques to sportspeople. Travel is also possible – even probable – in this job.

THE ROUTE

Some sports coaches don't have a degree but it is becoming common for people interested in a career in this area to study for one in a related area. However, this alone will not make you eligible to become a coach; you will need to obtain the appropriate coaching qualification by your chosen sport's national governing body. Some degrees incorporate coaching qualifications into them, so it's worth trying to find this out when applying.

Practice is as important as theory though so you will need to show a commitment to sports coaching by taking part in it. Voluntary opportunities, such as coaching a children's football team, are a good place to start.

THE UPSIDE

If you love sport and working with people, what better combination could you hope for?

THE DOWNSIDE

The salary – if you're not working with the big shots you might need another job to pay the bills.

FURTHER INFORMATION

- SkillsActive
  www.skillsactive.com
- Sports Coach UK
  www.sportscoachuk.org

Sports development officer (SDO)

THE WORK

As concern over levels of obesity in the UK grows, health professionals want to ensure that both adults and children have access to sports and other physical activities in their area to help keep them healthy. This is where a sports development officer comes in. He or she will work alongside local councils, schools, clubs and other organisations, such as the police and national governing bodies, to ensure that opportunities are available and that everyone knows about them.

A large part of their job will be identifying the different sectors of society that might need extra help and support in getting involved, including people from disadvantaged backgrounds, individuals with physical or emotional disabilities, the elderly and the very young. This will normally mean coming up with suitable ways to reach out to them, such as liaising with the police,

social workers, health professionals, teachers and local charities so their message gets out.

Additionally, SDOs recruit and train volunteers to help out on schemes, such as after-school clubs and holiday activities, and try to source funding to enable these groups to run. Much of the work tends to be administrative rather than sporty in nature, as the latter is left to the volunteers and any coaches who come on board. Therefore, SDOs can often be found writing reports, maintaining databases, assessing projects, marketing opportunities and finding funding. A suit would probably be worn more often than a tracksuit!

THE CONDITIONS

Working hours depend on who your employer is. If you land a job with a local authority, it's standard to work a 36-hour week, although you may have to attend meetings or events outside of these. The good news is that extra work will probably be paid or time in lieu given. You will normally be office based though you will also have meetings out and about with people who are either supporting or using your schemes and initiatives, often in schools and other clubs. Be ready to work in all sorts of weathers and conditions too, especially if you are attending a rainy Bank Holiday footie match!

THE ROUTE

There is no set degree requirement to get into this area but admittedly employers might find you a more attractive candidate if you can offer a degree in a related subject such as sports science or management. You won't need to go on to further postgraduate study (unless you want to, of course!) but work experience is vital to show commitment and knowledge of what's entailed. Voluntary work is often a great way in, so check out local opportunities at home and at university to help with coaching or teaching sports.

THE UPSIDE

Using your knowledge of and commitment to sport to help people become healthier and happier in life.

THE DOWNSIDE

Don't expect to be driving a Ferrari on this salary (but with your interest in health promotion, you'll be cycling anyway, right?)

FURTHER INFORMATION

- Sports Leaders UK
  www.sportsleaders.org
- The Institute for the Management of Sport and Physical Activity (IMSPA)
  www.imspa.co.uk

www.ucas.com

at the heart of connecting people to higher education

The career for you?

Is sports science and physiotherapy for you?

Being successful – in whatever specialism – calls for more than an in-depth understanding of the relevant discipline; it also requires certain skills and personal qualities or attributes.

To help you decide if a career in a sports science-related area is for you, we suggest you consider the following questions:

- What do you want from your future work?
- What does the course typically involve?
- Which skills do professionals in sports science-related areas and physiotherapy typically need?

WHAT DO YOU WANT FROM YOUR FUTURE CAREER?

You may not have an instant answer for this, but your current studies, work experience to date and even your hobbies can give you clues about the kind of work you enjoy, and the skills you have already started to develop. Start with a blank sheet of paper and note down your answers to the questions we've asked below to help get you thinking. Be as brutally honest with yourself as you can. Don't write what you think will impress your teachers or parents; write what really matters to you and you'll start to see a pattern emerging.

ANSWER THESE QUESTIONS TO HELP YOU CHOOSE YOUR CAREER

- When you think of your future, in what kind of environment do you see yourself working: office, outdoor, 9am to 5pm, high-pressure, regular routine?
- What are your favourite hobbies outside school?
- What is it about them you enjoy? Working with people, figuring out how things work?
- What are your favourite subjects at school?
- What is it about them that you enjoy most? Being able to create something, debating, problem-solving, practical hands-on work?
- What do you dislike about the other subjects you're studying? (Writing 'the teacher' doesn't count!)
- Which aspects of your work experience have you most enjoyed?

WHICH SKILLS WILL YOU TYPICALLY NEED?

Without doubt, admissions tutors in sports science look for applicants who love sport and who want to learn about how it can improve people's lives. Therefore, clear **evidence of a commitment to sports** as a career is essential, which can usually be demonstrated through work experience placements with charitable organisations, for example, and participation in individual and/or team sports. This will also provide proof of your **ability to work well and get on with a wide variety of people**. Teamwork is an essential part of any sports science-related career, whether working with sportspeople or with other professionals supporting them, so you will need to show that you relish opportunities to work as part of a wider initiative. However, an interest in sports and people won't cut it without a **good academic record**. People often believe that they don't need high GCSE and A level grades to get on in sports. However, this is not the case and it is very likely that offers will become even higher in the future with more applicants fighting for places.

This is also true for careers in podiatry and physiotherapy. When people come to you with physical problems, they may also want to talk more generally about their lives and how any disabilities or illnesses they may have impact on that. Therefore, a **sympathetic nature and good listening skills** are vital. This is equally applicable for sports and exercise psychologists, who spend much of their time listening and relating to their clients in order to work out how best to help them through their issues. Therefore (as is also the case with all other sports science-related areas), an **analytical approach** is indispensable – you will need some sort of distance from the problems and puzzles you face to come up with workable solutions.

Finally, you must not forget that sports science, physiotherapy, podiatry and psychology are very much **science-based subjects**, so an interest in the relevant fields is essential. It is not uncommon for universities offering these subjects to ask for at least one A level in a science subject such as biology, chemistry or physics. Sciences also demand a very particular approach to their study, and the following 'hard' skills will be vital:

- excellent problem-solving
- a logical approach to looking at issues
- an analytical outlook to cope with statistical information
- a methodical approach to your work
- computer literacy.

ALTERNATIVE CAREERS

While many graduates progress into a sports-related field after university, some will decide to change direction. A sports science degree will develop your analytical thinking abilities and problem-solving skills, which are in demand in many different professions, including management, sales, marketing and other related fields within the leisure industry and beyond. Your people skills and teamworking ability will make you an attractive candidate for a career in personnel and human resources, should that area appeal to you. Sports might be the 'be all' for you at the moment but if you change your mind during your degree they need not be the 'end all'.

Professional bodies

Professional bodies are responsible for overseeing a particular profession or career area, ensuring that people who work in the area are fully trained and meet ethical guidelines. Professional bodies may be known as institutions, societies and associations. They generally have regulatory roles; they make sure that members of the profession are able to work successfully in their jobs without endangering lives or abusing their position.

Professional bodies are often involved in training and career development, so courses and workplace training may have to follow the body's guidelines. In order to be fully qualified and licensed to work in your profession of choice, you will have to follow the professional training route. In many areas of work, completion of the professional training results in gaining chartered status – and the addition of some extra letters after your name. Other institutions may award other types of certification once certain criteria have been met. Chartered or certified members will usually need to take further courses and training to ensure their skills are kept up to date.

WHAT PROFESSIONAL BODIES ARE THERE?

Not all career areas have professional bodies. Those jobs that require extensive learning and training are likely to have bodies with a regulatory focus. This includes careers such as engineering, law, construction, health and finance. If you want to work in one of these areas, it's important to make sure your degree course is accredited by the professional body – otherwise you may have to undertake further study or training later on.

Other bodies may play more of a supportive role, looking after the interests of people who work in the sector. This includes journalism, management and arts-based careers. Professional bodies may also be learned bodies, providing opportunities for further learning and promoting the development of knowledge in the field.

CAN I JOIN AS A STUDENT?

Many professional bodies offer student membership – sometimes free or for reduced fees. Membership can be extremely valuable as a source of advice, information and resources. You'll have the opportunity to meet other students in the field, as well as experienced professionals. It will also look good on your CV, when you come to apply for jobs.

See below for a list of professional bodies in the field of sports science and physiotherapy.

The British Association of Sport & Exercise Sciences (BASES)
www.bases.org.uk

The Institute for the Management of Sport and Physical Activity (IMSPA)
www.imspa.co.uk

The Royal Society for Public Health
www.rsph.org.uk

The British Psychological Society
www.bps.org.uk

British Association of Occupational Therapists and College of Occupational Therapists
www.cot.co.uk

The Chartered Society of Physiotherapy
www.csp.org.uk

The Society of Chiropodists and Podiatrists
www.feetforlife.org

Graduate destinations

Each year, comprehensive statistics are collected on what graduates are doing six months after they complete their course. The survey is coordinated by the Higher Education Statistics Agency (HESA) and provides information about how many graduates move into employment (and what type of career) or further study and how many are believed to be unemployed.

The full results across all subject areas are published by the Higher Education Careers Service Unit (HECSU) and the Association of Graduate Careers Advisory Services (AGCAS) in *What Do Graduates Do?*, which is available from **www.ucasbooks.com**.

	Sports Science and Physiotherapy
In UK employment	66.5%
In overseas employment	1.4%
Working and studying	6.6%
Studying in the UK for a higher degree	4.9%
Studying in the UK for a teaching qualification	3.9%
Undertaking other further study or training in the UK	2.3%
Studying overseas	0.1%
Assumed to be unemployed	6.7%
Not available for employment, study or training	4.0%
Other	3.6%

> THE CAREER FOR YOU?

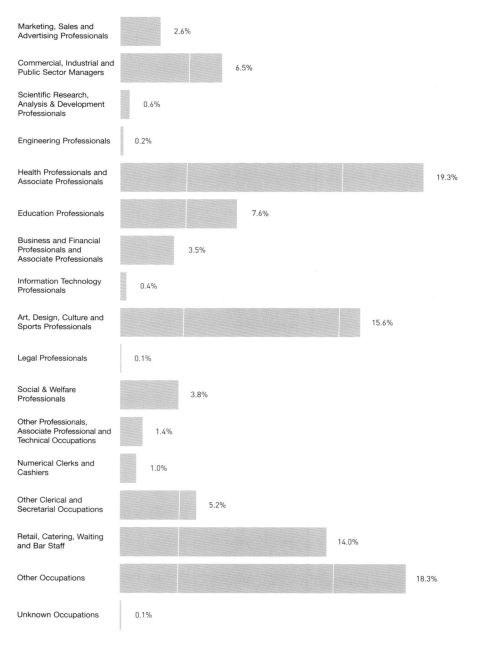

Marketing, Sales and Advertising Professionals — 2.6%

Commercial, Industrial and Public Sector Managers — 6.5%

Scientific Research, Analysis & Development Professionals — 0.6%

Engineering Professionals — 0.2%

Health Professionals and Associate Professionals — 19.3%

Education Professionals — 7.6%

Business and Financial Professionals and Associate Professionals — 3.5%

Information Technology Professionals — 0.4%

Art, Design, Culture and Sports Professionals — 15.6%

Legal Professionals — 0.1%

Social & Welfare Professionals — 3.8%

Other Professionals, Associate Professional and Technical Occupations — 1.4%

Numerical Clerks and Cashiers — 1.0%

Other Clerical and Secretarial Occupations — 5.2%

Retail, Catering, Waiting and Bar Staff — 14.0%

Other Occupations — 18.3%

Unknown Occupations — 0.1%

Reproduced with the kind permission of HECSU/AGCAS, *What Do Graduates Do? 2010*.
Data from the HESA Destinations of Leavers of Higher Education Survey 09/10

Case studies

JUST WHAT DOES A CAREER IN SPORTS SCIENCE AND RELATED FIELDS OFFER YOU?

The following profiles show the wealth of exciting opportunities that are yours for the taking.

Biomechanics laboratory technician

Kingston University

ANDREW STRONG

Route into sports science:
Foundation degree in sports science and business (2006); BSc sports science with business, (2010), both at Kingston University

WHY SPORTS SCIENCE?

I've always enjoyed most sports, whether watching or playing, and science was also one of my strong subjects. Since leaving school I've become increasingly interested in fitness and fascinated by the human body, and sports science therefore seemed an obvious choice. I also studied business as I felt it would open further opportunities to me in future.

HOW DID YOU GET WHERE YOU ARE TODAY?

When I was 15, I undertook a work experience placement at a leisure centre that specialised in gymnastics. I really took to the coaching aspect and enjoyed working with children, and undertook courses in gymnastics coaching and fitness instruction. My part-time role became full time and a few years later I became head of gymnastics for the special needs and recreational departments and was coaching my own group of regionally competitive gymnasts.

I then travelled the world for a year and lived in Sweden for six months after meeting my girlfriend. I struggled to find work and decided I wanted to do a degree. Aged 23, I moved back to the UK to start a foundation degree in science, which then led onto the university degree course. After completing my course, I started work as a health and wellbeing physiologist with Nuffield Health and Wellbeing.

A couple of months into the role, I received an offer from Kingston University to return as biomechanics technician on a temporary contract. This appealed to me as my final-year undergraduate project focused on biomechanics techniques and I excelled in this area, partly due to my gymnastics experience. I was also attracted because I could stop commuting into central London, I'd have an increased salary, and would be able to take a masters by research while working full time. In September 2011 my role finally became permanent and I'm hoping to begin my masters soon.

WHAT DOES YOUR JOB INVOLVE?

My role predominantly involves looking after the biomechanics equipment within the sports science department; I set up for practicals and seminars as well as coordinating the laboratory bookings for undergraduate and postgraduate students performing research. I have also been offered teaching opportunities and have taken practical sessions and lectures. I will soon be assessed for a short course in undergraduate teaching, which will help towards a career in lecturing if I choose that direction.

I generally work from 8.30am to 5pm, Monday to Friday, although when seminars continue until 6pm or research is being performed outside of these hours I work longer. I mainly deal with undergraduate and postgraduate students, as well as external individuals and groups who request consultancy services such as fitness testing.

WHAT HAS BEEN YOUR BIGGEST CHALLENGE?

Learning about how to operate the equipment in depth, rather than just having a working knowledge of how to use it. When equipment works my job goes quite smoothly but inevitably things sometimes go wrong and it's then that you develop a more involved understanding.

AND THE BEST BITS?

Being around academics and research, I am constantly learning new things. I also love helping students produce better research and being part of projects that develop over time.

ANDREW'S TOP TIPS

Study something you enjoy and have a real interest in as this helps to maintain your motivation when work becomes harder. Gain as much practical experience as possible through work placements – this will help with job-hunting and develops an understanding beyond the taught aspects of studying. There are always opportunities to further yourself – you just need to put yourself in a position to take them.

Partnership officer

Sport Cheshire (Cheshire and Warrington County Sports Partnership)

SARAH TILLING

Route into sports science:
A levels – biology, sport, travel and tourism (2006); BSc sport and exercise sciences, University of Chester (2009)

WHY SPORTS SCIENCE?

At school I was interested in a variety of sports and played to a reasonable standard, but an injury made me think about what else I could do other than play. I started volunteering for local authority initiatives, working with a variety of people, and soon realised that I definitely wanted to have a career in a sports-related field. Sport and exercise science seemed to be the best option, especially given my desire to develop and enhance opportunities for other people.

HOW DID YOU GET TO WHERE YOU ARE TODAY?

I continued to volunteer while at university, which led me into paid part-time work as a multi-sports coach and volunteer mentor, during which I learned some valuable lessons and gained essential knowledge that helped with my degree. For my work experience I chose to do something different to coaching so I could see what other things were like, although all this did was cement my feelings for developing sport!

After graduating I worked as a coach and teaching assistant to support myself financially and to see what teaching was all about. Teaching was something I had always considered but I wasn't 100 per cent sure if it was for me. Within two weeks of starting as a teaching assistant an opportunity came up within the local sports development team and I was offered the role. I worked on various projects, developing opportunities for individuals to take part in sport regardless of age or ability. This involved working with a variety of target groups and partners to achieve better provision and all-round access to local facilities and groups. Following this, the sports development team was moved to Sport Cheshire, where I now work.

WHAT DOES YOUR JOB INVOLVE?

My main role is to develop the local infrastructure for people to participate in sport and to support National Governing Bodies (NGBs) to develop and achieve their local priorities. I also lead and develop national projects set by Sport England and deliver them locally across Cheshire and Warrington. Within my role, I connect, lead, advocate and deliver on a variety of projects, and am responsible for line management of staff and basic communications with the public. This involves working with a variety of people including NGBs, Sport England, leisure centres, schools, universities, health practitioners, parish councils, local authorities, the general public and many more. Part of my role involves continuous professional development in the form of training, conferences, talks and educational courses. I work full time.

WHAT HAS BEEN YOUR BIGGEST CHALLENGE?

I think my biggest challenge was to make myself stand out – being different and having your own unique selling point makes a massive difference. It's important to think beyond the norm and really show what you can bring to your chosen career. This means having the confidence to believe you are more than capable of delivering targets.

AND THE BEST BITS?

My biggest enjoyment is helping others to access and develop in their chosen sport – it's a real buzz. There is nothing better than helping someone else achieve their goals and knowing that they wouldn't have managed it without my help.

SARAH'S TOP TIPS

You don't need to know what you want to do when you start university – just watch yourself evolve within your chosen area. Immerse yourself in the world of sport, as it opens so many doors when people know you and what you do.

Science officer

UK Anti-Doping

AMY DYER

Route into anti-doping:
A levels – biology, chemistry, physical education, general studies (2004); BSc sport and exercise science, University of Bath (2008); MSc human and applied physiology, King's College London (2009)

WHY SPORTS SCIENCE?

I've always been interested in sport and had the academic background and interest in science so it seemed logical to pursue both (and I didn't want to give up either one!)

HOW DID YOU GET TO WHERE YOU ARE TODAY?

In my third year I undertook a 12-month placement with Lucozade Sport, as well as additional fitness qualifications, including personal training and massage. This gave me an invaluable insight into the commercial world of sport science. My placement year also really cemented my interest in biomechanics and physiology, and opened my eyes to potential career opportunities. Through this I realised that a postgraduate qualification was essential so I undertook an MSc at King's College London.

Throughout both degrees I volunteered and took part in numerous 'sport science' positions, including assisting with fitness testing of athletes and other professionals such as the police. All of these experiences developed my interest in working as an applied physiology practitioner in elite sport to maximise athletes' and coaches' performances through assessment and analysis of various physiological components.

This led me into the position of junior rehabilitation scientist with the English Institute for Sport (EIS) and the British Olympic Medical Institute and I got to work with athletes from a range of sports. I then left to take up my current position.

WHAT DOES YOUR JOB INVOLVE?

My job involves liaising with colleagues within UK Anti-Doping (such as testing officers and members of the education team), national governing bodies (eg England Hockey, GB Rowing, etc), researchers and medical staff, the World Anti-Doping Agency (WADA) and other key stakeholders involved in sport and anti-doping.

I provide anti-doping information and support to athletes of all ages and levels, as well as supporting coaches, medics, physiotherapists and parents on issues regarding prohibited substances: particularly how athletes can avoid unintentional doping charges. I manage, maintain and develop the Global DRO service (an online database for checking medications) with national anti-doping agencies in the United States and Canada.

Much of my work involves multidisciplinary communication and development with internal colleagues and key stakeholders. I also work with the education team to coordinate and deliver science and medicine education meetings, workshops and discussions. My job requires me to work internally and externally with anti-doping laboratories and researchers to advise on scientific methods and substances that may enhance testing knowledge and procedures, and develop new strategies to ensure effective testing programmes.

WHAT HAS BEEN YOUR BIGGEST CHALLENGE?

Coordinating the annual UK Anti-Doping submission to WADA on the Prohibited List International Standard. This requires consultation with key stakeholders regarding the previous year's changes, research on new and existing prohibited substances and methods, and discussions on potential developments. Coordinating these comments and developing a submission to tight deadlines is very challenging.

AND THE BEST BITS?

UK Anti-Doping is a very young organisation and working in such a vibrant environment, particularly in the lead-up to the London Olympics, is a great experience. As well as the day-to-day duties, the role allows freedom to work independently and direct new projects. Finally, it's a great learning environment and a wonderful opportunity to interact with athletes, support personnel and scientists alike.

AMY'S TOP TIPS

Volunteer as much as you can in areas that interest you. Not only will this build up your CV but it will also help you narrow down what you are interested in and potential careers to match

Third-year student, sports and exercise sciences

University of Leeds

KENDAL BARRETT-BROWN

Route into sports and exercise sciences:
A levels – biology, physical education, art (2009); BSc sports and exercise sciences, University of Leeds (graduating 2012)

WHY SPORTS SCIENCE?

I knew from studying my GCSEs that I wanted to do a degree in sports science, so I tailored my A levels to reach the specifications. I chose this particular university because Leeds is both a campus and a city university. It looked impressive and the school was welcoming and has a reputation for being a platform for a future profession in physiotherapy.

WHAT DOES YOUR COURSE INVOLVE?

While we do not have seminars, there are numerous practical sessions which give you hands-on experience such as in our anatomy modules. We learn mainly through lectures, due to the extensive science content that must be covered.

I study for approximately eight hours per day, five days a week. What I do depends on what I am working on – I might be covering extra reading material, writing down lecture notes or planning my essays. It's not an easy course because it is extremely research based and science led. Although it is hard work it is definitely worth it in the end. Luckily I've always been good at working hard and playing hard, as getting that balance is vital – otherwise you're constantly playing catch-up.

The best part of the course so far has been the yearly debate, which is assessed by your classmates. It's always an enjoyable experience. I also enjoy the group work – you get to know how other people work and discover their strengths and weaknesses.

Our tutors are very supportive. I can see mine either at drop-in hours, specific times that they set aside for students to ask for help, or via email. There's also good camaraderie amongst students in all the years – we all help each other.

TELL US ABOUT YOUR WORK PLACEMENT

As part of my course I had to complete a period of work experience, and chose to attend a local physiotherapist's practice in Leeds. I was there for seven days, learning how physiotherapists treat their patients. Because the job entails physical contact with members of the public, I wasn't allowed to 'treat' clients, but watching the professionals at work and being allowed to take notes has proved very useful for my degree and was an eye-opening experience.

WHAT'S THE TOUGHEST CHALLENGE YOU HAVE FACED ON YOUR COURSE?

As a student my biggest challenge has been the biomechanics module. Having to take maths as a core module for the first two years was challenging.

AND THE BEST BITS?

The lecturers are all really friendly and willing to help. The content is interesting, engaging and relevant to sport rehabilitation and exercise in the community today. When I graduate, although I no longer want to be a physiotherapist, I know that the course has provided a wide enough platform to consider any other future career prospects.

KENDAL'S TOP TIPS

Be aware that sports and exercise science degrees are very different at each university. Here at the University of Leeds it is very much research and science-led, with no lectures on the role of coaching in sport, marketing/business, media or actual participation in sport. It's much harder to change universities once you've started your degree so make sure you choose the course to suit you rather than the university.

Account manager and senior academy assessor

The Training Room

REBECCA TAYLOR

Route into sports science:
A levels – PE, psychology, human biology, English language (2005); BSc sports psychology and coaching sciences, University of Bournemouth (2009).

WHY SPORTS SCIENCE?

Since I've always been keen on fitness and sports, and fascinated by psychology, combining the two seemed like the perfect course for me.

HOW DID YOU GET TO WHERE YOU ARE TODAY?

Studying for my degree was a fantastic experience all round; I was in a great location and at a great university. My third year was a placement year and I worked at a golf company, which provided me with a lot of valuable experience and a nice break before my last year of study!

After graduating, I decided to stay in Bournemouth as I'd had such a great time. My first job was with The Training Room. Although this was only meant to be for a few months while I tried to work out what I wanted to do with my career, I soon realised that I had landed on my feet by working with such a young company. The company specialises in running personal training courses and this opened up opportunities for me to gain personal training qualifications a few years later. I have moved from being an academy assessor to team leader, and now I've become an account manager for Pure Gym. I also coach swimming in my spare time as I had some experience while at university doing this, and decided to keep going in my spare time.

This has been a great experience for me, and I can't wait to see what will happen over the next few years.

WHAT DOES YOUR JOB INVOLVE?

My job involves managing a small team of academy assessors who talk to people looking to become personal trainers, deciding on the right route for them and discussing the job opportunities available once they are qualified. My main responsibility is to ensure that my team is productive and providing a fantastic service to every applicant. My main hours are 10am to 6pm Monday to Friday; however we have do have a flexi-time options if necessary. The company and my colleagues are all still quite young, which makes for a great working environment.

WHAT HAS BEEN YOUR BIGGEST CHALLENGE?

Learning to manage different types of people has been quite difficult as I'm not so experienced in this area. However, as time goes on, I am learning more about how to do this and growing in confidence.

AND THE BEST BITS?

I work in a very laid-back and fun environment with a great atmosphere. The people I work with are similar to me as well which means it's a great office to work in five days a week.

REBECCA'S TOP TIPS

It's fine to want to choose sport as a degree – especially if you want to make a career out of a hobby. When applying for jobs, don't underestimate the smaller companies as they have the greatest potential to grow and offer you fantastic opportunities. Always apply for the jobs and promotions you want, even if you think they are out of reach. Employers like seeing that you want to progress and if you are working hard and applying yourself then this will give you a big advantage.

The
UCAS Guide
to getting into
University
and College

UCAS

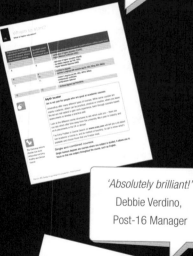

What would 650,000 potential students like to know about UCAS? Everything!

- With rising costs and high competition for places, thorough research and preparation have never been more crucial for future students.

- Relevant throughout the whole year.

- Published by UCAS, a well-known and respected brand with direct access to the most up-to-date information.

- Written in a friendly, step-by-step format, with myth busters, checklists and helpful tips from students and experts at universities and colleges.

'...the most comprehensive guide... completely impartial... offers fabulous tips and advice...'
David Fullerton, Head of Careers

'Absolutely brilliant!'
Debbie Verdino,
Post-16 Manager

Order your copy now...

t +44 (0)1242 544 610

f +44(0)1242 544 806

e publicationservices@ucas.ac.uk

Price: £11.99

Entry routes

Routes to qualification

Sports science-related subjects are many and varied, making it impossible to cover all the various routes to qualifications here. The **Areas of work** profiles on pages 14 to 35 give a brief summary of what is required in each of the highlighted professions, so take a look at these for more in-depth information.

Generally speaking, if you graduate with a degree in sports science or a related area, you should be able to enter a job after university without having to do a postgraduate qualification. However, some people choose to continue studying either to become more specialised (for example, in biomechanics) or to improve their job prospects. Careers in research and academia normally require extra time in postgraduate study, either on an MSc course or a PhD. To research and apply for postgraduate courses at a range of higher education institutions, go to **www.ukpass.ac.uk**.

At the end of their degree course, trainee podiatrists and physiotherapists will have undertaken sufficient study to qualify them to register with the Health Professions Council which, in turn, allows them to apply for work with such employers as the NHS. On-the-job training, however, is part of the job in both of these fields, as personal and professional development is essential to keep skills and knowledge of practice up to date.

For sports and exercise psychologists, gaining their undergraduate degree is just the first step on the career ladder. After graduating, they will need to undertake a further three years of postgraduate study, which will involve specialising in their chosen area, and carrying out supervised clinical placements, in order to reach chartered status. At this point, the job search normally begins.

What does a degree in these areas normally involve?

Again, the answer to this question will depend on what area of study you are hoping to go into. Below is a brief summary of the main degree subjects covered in this publication.

PODIATRY

Podiatry degrees cover everything you will need to know to enable you to practise as a podiatrist upon completion of the three-year course. This includes the anatomy, physiology, pathology, life sciences and body systems relating to the feet and lower limbs, as well as issues surrounding clinical practice, research, medicine and pharmacology. Often, certain subjects are studied alongside students in other disciplines, such as midwifery, pharmacology, nursing and physiotherapy, as this helps to introduce undergraduates to the multidisciplinary approach adopted in the healthcare professions as a whole.

Practical experience is vital in this degree, so students will find themselves working on patients, with supervision, to learn about how to conduct examinations, diagnoses, treatment and the use of appropriate equipment. The final year normally involves clinical placements in NHS settings such as hospital wards, outpatients and even in orthopaedic surgery.

PHYSIOTHERAPY

Physiotherapy students normally start off learning about the theory of practice. This involves studying aspects of anatomy, physiology, pathology and the musculoskeletal system. Other specialisms can be incorporated into this, including how health and illness affect the body, as well as neurological and cardio-respiratory problems. Some of the study will be combined with students on other related courses, particularly looking at aspects relating to ethics, the law and research. As with all healthcare courses, the chance to specialise is offered and you may be interested in taking up such options as acupuncture, sports medicine or hydrotherapy.

Practical experience is gained firstly by practising on your fellow students before you are allowed to try your skills out on the general public! Further into your training, you will be able to access clinical placements, often in each year of study.

SPORTS SCIENCE

Sports science involves looking (albeit probably in a more general way than physiotherapy and podiatry) at various biological areas of study – including anatomy, biomechanics, psychology, physiology, nutrition and metabolism, and relating them to how people perform physically. These biological subjects will be studied at a basic level at the start of any sports science degree, and will be looked at in more depth and detail in years two and three. Additionally, sports science undergraduates look at other aspects relating to the sporting arena, including management, business, technology, coaching and the analysis of performance.

SPORTS AND EXERCISE PSYCHOLOGY

All accredited psychology degrees cover the necessary theories and methods of psychology for you to attain the Graduate Basis for Registration (GBR), which is required by the British Psychological Society before you can progress further – if you so wish – with your training in this field. Courses usually last for three years, full time, though some four-year courses – with a year's work placement – are available. In the first year or two, students normally look at a wide range of psychological areas, such as cognitive psychology, use of statistics in analysis, research methods, language acquisition and development, and thinking and reasoning. In the final year, you will be able to specialise in your chosen topic, while carrying out a piece of research. Specialisms can range from the psychology of pain to looking at language disorders in children.

TEACHING METHODS

Most degree courses adopt a variety of different teaching methods: lectures, smaller group seminars, tutorials (often on a one-to-one basis), and practical workshops. This is something to consider when applying for courses as teaching methods can vary. Equally assessment methods differ between universities. Some of the more traditional institutions rely on final examinations, while others assess students through either continuous assessment or a mixture of final exams and coursework.

ENTRY REQUIREMENTS

While you don't need to have all three sciences at A level for sports science and related areas, admissions tutors normally prefer at least one out of chemistry, physics, biology or maths, and some will not accept physical education as a substitute for one of these, although it is welcomed as an additional A level. Psychology A level is not a prerequisite for a psychology degree, although it can be a useful introduction to the subject area. Normally a combination of good results in academic A level subjects are accepted, but sometimes general studies is not considered worthy of an offer.

Competition for places on UK sports science and related courses is very tough, and it is thought that it will become even fiercer with interest in these areas peaking as a result of the London 2012 Olympics. Therefore, it is not uncommon for admissions tutors to request high grades or UCAS Tariff points. Check with each institution for their entry requirements. Tutors may also take GCSE grades into account as another way to filter the growing number of straight-A students.

TOP TIP

Don't be afraid to pick up the phone – university admissions offices welcome enquiries directly from students, rather than careers officers on your behalf. It shows you're genuinely interested and committed to your career early on.

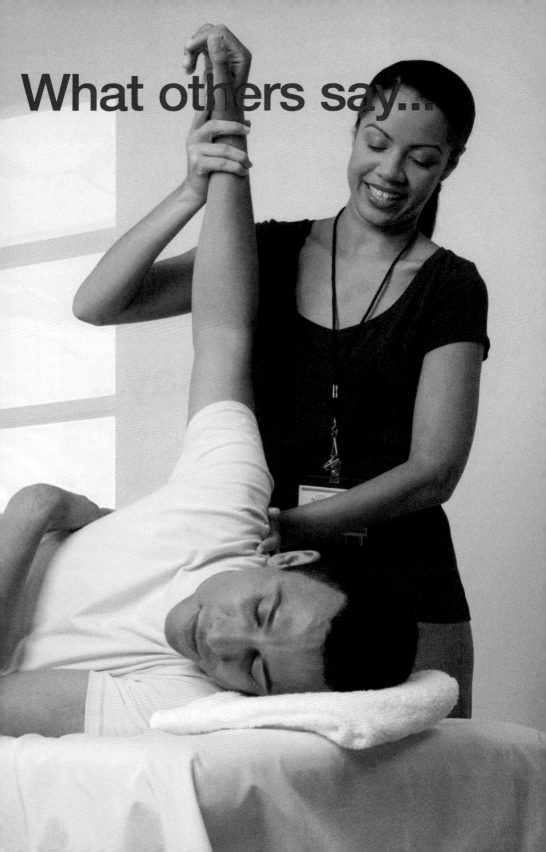

What others say...

What others say...

These are extracts from case studies in previous editions of this book. They give some insights into the experiences and thoughts of people who were once in the same position as you.

DUNCAN MARCHBANKS – ORTHOTIST

I enjoyed physics and maths at college, and was interested in a degree in prosthetics and orthotics because I knew it would enable me to combine the subject areas I liked – as it involves the study of the human body with engineering principles. I also knew there were excellent graduate job opportunities and exciting developments in the field.

Orthotics is a vast subject, and as a graduate orthotist there is so much to learn. I am sometimes faced with clinical problems that I am uncertain about, but I expand my knowledge by working and sharing ideas with colleagues from different disciplines. Continual

professional development is essential for prosthetists and orthotists, so I regularly attend conferences, scientific meetings and courses, and research the literature.

Find out as much about your prospective degree course as possible to ensure it will suit you; take every opportunity to talk to course tutors and current students and to attend open days. Try to arrange work experience to see what it is like to work within a clinical environment. Work hard for your A levels, as the principles you learn at this stage are vital foundations for later study.

JON CREE – LECTURER, SPORT EXERCISE AND SCIENCE

Middlesex was the only university that offered studies in rehabilitation and injury prevention, so it was ideal for me. The course lasted four years and was a good mix of theory, practice and placements – I did three months in Australia for one of mine, while the others were mainly in private rehabilitation and physiotherapy clinics.

I then realised there was a big gap between athletes becoming rehabilitated and reaching elite status once again, and it was an area I wanted to explore further. Luckily Middlesex was launching the only MSc of its kind in this area so I went back to continue my education. When my MSc ended, I was offered a position in the sports science teaching team.

I enjoy being part of the teaching team. I meet lots of very interesting people. Because of my age, I develop good relationships with my students, who feel they can relate to me and see how what they are studying can translate into a career. The opportunities that come my way are fantastic and my colleagues are a great bunch to work with.

PETER NUNN – PERSONAL TRAINER

I had worked as a life guarding and fitness instructor before deciding that I wanted a more intellectually demanding and exciting work life. So I decided to investigate university courses that would help me achieve this. I found the perfect course and enrolled.

I wanted to have the opportunity to work with athletes at the highest level, but also wanted to work in the area of health related fitness in a gym or studio environment. I thought that this would be more likely if I took the route of personal trainer, rather than a sport coach or a physiologist.

My undergraduate degree had given me all the theory I needed. I now needed the practical element, so I enrolled on my personal training diploma in London and completed a two-week intensive course. I now work as a self-employed personal trainer in a large gym organisation.

Make sure you choose a subject you are passionate about for your degree and that you can enter into your chosen career with that course. Get a few years experience as a gym instructor or an employed personal trainer before venturing into self-employment, and be 100% committed to the job or you will not succeed.

ROWENA TASSELL – HEALTHY LIFESTYLES DEVELOPMENT OFFICER

I am responsible for promoting healthy lifestyles, particularly trying to reach sections of the community that might find this more challenging for various reasons. I target areas such as physical activity, healthy eating and obesity, drugs and alcohol, and mental health.

The job is very much about keeping existing projects going and starting up new initiatives, so I have had to learn to be very disciplined about not taking on too much work. I do generally manage to work requests into my plans, but if I can't I will direct people to somewhere or someone they can get help from.

Work experience, voluntary or paid, sets you apart from other graduates. It shows that you are committed and helps you to find out what really interests you. It's also a great way of making contacts, which may help you with employment when you leave university.

SITAL VARA – PODIATRIST

I enjoyed every minute of my three-year podiatry degree – shadowing podiatrists, observing clinics, and treating all sorts of patients and conditions. This meant we were exposed to general clinics, nail surgery, high-risk patient clinics, biomechanics, orthopaedics, wound care and children's clinics.

Seven months ago, I started a private practice with another podiatrist who I knew from university. We work privately part time and with the NHS for the rest of the time, mainly treating patients with general and biomechanical foot problems.

I absolutely love wound care and treating high-risk patients; it is so rewarding seeing a chronic wound finally heal. It is brilliant to see the wound eventually heal up and how happy that made the patient.

Spend time researching what it is we do and to make sure it is for you. I'd also recommend not taking a year out after studying like I did. Get straight into working; it is not as scary as you might think. Finally, starting in the NHS is a great way to start; you get lots of experience in a number of different settings and that really builds your confidence.

JENNIFER RILEY – JUNIOR PHYSIOTHERAPIST

I work with patients to help with their rehabilitation and I also teach physiotherapy students. It is a very diverse career with many differing prospects, and the career progression and development opportunities attracted me.

On a daily basis I work with senior physiotherapists and technical instructors within the hospital's orthopaedic in-patient department. I help with patients' rehabilitation when they are recovering from joint replacements and other orthopaedic surgeries, in both gym and ward sessions. This includes gait re-education, exercises and mobility aid assessments. I am responsible for safely progressing patients with their treatments so they can be discharged from hospital. I also refer patients for further treatment if required.

Try to get as much pre-application experience as you can. Universities want to see that you're truly interested in this profession, so write to hospitals, private practices, sports teams and care centres to gain all the voluntary or paid experience that you can. This will also help you decide if physiotherapy is the career for you.

JENNY PAGE – SENIOR LECTURER, SPORT AND EXERCISE PSYCHOLOGY

I really enjoyed the sports psychology part of my sports science degree; it allowed me to think about factors that I had not previously considered to be very important in performing well, such as being confident, motivated and focused when performing. I then wanted to use my knowledge to help sports performers so I trained to become a sports psychologist.

As a sports psychologist I have completed workshops with a rugby league academy, Hampshire Gymnastics and the Independent Schools Football Association for Girls. I have also delivered one-to-one consultancy with a rugby union player, rugby league players, shooters and a football referee, amongst other performers.

As a lecturer, I teach students from college right through to MSc level, through lectures, seminars and laboratories – and my regular working day is normally from 8.00am until 5.30pm during term time. However, both my research and the work I do with athletes are often completed in the evenings and at weekends.

If you want to become a lecturer, once you have your degree and are undertaking an MSc, ask your institution if you can help deliver some of the lectures, seminars or laboratories. If you would like to be a sports psychologist, you will need to obtain a postgraduate qualification in the area.

CHRISTINA ERIKSTRUP – PROSTHETIST

At university I really enjoyed the science and thinking which went into making and developing prostheses/orthoses, so I was tempted to go into research. But after my two placements, I realised it was the work in the clinic with patients that I enjoyed the most.

I undertook two six-month placements in my final year: one at an orthotics centre in Sweden and the other in a prosthetics centre in London. On both, I followed a supervisor and helped make patients' prostheses or orthoses. After graduating, I was offered a permanent position in the company where I did my prosthetic placement, which is where I work today.

My main responsibility is to assess a patient's suitability for a prosthesis. I then take a cast of their residual limb (stump) which I use as a mould to make an individually fitted prosthesis, and technicians help manufacture it. I then have to ensure that the prosthesis fits well and is safe for the patient to use on a daily basis. Most enjoyable is the creative side of my job; a patient may want to do a specific activity with their prosthesis, and I then have to work out how to make the prosthesis so that this can be achieved.

CHRIS PEACH – SPORTS DEVELOPMENT OFFICER

After graduating in human geography and sports science, I was offered the chance to do an MA in sports development as part of a scholarship scheme. During this I worked on a coaching and volunteering scheme, placing students into the community and gaining project management skills. I continued to work hard, gained

some great experience and eventually found my ideal role as a sports development officer.

I love my job. Working with people who also love sport, setting things up and delivering activities for children and adults is great. I normally work 9am to 5pm but sometimes there are weekend events, evening coaching sessions or special events to attend so it can vary.

Many people come out of university with a degree but they don't necessarily know how to stand out from other potential employees when applying for jobs. Set yourself apart by volunteering and showing what makes you different and more employable than anyone else!

SAMANTHA FENNELL – REGISTERED OSTEOPATH AND BSO CLINICAL TUTOR

During my degree, there was a lot of valuable patient contact in the Bristish School of Osteopathy's (BSO) busy clinical centre. I then went straight on to do a master's degree in paediatrics to enhance my knowledge – also working at an osteopathic practice with a very strong paediatric patient base.

This expertise then led to a job as a clinical tutor at the BSO, with further responsibilities in a BSO community outreach clinic and for a charity providing free osteopathic treatments to those who are homeless.

On other days I work privately, seeing members of the general public with a vast variety of problems. Diagnosing someone involves listening to their medical history, examining muscles and joints, observing movements and considering relevant psychological and social factors. X-rays, scans and other clinical investigations are also used, if required. Osteopaths deploy a wide range of gentle, safe, non-invasive manual techniques such as deep-tissue massage, joint articulation and manipulation. I may also advise patients on exercise, posture and diet.

Connect with us...

 www.facebook.com/ucasonline

 www.twitter.com/ucas_online

 www.youtube.com/ucasonline

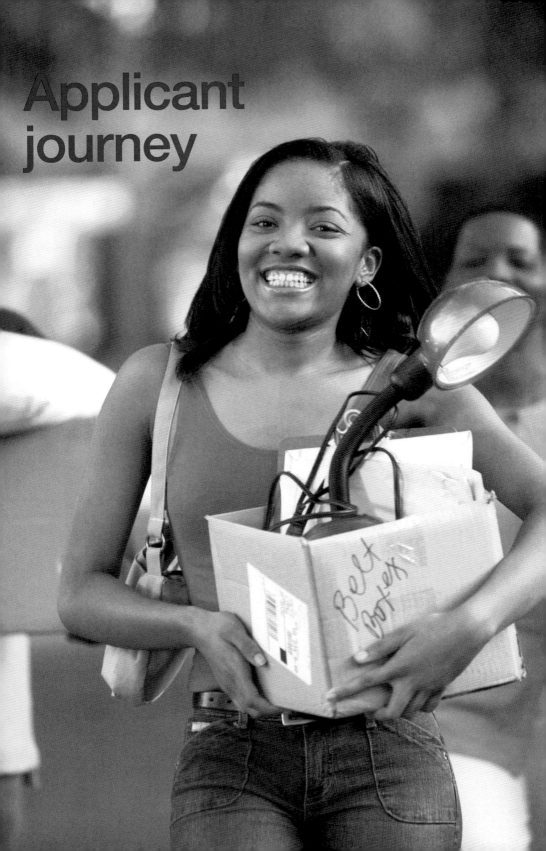

Applicant journey

SIX EASY STEPS TO UNIVERSITY AND COLLEGE

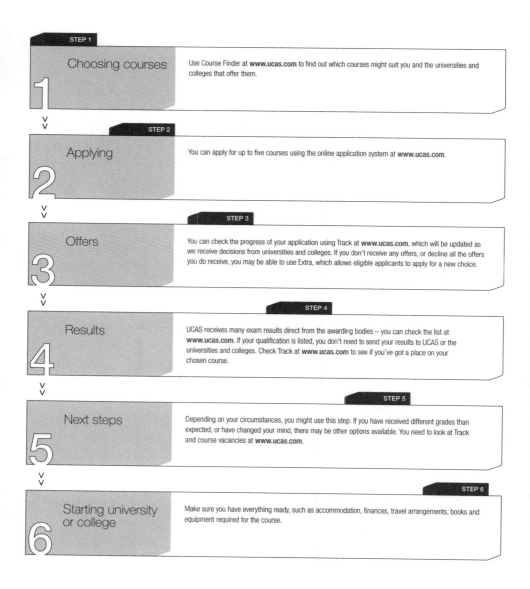

STEP 1

Choosing courses

Use Course Finder at **www.ucas.com** to find out which courses might suit you and the universities and colleges that offer them.

STEP 2

Applying

You can apply for up to five courses using the online application system at **www.ucas.com**.

STEP 3

Offers

You can check the progress of your application using Track at **www.ucas.com**, which will be updated as we receive decisions from universities and colleges. If you don't receive any offers, or decline all the offers you do receive, you may be able to use Extra, which allows eligible applicants to apply for a new choice.

STEP 4

Results

UCAS receives many exam results direct from the awarding bodies – you can check the list at **www.ucas.com**. If your qualification is listed, you don't need to send your results to UCAS or the universities and colleges. Check Track at **www.ucas.com** to see if you've got a place on your chosen course.

STEP 5

Next steps

Depending on your circumstances, you might use this step. If you have received different grades than expected, or have changed your mind, there may be other options available. You need to look at Track and course vacancies at **www.ucas.com**.

STEP 6

Starting university or college

Make sure you have everything ready, such as accommodation, finances, travel arrangements, books and equipment required for the course.

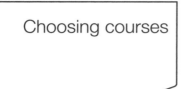

Choosing courses

Step 1 – Planning your application for sports science and physiotherapy

Planning your application is the start of your journey to finding a place at a university or college.

This section will help you decide what course to study and how to choose a university or college where you'll enjoy living and studying. Find out about qualifications, degree options, how they'll assess you, and coping with the costs of higher education.

UCAS CARD

At its simplest, the UCAS Card scheme is the start of your UCAS journey. It can save you a packet on the high street with exclusive offers to UCAS Card holders, as well as providing you with hints and tips about finding the best course at the right university or college. If that's not enough you'll also receive these benefits:

- frequent expert help from UCAS, with all the essential information you need on the application process
- free monthly newsletters providing advice, hints, tips and exclusive discounts
- tailored information on the universities and courses you're interested in
- and much more.

If you're in Year 12, S5 or equivalent and thinking about higher education for autumn 2013, sign up for your FREE UCAS Card today to receive all these benefits at **www.ucas.com/ucascard**.

---

1 Choosing courses

Choosing courses

USE COURSE FINDER AT WWW.UCAS.COM TO FIND OUT WHICH COURSES MIGHT SUIT YOU, AND THE UNIVERSITIES AND COLLEGES THAT OFFER THEM

Use the UCAS website – www.ucas.com has lots of advice on how to find a course. Go to the students' section of the website for the best advice or go straight to Course Finder to see all the courses available through UCAS. Our map of the UK at **www.ucas.com/students/choosingcourses/choosinguni/map/** shows you where all the universities and colleges are located.

Watch UCAStv – at **www.ucas.tv** there are videos on *How to choose your course, Attending events* and *Open days*, as well as case studies from students talking about their experiences of finding a course at university or college.

Attend UCAS conventions – UCAS conventions are held throughout the UK. Universities and colleges have exhibition stands where their staff offer information about courses and institutions. Details of when the conventions are happening, and a convention planner to help you prepare, are shown at **www.ucas.com/conventions**.

Look at university and college websites and prospectuses – universities and colleges have prospectuses and course-specific leaflets on their undergraduate courses. Your school or college library may have copies or go to the university's website to download a copy, or ask them to send one to you.

Go to university and college open days – most institutions offer open days to anyone who wants to attend. See the list of universities and colleges on **www.ucas.com** and the *UCAS Open Days* publication (see the Essential Reading chapter on page 120) for information on when they are taking place. Aim to visit all of the universities and colleges you are interested in before you apply. It will help with your expectations of university life and make sure the course is the right one for you.

League tables – these can be helpful but bear in mind that they attempt to rank institutions in an overall order reflecting the views of those that produce them. They may not reflect your views and needs. Examples can be found at **www.thecompleteuniversityguide.co.uk**, **www.guardian.co.uk/education/universityguide**, **www.thetimes.co.uk** (subscription service) and **www.thesundaytimes.co.uk** (subscription service). See page 76 for more information about league tables.

Do your research – speak and refer to as many trusted sources as you can find. Talk to someone already doing the job you have in mind. The section 'A career in sports science and physiotherapy' on pages 13 to 35 will help you identify the different areas you might want to enter.

DECIDING ON YOUR COURSE CHOICES

Through UCAS you can initially apply for up to five courses. How do you find out more information to make an informed decision?

Remember you don't have to make five course choices. Only apply for a course if you're completely happy with both the course and the university or college and you would definitely be prepared to accept a place.

How do you narrow down your course choices? First of all, look up course details in this book or on Course Finder at **www.ucas.com**. This will give you an idea of the full range of courses and topics on offer. You'll quickly be able to eliminate institutions that don't offer the right course, or you can choose a 'hit list' of institutions first, and then see what they have to offer.

Once you've made a short(er) list, look at university or college websites, and generally find out as much as you can about the course, department and institution. Don't be afraid to contact them to ask for more information, request their prospectus or arrange an open day visit.

Choosing courses

1

Choosing your institution

Different people look for different things from their university or college course, but the checklist on the next page sets out the kinds of factors all prospective students should consider when choosing their university. Keep this list in mind on open days, when talking to friends about their experiences at various universities and colleges, or while reading prospectuses and websites.

WHAT TO CONSIDER WHEN CHOOSING YOUR SPORTS SCIENCE AND PHYSIOTHERAPY COURSE

Location	Do you want to stay close to home? Would you prefer to study at a city or campus university or college?
Grades required	Use the Course Finder facility on the UCAS website, **www.ucas.com**, to view entry requirements for courses you are interested in. Also, check out the university or college website or call up the admissions office. Some institutions specify grades required, eg AAB, while others specify 'points' required, eg 340. If they ask for points, it means they're using the UCAS Tariff system, which awards points to different types and levels of qualification. For example, an A grade at A level = 120 points; a B grade at A level = 100 points. The full Tariff tables are available on pages 100 -109 and at **www.ucas.com**.
Employer links	Ask the course tutor or department about links with employers, especially for placements or work experience.
Graduate prospects	Ask the careers office for their list of graduate destinations.
Cost	Ask the admissions office about variable tuition fees and financial assistance.
Sports science and physiotherapy or non-sports science and physiotherapy degree?	Is there another subject that you enjoy that you could study first, that might help give you an edge in employers' eyes?
Degree type	Do you want to study sports science and physiotherapy on its own (single honours degree) or 50/50 with another subject (joint) or as one of a few subjects (combined degree)? If you opt for a joint or combined course, check that you won't need to do a conversion course to pursue your chosen career.
Teaching style	How many lectures per week, number of tutorials or amount of one-to-one work, etc?
Course assessment	Can you see yourself writing essays throughout the year?
Facilities for students	Check out the library and sporting facilities, and find out if there is a careers adviser dedicated to your subject.
'Fit'	Even if all the above criteria stack up, this one relies on gut feel – go and visit the institution if you can and see if it's 'you'.

1 Choosing courses

League tables

The information that follows has been provided by Dr Bernard Kingston of *The Complete University Guide*.

League tables are worth consulting early in your research and perhaps for confirmation later on. But never rely on them in isolation – always use them alongside other information sources available to you. Universities typically report that over a third of prospective students view league tables as important or very important in making their university choices. They give an insight into quality and are mainly based on data from the universities themselves. Somewhat confusingly, tables published in, say, 2012 are referred to as the 2013 tables because they are aimed at applicants going to university in that following year. The well known ones - *The Complete University Guide*, *The Guardian*, *The Times*, and *The Sunday Times* - rank the institutions and the subjects they teach using input measures (eg entry standards), throughput measures (eg student : staff ratios) and output measures (eg graduate prospects). Some tables are free to access whilst others are behind pay walls. All are interactive and enable users to create their own tables based on the measures important to them.

The universities are provided with their raw data for checking and are regularly consulted on methodology. But ultimately it is the compilers who decide what measures to use and what weights to put on them. They are competitors and rarely consult amongst themselves. So, for example, *The Times* tables differ significantly from *The Sunday Times* ones even though both newspapers belong to the same media proprietor.

Whilst the main university rankings tend to get the headlines, we would stress that the individual subject tables are as least as important, if not more so, when deciding where to study. All universities, regardless of their overall ranking, have some academic departments that rank highly in their subjects. Beware also giving much weight to an institution being a few places higher or lower in the tables – this is likely to be of little significance. This is particularly true in the lower half of the main table where overall scores show considerable bunching.

Most of the measures used to define quality come from hard factual data provided by the Higher Education Statistics Agency (HESA) but some, like student satisfaction and peer assessment, are derived from surveys of subjective impressions where you might wish to query sample size. We give a brief overview of the common measures here but please go to the individual websites for full details.

- **Student satisfaction** is derived from the annual National Student Survey (NSS) and is heavily used by *The Guardian* and *The Sunday Times*.
- **Research assessment** comes from a 2008 exercise (RAE) aimed at defining the quality of a university's research (excluded by *The Guardian*).
- **Entry standards** are based on the full UCAS Tariff scores obtained by new students.
- **Student : staff** ratio gives the number of students per member of academic staff.
- **Expenditure** figures show the costs of academic and student services.
- **Good honours** lists the proportion of graduates gaining a first or upper second honours degree.
- **Completion** indicates the proportion of students who successfully complete their studies.

- **Graduate prospects** usually reports the proportion of graduates who obtain a graduate job – not any job – or continue studying within six months of leaving.
- **Peer assessment** is used only by *The Sunday Times* which asks academics to rate other universities in their subjects.
- **Value added** is used only by *The Guardian* and compares entry standards with good honours.

All four main publishers of UK league tables (see Table 1) also publish university subject tables. *The Complete University Guide* and *The Times* are based on four measures: student satisfaction, research quality, entry standards and graduate destinations. *The Sunday Times* uses student satisfaction, entry standards, graduate destinations, graduate unemployment, good degrees and drop-out rate, while *The Guardian* uses student satisfaction (as three separate measures), entry standards, graduate destinations, student-staff ratio, spend per student and value added. This use of different measures is one reason why the different tables can yield different results (sometimes very different, especially in the case of *The Guardian* which has least in common with the other tables).

League tables compiled by *The Complete University Guide* (**www.thecompleteuniversityguide.co.uk**) and *The Guardian* (**www.guardian.co.uk**) are available in spring, those by *The Times* (**www.thetimes.co.uk**) and *The Sunday Times* (**www.thesundaytimes.co.uk**) in the summer.

Table 1 – measures used by the main publishers of UK league tables

	Universities	Measures	Subjects	Measures
The Complete University Guide	116	9	62	4
The Guardian	119	8	46	8
The Sunday Times	122	8	39	6
The Times	116	8	62	4

THINGS TO WATCH OUT FOR WHEN READING SUBJECT LEAGUE TABLES

- Physiotherapy will usually be included within a more general table covering subjects allied to medicine.

WHO PUBLISHES ECONOMICS, FINANCE AND ACCOUNTANCY LEAGUE TABLES?

The Complete University Guide	Other Subjects Allied to Medicine Sports Science
The Guardian	Nursing and Paramedical Studies Sports Science
The Sunday Times	Subjects Allied to Medicine Sports Science
The Times	Other Subjects Allied to Medicine Sports Science

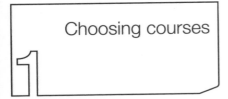

Choosing courses

How will they choose you?

Most admissions departments will have different entry criteria, so make sure that you check prospectuses, websites and all other materials thoroughly before you apply. Even better, why not give them a call and discuss it with them directly? Not only will it leave you better prepared to submit a targeted application, but it will also demonstrate that you're self-motivated.

ACADEMIC ABILITY

Many courses in sports science and physiology are intellectually demanding. Not only may you be learning about the basics of these disciplines for the very first time, but you'll also be required to work in much greater analytical depth than you previously have at GCSE or A level (or equivalent). Therefore in order for admissions tutors to be sure you have what it takes to cope with the course, you'll need to show that you have the academic ability to take on new ideas.

SELF-MOTIVATION AND SELF-DISCIPLINE

Studying at university is very different from school and sixth form. In those settings, you will have a set course, normally following a study pattern suggested by your teachers. The homework set for you will have ensured that you studied regularly and on time.

At university, tutors and lecturers don't have time to keep tabs on their students in the same way. Whereas at A level your teachers will have helped motivate you to finish work on time, university tutors will simply hand out reading lists and essay titles in advance and expect you to complete assignments on time without constant reminders.

Understandably this can be daunting for some people. Certainly, time management and self-motivation are skills you hone at university, but it will help if your referee can write about any instances where you've shown an ability to work well on your own, as this is how you will be studying on your undergraduate course.

DEVOTION TO YOUR SUBJECT

A good way to prove to admissions tutors that you have a genuine interest in the subject you're applying for is to do some reading into the area, potentially from books they have written. Additionally, contact the relevant department and ask for their first-year reading list, if this is not available online. You don't need to read everything on it, but if you choose two or three books that appeal to you and read them in some depth it will show commitment to both the subject and the relevant university's course.

Be warned though – don't think that merely mentioning a few key books will automatically get you through. Unless you can make a few valid points about what interested you in what you've read, don't bother; it could do more harm than good.

WORK EXPERIENCE

Relevant work experience is not essential to gain a university place in sports science or physiotherapy, but it will certainly help your application. Not only will you convince admissions tutors that you are enthusiastic about the subject, but you'll also have the chance to develop useful skills that are transferable to your university course – such as time management and communication skills.

For more help on how to get work experience and what work experience counts, see page 94.

YOUR PERSONAL STATEMENT

Your personal statement can really enhance your application. It's here that you can show evidence of all the above issues – academic ability, self-motivation and self-discipline, and an interest in and insight into your subject through reading and work experience. Most universities consider personal statements to be very important as this is where your own voice comes through and can set you apart from the crowd. Make the most of it and use it to your advantage. Be honest but not over-friendly and give well reasoned statements. And above all make sure it's free from mistakes and easy to read. There's nothing more offputting for an admissions tutor than applications and personal statements that are badly written and have glaring grammatical errors or spelling mistakes.

As this is such an important part of your application, it's worth drafting it a few times before sending it to UCAS. Ask family, friends and teachers to check it, not only for mistakes but also to see if you're leaving anything out that should be in, or equally if there's anything that should come out.

For more hints and tips on personal statements, see page 92.

THE INTERVIEW

It's unlikely that you'll have to sit an entry test. This means that if there is an interview (and in many cases there will be) it is particulary important.

Talk to someone who has been – or is currently – on the course that you are applying for. What was their interview like? What kinds of questions were they asked? Be prepared and if possible do a mock interview with a friend, relative or school careers adviser before you go for the real thing.

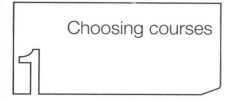

Choosing courses

The cost of higher education

The information in this section was up-to-date when this book was published. You should visit the websites mentioned in this section for the very latest information.

THE COST OF STUDYING IN THE UK

As a student, you will usually have to pay for two things: tuition fees for your course, which for most students do not need to be paid for up front, and living costs such as rent, food, books, transport and entertainment. Fees charged vary between courses, between universities and colleges, and also according to your normal country of residence, so it's important to check these before you apply. Course fee information is supplied to UCAS by the universities and is displayed in Course Finder at **www.ucas.com**.

If you're studying in Scotland and already live there, check the Student Awards Agency for Scotland (SAAS) website **www.saas.gov.uk** for further information.

STUDENT LOANS

The purpose of student loans from the Government is to help cover the costs of your tuition fees and basic living costs (rent, bills, food and so on). Two types are available: a tuition fee loan to cover the tuition charges and a maintenance loan to help with accommodation and other living costs. Both types of student loan are available to all students who meet the basic eligibility requirements. Interest will be charged at inflation plus a fixed percentage while you are studying. In addition, many other commercial loans are available to students studying at university or college but the interest rate can vary considerably. Loans to help with costs will be available for all eligible students, irrespective of family income.

Find out more information from the relevant sites below:

England: Student Finance England –
www.direct.gov.uk/studentfinance
Northern Ireland: Student Finance Northern Ireland –
www.studentfinanceni.co.uk
Scotland: Student Awards Agency for Scotland –
www.saas.gov.uk
Wales: Student Finance Wales –
www.studentfinancewales.co.uk
www.cyllidmyfyrwyrcymru.co.uk

BURSARIES AND SCHOLARSHIPS

- The National Scholarships Programme give financial help to students studying in England. The scheme is designed to help students whose families have lower incomes.
- Students from families with lower incomes will be entitled to a non-repayable maintenance grant to help with living costs.
- Many universities and colleges also offer non-repayable cholarships and bursaries to help students cover tuition and living costs whilst studying.
- All eligible part-time undergraduates who study for at least 25% of their time will be able to apply for a loan to cover the costs of their tuition, which means they no longer have to pay up front.

There will be extra support for disabled students and students with child or adult dependants. For more information, visit the country-specific websites listed above.

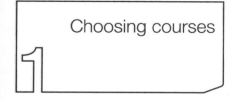

1 Choosing courses

International students

APPLYING TO STUDY IN THE UK

Deciding to go to university or college in the UK is very exciting. You need to think about what course to do, where to study, and how much it will cost. The decisions you make can have a huge effect on your future but UCAS is here to help.

HOW TO APPLY

Whatever your age or qualifications, if you want to apply for any of the 35,000 courses listed at 300 universities and colleges on the UCAS website, you must apply through UCAS at **www.ucas.com**. If you are unsure, your school, college, adviser, or local British Council office will be able to help. Further advice and a video guide for international students can be found on the non-UK students' section of the UCAS website at **www.ucas.com/international**

Students may apply on their own or through their school, college, adviser, or local British Council if they are registered with UCAS to use Apply. If you choose to use an education agent's services, check with the British Council to see if they hold a list of certificated or registered agents in your country. Check also on any charges you may need to pay. UCAS charges only the application fee (see page 84) but agents may charge for additional services.

HOW MUCH WILL MY APPLICATION COST?

If you choose to apply to more than one course, university or college you need to pay UCAS £23 GBP when you apply. If you only apply to one course at one university or college, you pay UCAS £12 GBP.

WHAT LEVEL OF ENGLISH?

UCAS provides a list of English language qualifications and grades that are acceptable to most UK universities and colleges, however you are advised to contact the institutions directly as each have their own entry requirement in English. For more information go to **www.ucas.com/students/wheretostart/ nonukstudents/englangprof**.

INTERNATIONAL STUDENT FEES

If you study in the UK, your fee status (whether you pay full-cost fees or a subsidised fee rate) will be decided by the UK university or college you plan to attend. Before you decide which university or college to attend, you need to be absolutely certain that you can pay the full cost of:

- your tuition fees (the amount is set by universities and colleges, so contact them for more information – visit their websites where many list their fees). Fee details will also be included on Course Finder at **www.ucas.com**
- the everyday living expenses for you and your family for the whole time that you are in the UK, including accommodation, food, gas and electricity bills, clothes, travel and leisure activities
- books and equipment for your course
- travel to and from your country.

You must include everything when you work out how much it will cost. You can get information to help you do this accurately from the international offices at

universities and colleges, UKCISA (UK Council for International Student Affairs) and the British Council. There is a useful website tool to help you manage your money at university – **www.studentcalculator.org.uk**.

Scholarships and bursaries are offered at some universities and colleges and you should contact them for more information. In addition, you should check with your local British Council for additional scholarships available to students from your country who want to study in the UK.

LEGAL DOCUMENTS YOU WILL NEED

As you prepare to study in the UK, it is very important to think about the legal documents you will need to enter the country.

Everyone who comes to study in the UK needs a valid passport, details of which will be collected either in you UCAS application or later through Track. If you do not yet have a passport, you should apply for one as soon as possible. People from certain countries also need visas before they come into the UK. They are known as 'visa nationals'. You can check if you require a visa to travel to the UK by visiting the UK Border Agency website and selecting 'Studying in the UK', so please check the UK Border Agency website at **www.ukba.homeoffice.gov.uk** for the most up-to-date guidance and information about the United Kingdom's visa requirements.

When you apply for your visa you need to make sure you have the following documents:

- a confirmation of acceptance for studies (CAS) number from the university of college where you are going to study. The institution must be on the UKBA Register of Sponsors in order to accept international students

- a valid passport
- evidence that you have enough money to pay for your course and living costs
- certificates for all qualifications you have that are relevant to the course you have been accepted for and for any English language qualifications.

You will also have to give your biometric data.

Do check for further information from your local British Embassy or High Commission. Guidance information for international students is also available from UKCISA and from UKBA.

ADDITIONAL RESOURCES

There are a number of organisations that can provide further guidance and information to you as you prepare to study in the UK:

- British Council
  www.britishcouncil.org
- Education UK (British Council website dealing with educational matters)
  www.educationuk.org
- English UK (British Council accredited website listing English language courses in the UK)
  www.englishuk.com
- UK Border Agency (provides information on visa requirements and applications)
  www.ukba.homeoffice.gov.uk
- UKCISA (UK Council for International Student Affairs)
  www.ukcisa.org.uk
- Directgov (the official UK Government website)
  www.direct.gov.uk
- Prepare for Success
  www.prepareforsuccess.org.uk

Applying

2

Step 2 –
Applying

You apply through UCAS using the online application system, called Apply, at **www.ucas.com**. You can apply for a maximum of five choices, but you don't have to use them all if you don't want to. If you apply for fewer than five choices, you can add more at a later date if you want to. But be aware of the course application deadlines (you can find these in Course Finder at **www.ucas.com**).

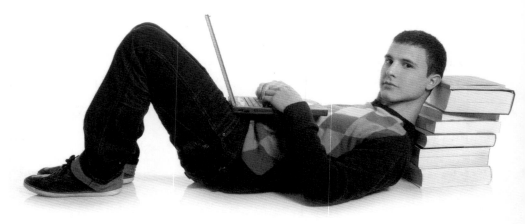

IMPORTANT DATES FOR 2012 ENTRY

Early June 2012	UCAS Apply opens for 2013 entry registration.
Mid-September 2012	Applications can be sent to UCAS.
15 October 2012	Application deadline for the receipt at UCAS of applications for all medicine, dentistry, veterinary medicine and veterinary science courses and for all courses at the universities of Oxford and Cambridge.
15 January 2013	Application deadline for the receipt at UCAS of applications for all courses except those listed above with a 15 October deadline, and some art and design courses with a 24 March deadline.
25 February 2013	Extra starts (see page 98 for more information about Extra).
24 March 2013	Application deadline for the receipt at UCAS of applications for art and design courses except those listed on Course Finder at **www.ucas.com** with a 15 January deadline.
31 March 2013	If you apply by 15 January, the universities and colleges should aim to have sent their decisions by this date (but they can take longer).
9 May 2013	If you apply by 15 January, universities and colleges need to send their decisions by this date. If they don't, UCAS will make any outstanding choices unsuccessful on their behalf.
30 June 2013	If you send your application to us by this date, we will send it to your chosen universities and colleges. Applications received after this date are entered into Clearing (see page 112 for more information about Clearing).
3 July 2013	Last date to apply through Extra.
August 2013 (date to be confirmed)	Scottish Qualifications Authority (SQA) results are published.
15 August 2013	GCE and Advanced Diploma results are published (often known as 'A level results day'). Adjustment opens for registration (see page 113 for more information about Adjustment).

DON'T FORGET...

Universities and colleges guarantee to consider your application only if we receive it by the appropriate deadline. Check application deadlines for your courses on Course Finder at **www.ucas.com**.

If you send it to UCAS after the deadline but before 30 June 2013, universities and colleges will consider your application only if they still have places available.

Applying

2

How to apply

You apply online at **www.ucas.com** through Apply – a secure, web-based application service that is designed for all our applicants, whether they are applying through a UCAS-registered centre or as an individual, anywhere in the world. Apply is:

- easy to access – all you need is an internet connection
- easy to use – you don't have to complete your application all in one go: you can save the sections as you complete them and come back to it later
- easy to monitor – once you've applied, you can use Track to check the progress of your application, including any decisions from universities or colleges. You can also reply to your offers using Track.

Watch the UCAStv guide to applying through UCAS at **www.ucas.tv**.

APPLICATION FEE
The fee for applying through UCAS is £23 for two or more choices and £12 for one choice.

You can submit only one UCAS application in each year's application cycle.

DEFERRED ENTRY

If you want to apply for deferred entry in 2014, perhaps because you want to take a year out between school or college and higher education, you should check that the university or college will accept a deferred entry application. Occasionally, tutors are not happy to accept students who take a gap year, because it interrupts the flow of their learning. If you apply for deferred entry, you must meet the conditions of any offers by 31 August 2013 unless otherwise agreed by the university or college. If you accept a place for 2014 entry and then change your mind, you cannot reapply through us in the 2014 entry cycle unless you withdraw your original application.

INVISIBILITY OF CHOICES

Universities and colleges cannot see details of the other choices on your application until you reply to any offers or you are unsuccessful at all of your choices.

APPLYING THROUGH YOUR SCHOOL OR COLLEGE

1 GET SCHOOL OR COLLEGE 'BUZZWORD'

Ask your UCAS application coordinator (may be your sixth form tutor) for your school or college UCAS 'buzzword'. This is a password for the school or college.

2 REGISTER

Go to **www.ucas.com/students/apply** and click on **Register/Log in to use Apply** and then **register**. After you have entered your registration details, the online system will automatically generate a username for you, but you'll have to come up with a password and answers to security questions.

3 COMPLETE SEVEN SECTIONS

Complete all the sections of the application. To access any section, click on the section name at the left of the screen and follow the instructions. The sections are:

Personal details – contact details, residential status, disability status

Additional information – only UK applicants need to complete this section

Student finance – UK students can share some of their application details with their student finance company. Finance information is provided for other EU and international applicants.

Choices – which courses you'd like to apply for

Education – your education and qualifications

Employment – for example, work experience, holiday jobs

Statement – see page 92 for personal statement advice.

Before you can send your application you need to go to the **View all details** screen and tick the **section completed** box.

4 PASS TO REFEREE

Once you've completed all the sections, send your application electronically to your referee (normally your form tutor). They'll check it, approve it and add their reference to it, and will then send it to UCAS on your behalf.

USEFUL INFORMATION ABOUT APPLY

- Important details like date of birth and course codes will be checked by Apply. It will alert you if they are not valid.
- We strongly recommend that the personal statement and reference are written in a word-processing package and pasted into Apply.
- If you want to, you can enter European characters into certain areas of Apply.
- You can change your application at any time before it is completed and sent to UCAS.
- You can print and preview your application at any time. Before you send it you need to go to the **View all details** screen and tick the **section completed** box.
- Your school, college or centre can choose different payment methods. For example, they may want us to bill them, or you may be able to pay online by debit or credit card.

NOT APPLYING THROUGH A SCHOOL OR COLLEGE

If you're not currently studying, you'll probably be applying as an independent applicant rather than through a school, college or other UCAS-registered centre. In this case you won't be able to provide a 'buzzword', but we'll ask you a few extra questions to check you are eligible to apply.

If you're not applying through a UCAS-registered centre, the procedure you use for obtaining a reference will depend on whether or not you want your reference to be provided through a registered centre. For information on the procedures for providing references, visit **www.ucas.com/students/applying/howtoapply/reference**.

APPLICATION CHECKLIST

We want this to run smoothly for you and we also want to process your application as quickly as possible. You can help us to do this by remembering to do the following:

✓ check the closing dates for applications – see page 87
✓ check the student finance information at **www.ucas.com/students/studentfinance/** and course fees information in Course Finder at **www.ucas.com**
✓ start early and allow plenty of time for completing your application – including enough time for your referee to complete the reference section
✓ read the online instructions carefully before you start
✓ consider what each question is actually asking for – use the 'help'
✓ pay special attention to your personal statement (see page 92) and start drafting it early
✓ ask a teacher, parent, friend or careers adviser to review your draft application – particularly the personal statement
✓ if you get stuck, watch our videos on YouTube, where we answer your frequently asked questions on completing a UCAS application at **www.youtube.com/ucasonline**
✓ if you have extra information that will not fit on your application, send it direct to your chosen universities or colleges after we have sent you your Welcome letter with your Personal ID – don't send it to us
✓ print a copy of the final version of your application, in case you are asked questions on it at an interview.

Applying

2

The personal statement

Next to choosing your courses, this section of your application will be the most time-consuming. It is of immense importance as many colleges and universities make their selection solely on the information in the UCAS application, rather than interviews and admissions tests. The personal statement can be the deciding factor in whether or not they offer you a place. If it is an institution that interviews, it could be the deciding factor in whether you get called for interview.

Keep a copy of your personal statement – if you are called for interview, you will almost certainly be asked questions based on it.

Tutors will look carefully at your exam results, actual and predicted, your reference and your own personal statement. Remember, they are looking for reasons to offer you a place – try to give them every opportunity to do so!

A SALES DOCUMENT

The personal statement is your opportunity to sell yourself, so do so. The university or college admissions tutor wants to get a rounded picture of you to decide whether you will make an interesting member of the university or college both academically and socially. They want to know more about you than simply the subjects you are studying at school.

HOW TO START

At **www.ucas.com** you'll find several tools to help you write a good personal statement.
- Personal statement timeline, to help you do all your research and plan your statement over several drafts and checks.
- Personal statement mind map, which gives you reminders and hints on preparation, content and presentation, with extra hints for mature and international applicants.

- Personal statement worksheet, which gets you to start writing by asking relevant questions so that you include everything you need. You can also check your work against a list of dos and don'ts.

Include things like hobbies, and try to link the skills you have gained to the type of course you are applying for. Describe your career plans and goals. Have you belonged to sports teams or orchestras or held positions of responsibility in the community? Try to give evidence of your ability to undertake higher level study successfully by showing your commitment and maturity. If you left full-time education a while ago, talk about the work you have done and the skills you have gathered or how you have juggled bringing up a family with other activities – that is solid evidence of time management skills. Whoever you are, make sure you explain what appeals to you about the course you are applying for.

For physiotherapy courses it is important that you demonstrate excellent interpersonal skills and provide evidence that you have considered deeply your reasons for your choice of course. You should arrange to observe a physiotherapist at work and describe what you have gained from this experience.

For sports science courses provide details of all the sports you have played competitively and the level at which you have played. Include information about coaching qualifications you have gained and any coaching courses you have run.

Visit **www.ucas.tv** to view the video to help guide you through the process and address the most common fears and concerns about writing a personal statement.

WHAT ADMISSIONS TUTORS LOOK FOR

- Your reasons for wanting to take this subject in general and this particular course.
- Your communication skills – not only what you say but how you say it. Your grammar and spelling must be perfect.
- Relevant experience – practical things you've done that are related to your choice of course.
- Evidence of your teamworking ability, leadership capability, independence.
- Evidence of your skills, for example: IT skills, empathy and people skills, debating and public speaking, research and analysis.
- Other activities that show your dedication and ability to apply yourself and maintain your motivation.

WHAT TO TELL THEM

- Why you want to do this subject – how you know it is the subject for you.
- What experience you already have in this field – for example work experience, school projects, hobbies, voluntary work.
- The skills and qualities you have as a person that would make you a good student, for example anything that shows your dedication, communication ability, academic achievement, initiative.
- Examples that show you can knuckle down and apply yourself, for example running a marathon or your Extended Project.
- If you're taking a gap year, why you've chosen this and (if possible) what you're going to do during it.
- About your other interests and activities away from studying – to show you're a rounded person. (But remember that it is mainly your suitability for the particular course that they're looking to judge.)

WORK EXPERIENCE

How much does it count? Ask any admissions tutor or recruiter about the importance of work experience on a candidate's application and they'll all agree – work experience shows a real, rather than theoretical, interest in your chosen field. An absence of work experience might make tutors question your commitment to your choice of career.

In your personal statement you'll need to set out which subject you'd like to study, why you'd like to study it, and what skills and experience you bring that would make you a great student for the course. This is where your work experience will help you stand out by allowing you to describe where you've worked, what it taught you and the skills it helped you develop.

Work experience will also help you to be sure you're on the right track with your interest in a particular degree or career, and increasing your general skill set (eg learning quickly, communication skills and teamwork). Since sports science and related areas are involved in people-centred professions, work experience in a setting where you're dealing with a variety of individuals could help you to find out early on whether a career in this area is really for you.

WHAT WORK EXPERIENCE COUNTS

If you are looking to study a specific vocational course, such as podiatry or physiotherapy, try to get experience in a relevant setting – eg observing a podiatrist or physiotherapist at work in a hospital or private clinic. If you're hoping to do a sports science degree, get in touch with leisure centres, sports and other health charities, the relevant departments in city and county councils and schools to see if there are any opportunities where you could get involved. Paid and voluntary work are equally useful. For potential sports scientists, it goes without saying that participation in sports will be looked for, so make the most of any activities you enjoy, from dancing and darts to swimming and shot-put.

Remember that regular experience, paid or voluntary, even if only for two or three hours a week, over a longer period of time will be more beneficial than a concentrated stint of one week in the holidays – and it shows commitment, too.

If you only have non-sports science or physiotherapy work experience, it will still be useful to include in your personal statement. The trick is to pull out the personal and professional skills you developed that are relevant to the work or skills required in art and design – for example interpersonal skills, working in teams, or coaching skills.

WHERE TO LOOK

You'll need to be proactive; contact your local NHS trust, private clinics, schools, leisure centres and so on, explain what you want to study and ask if there is any way you could come in and help or observe, in any capacity, for a few days or over a longer period of time. For would be sports and exercise scientists, contact junior sports clubs and see if you can get involved. Use your contacts; do you or does anyone in your family or your friends' families know someone who works in sports science or physiotherapy and could help you out?

Also, find out about work experience routes for the dedicated A level student, including taster days and introductory courses offered by universities and colleges.

HOW TO MAKE THE MOST OF IT

Wherever you find yourself, here are a few tips to help you make the most of your work experience:
- Work hard and do what's asked of you willingly
- Ask for feedback on how you're doing – it shows your enthusiasm and helps you develop your skills
- Write down everything you have done and what you learned. This will help you write your personal statement and give you valuable real examples to use at interview
- Make yourself useful – offer to help out.

Offers

3

Step 3 – Offers

Once we have sent your application to your chosen universities and colleges, they will each consider it independently and tell us if they can offer you a place. Some universities and colleges will take longer to make decisions than others. You may be asked to attend an interview, sit an additional test or provide a piece of work, such as an essay, before a decision can be made.

INTERVIEWS

Many universities (particularly the more popular ones, running competitive courses) use interviews as part of their selection process. Universities will want to find out why you want to study your chosen course at their institution, and they want to judge whether the course is suitable for you and your future career plans. Interviews also give you an opportunity to visit the university and ask any questions you may have about the course or their institution.

If you are called for interview, the key areas they are likely to cover will be:

- evidence of your academic ability
- your capacity to study hard
- your commitment to a career in sports science or physiotherapy, best shown by work experience
- your logic and reasoning ability.

A lot of the interview will be based on information on your application, especially your personal statement. See pages 92 and 93 for tips about the personal statement.

Whenever a university or college makes a decision about your application, we record it and let you know. You can check the progress of your application using Track at **www.ucas.com**. This is our secure online service which gives you access to your application, using the same username and password you used when you applied. You use it to find out if you have been invited for an interview or need to provide an additional piece of work, and you can check to see if you have received any offers. Whenever there is any change in your application status, we email you to advise you to check Track.

TYPES OF OFFER

Universities can make two types of offer: conditional or unconditional.

Conditional offer

A conditional offer means the university or college offer you a place if you meet certain conditions – usually based on exam results. The conditions may be based on Tariff points (for example, 300 points from three A levels), or specify certain grades in named subjects (for example, A in sports science, B in biology, C in physics).

Unconditional offer

If you've met all the academic requirements for the course and the university or college wants to accept you, they will make you an unconditional offer. If you accept this you'll have a definite place.

However, for both types of offer, there might be other requirements, such as medical or financial conditions, that you need to meet before you can start your course.

REPLYING TO OFFERS

When you have received decisions for all your choices, you must decide which offers you want to accept. You will be given a deadline in Track by which you have to make your replies. Before replying, get advice from family, friends or advisers, but remember that you're the one taking the course so it's your decision.

Firm acceptance

- Your firm acceptance is your first choice – this is your preferred choice out of all the offers you have received. You can only have one firm acceptance.
- If you accept an unconditional offer, you are entering a contract that you will attend the course, so you must decline any other offers.
- If you accept a conditional offer, you are agreeing that you will attend the course at that university or college if you meet the conditions of the offer. You can accept another offer as an insurance choice.

Insurance acceptance

- If your firm acceptance is a conditional offer, you can accept another offer as an insurance choice. Your insurance choice can be conditional or unconditional and acts as a back-up, so if you don't meet the conditions for your firm choice but meet the conditions for your insurance, you will be committed to the insurance choice. You can only have one insurance choice.
- The conditions for your insurance choice would usually be lower than your firm choice.
- You don't have to accept an insurance choice if you don't want one, but if you do you need to be certain that it is an offer you would accept.

For more information watch our video guides *How to use Track*, *Making sense of your offers*, and *How to reply to your offers* at **www.ucas.tv**.

WHAT IF YOU HAVE NO OFFERS?

If you have used all five choices on your application and either received no offers, or decided to turn down any offers you have received, you may be eligible to apply for another choice through Extra. Find out more about Extra on page 98.

If you are not eligible for Extra, in the summer you can contact universities and colleges with vacancies in Clearing. See page 112 for more information.

Save with UCAS Card

If you're in Year 12, S5 or equivalent and thinking about higher education, sign up for the **FREE** UCAS Card to receive all these benefits:

- information about courses and unis
- expert advice from UCAS
- exclusive discounts for card holders

UCAS

Register today at
www.ucas.com/ucascard

find us on
Facebook

> Offers
>
> 3

Extra

Extra allows you to make additional choices, one at a time, without having to wait for Clearing in July. It is completely optional and free, and is designed to encourage you to continue researching and choosing courses if you are holding no offers. You can search for courses available through Extra on Course Finder, at **www.ucas.com**. The Extra service is available to eligible applicants from 25 February to early July 2013 through Track at **www.ucas.com**.

WHO IS ELIGIBLE?

You will be eligible for Extra if you have already made five choices and:

- you have had unsuccessful or withdrawal decisions from all five of your choices, or
- you have cancelled your outstanding choices and hold no offers, or
- you have received decisions from all five choices and have declined all offers made to you.

HOW DOES IT WORK?

We contact you and explain what to do if you are eligible for Extra. If you are eligible a special Extra button will be available on your Track screen. If you want to use Extra you should:

- tick the 'Available in extra' box in the study options section when looking for courses on Course Finder
- choose a course that you would like to apply for and enter the details on your Track screen.

When you have chosen a course the university or college will be able to view your application and consider you for its course.

WHAT HAPPENS NEXT?

We give the universities and colleges a maximum of 21 days to consider your Extra application. During this time, you cannot be considered by another university or college. If you have not heard after 21 days you can apply to a different university or college if you wish, but it is a good idea to ring the one currently considering you before doing so. If you are made an offer, you can choose whether or not to accept it.

If you accept any offer, conditional or unconditional, you will not be able to take any further part in Extra.

If you are currently studying for examinations, any offer that you receive is likely to be an offer conditional on exam grades. If you already have your examination results, it is possible that a university or college may make an unconditional offer. If you accept an unconditional offer, you will be placed. If you decide to decline the offer or the university or college decides they cannot make you an offer, you will be given another opportunity to use Extra, time permitting. Your Extra button on Track will be reactivated.

Once you have accepted an offer in Extra, you are committed to it in the same way as you would be with an offer through the main UCAS system. Conditional offers made through Extra will be treated in the same way as other conditional offers, when your examination results become available.

If your results do not meet the conditions and the university or college decides that they cannot confirm your Extra offer, you will automatically become eligible for Clearing if it is too late for you to be considered by another university or college in Extra.

If you are unsuccessful, decline an offer, or do not receive an offer, or 21 days have elapsed since choosing a course through Extra, you can use Extra to apply for another course, time permitting.

ADVICE

Do the same careful research and seek guidance on your Extra choice of university or college and course as you did for your initial choices. If you applied to high-demand courses and institutions in your original application and were unsuccessful, you could consider related or alternative subjects or perhaps apply for the subject you want in combination with another. Your teachers or careers advisers or the universities and colleges themselves can provide useful guidance. Course Finder at **www.ucas.com/coursefinder** is another important source of information. Be flexible, that is the key to success. But you are the only one who knows how flexible you are prepared to be. Remember that even if you decide to take a degree course other than sports science or physiotherapy, you may be able to take an alternative route into these professions.

Visit **www.ucas.tv** to watch the video guide on how to use Extra.

Offers

3

The Tariff

Finding out what qualifications are needed for different higher education courses can be very confusing.

The UCAS Tariff is the system for allocating points to qualifications used for entry to higher education. Universities and colleges can use the UCAS Tariff to make comparisons between applicants with different qualifications. Tariff points are often used in entry requirements, although other factors are often taken into account. Information on Course Finder at **www.ucas.com** provides a fuller picture of what admissions tutors are seeking.

The tables on the following pages show the qualifications covered by the UCAS Tariff. There may have been changes to these tables since this book was printed. You should visit **www.ucas.com** to view the most up-to-date tables.

FURTHER INFORMATION?

Although Tariff points can be accumulated in a variety of ways, not all of these will necessarily be acceptable for entry to a particular higher education course. The achievement of a points score therefore does not give an automatic entitlement to entry, and many other factors are taken into account in the admissions process.

Course Finder facility at **www.ucas.com** is the best source of reference to find out what qualifications are acceptable for entry to specific courses. Updates to the Tariff, including details on how new qualifications are added, can be found at **www.ucas.com/students/ucas_tariff/**.

HOW DOES THE TARIFF WORK?

- Students can collect Tariff points from a range of different qualifications, eg GCE A level with BTEC Nationals.
- There is no ceiling to the number of points that can be accumulated.
- There is no double counting. Certain qualifications within the Tariff build on qualifications in the same subject. In these cases only the qualification with the higher Tariff score will be counted. This principle applies to:
    - GCE Advanced Subsidiary level and GCE Advanced level
    - Scottish Highers and Advanced Highers
    - Speech, drama and music awards at grades 6, 7 and 8.
- Tariff points for the Advanced Diploma come from the Progression Diploma score plus the relevant Additional and Specialist Learning (ASL) Tariff points. Please see the appropriate qualification in the Tariff tables to calculate the ASL score.
- The Extended Project Tariff points are included within the Tariff points for Progression and Advanced Diplomas. Extended Project points represented in the Tariff only count when the qualification is taken outside of these Diplomas.
- Where the Tariff tables refer to specific awarding organisations, only qualifications from these awarding organisations attract Tariff points. Qualifications with a similar title, but from a different qualification awarding organisation do not attract Tariff points.

HOW DO UNIVERSITIES AND COLLEGES USE THE TARIFF?

The Tariff provides a facility to help universities and colleges when expressing entrance requirements and when making conditional offers. Entry requirements and conditional offers expressed as Tariff points will often require a minimum level of achievement in a specified subject (for example, '300 points to include grade A at A level chemistry', or '260 points including SQA Higher grade B in mathematics').

Use of the Tariff may also vary from department to department at any one institution, and may in some cases be dependent on the programme being offered.

In July 2010, UCAS announced plans to review the qualifications information provided to universities and colleges. You can read more about the review at **www.ucas.com/qireview**.

WHAT QUALIFICATIONS ARE INCLUDED IN THE TARIFF?

The following qualifications are included in the UCAS Tariff. See the number on the qualification title to find the relevant section of the Tariff table.

1   AAT NVQ Level 3 in Accounting
2   AAT Level 3 Diploma in Accounting (QCF)
3   Advanced Diploma
4   Advanced Extension Awards
5   Advanced Placement Programme (US and Canada)
6   Arts Award (Gold)
7   ASDAN Community Volunteering qualification
8   Asset Languages Advanced Stage
9   British Horse Society (Stage 3 Horse Knowledge & Care, Stage 3 Riding and Preliminary Teacher's Certificate)
10 BTEC Awards (NQF)
11 BTEC Certificates and Extended Certificates (NQF)
12 BTEC Diplomas (NQF)
13 BTEC National in Early Years (NQF)
14 BTEC Nationals (NQF)
15 BTEC QCF Qualifications (Suite known as Nationals)
16 BTEC Specialist Qualifications (QCF)
17 CACHE Award, Certificate and Diploma in Child Care and Education
18 CACHE Level 3 Extended Diploma for the Children and Young People's Workforce (QCF)
19 Cambridge ESOL Examinations
20 Cambridge Pre-U
21 Certificate of Personal Effectiveness (COPE)
22 CISI Introduction to Securities and Investment
23 City & Guilds Land Based Services Level 3 Qualifications
24 Graded Dance and Vocational Graded Dance
25 Diploma in Fashion Retail
26 Diploma in Foundation Studies (Art & Design; Art, Design & Media)
27 EDI Level 3 Certificate in Accounting, Certificate in Accounting (IAS)
28 Essential Skills (Northern Ireland)
29 Essential Skills Wales
30 Extended Project (stand alone)
31 Free-standing Mathematics
32 Functional skills
33 GCE (AS, AS Double Award, A level, A level Double Award and A level (with additional AS))
34 Hong Kong Diploma of Secondary Education (from 2012 entry onwards)
35 ifs School of Finance (Certificate and Diploma in Financial Studies)
36 iMedia (OCR level Certificate/Diploma for iMedia Professionals)
37 International Baccalaureate (IB) Diploma
38 International Baccalaureate (IB) Certificate
39 Irish Leaving Certificate (Higher and Ordinary levels)
40 IT Professionals (iPRO) (Certificate and Diploma)
41 Key Skills (Levels 2, 3 and 4)
42 Music examinations (grades 6, 7 and 8)
43 OCR Level 3 Certificate in Mathematics for Engineering
44 OCR Level 3 Certificate for Young Enterprise
45 OCR Nationals (National Certificate, National Diploma and National Extended Diploma)
46 Principal Learning Wales
47 Progression Diploma
48 Rockschool Music Practitioners Qualifications
49 Scottish Qualifications
50 Speech and Drama examinations (grades 6, 7 and 8 and Performance Studies)
51 Sports Leaders UK
52 Welsh Baccalaureate Advanced Diploma (Core)

Updates on the Tariff, including details on the incorporation of any new qualifications, are posted on **www.ucas.com**.

UCAS TARIFF TABLES

1

AAT NVQ LEVEL 3 IN ACCOUNTING

GRADE	TARIFF POINTS
PASS	160

2

AAT LEVEL 3 DIPLOMA IN ACCOUNTING

GRADE	TARIFF POINTS
PASS	160

3

ADVANCED DIPLOMA

Advanced Diploma = Progression Diploma plus Additional & Specialist Learning (ASL). Please see the appropriate qualification to calculate the ASL score. Please see the Progression Diploma (Table 47) for Tariff scores

4

ADVANCED EXTENSION AWARDS

GRADE	TARIFF POINTS
DISTINCTION	40
MERIT	20

Points for Advanced Extension Awards are over and above those gained from the A level grade

5

ADVANCED PLACEMENT PROGRAMME (US & CANADA)

GRADE	TARIFF POINTS
Group A	
5	120
4	90
3	60
Group B	
5	50
4	35
3	20

Details of the subjects covered by each group can be found at www.ucas.com/students/ ucas_tariff/tarifftables

6

ARTS AWARD (GOLD)

GRADE	TARIFF POINTS
PASS	35

7

ASDAN COMMUNITY VOLUNTEERING QUALIFICATION

GRADE	TARIFF POINTS
CERTIFICATE	50
AWARD	30

8

ASSET LANGUAGES ADVANCED STAGE

GRADE	TARIFF POINTS	GRADE	TARIFF POINTS
Speaking		Listening	
GRADE 12	28	GRADE 12	25
GRADE 11	20	GRADE 11	18
GRADE 10	12	GRADE 10	11
Reading		Writing	
GRADE 12	25	GRADE 12	25
GRADE 11	18	GRADE 11	18
GRADE 10	11	GRADE 10	11

9

BRITISH HORSE SOCIETY

GRADE	TARIFF POINTS
Stage 3 Horse Knowledge & Care	
PASS	35
Stage 3 Riding	
PASS	35
Preliminary Teacher's Certificate	
PASS	35

Awarded by Equestrian Qualifications (GB) Ltd (EQL)

10

BTEC AWARDS (NQF) (EXCLUDING BTEC NATIONAL QUALIFICATIONS)

GRADE	TARIFF POINTS		
	Group A	Group B	Group C
DISTINCTION	20	30	40
MERIT	13	20	26
PASS	7	10	13

Details of the subjects covered by each group can be found at www.ucas.com/students/ ucas_tariff/tarifftables

11

BTEC CERTIFICATES AND EXTENDED CERTIFICATES (NQF) (EXCLUDING BTEC NATIONAL QUALIFICATIONS)

GRADE	TARIFF POINTS				
	Group A	Group B	Group C	Group D	Extended Certificates
DISTINCTION	40	60	80	100	60
MERIT	26	40	52	65	40
PASS	13	20	26	35	20

Details of the subjects covered by each group can be found at www.ucas.com/students/ ucas_tariff/tarifftables

12

BTEC DIPLOMAS (NQF) (EXCLUDING BTEC NATIONAL QUALIFICATIONS)

GRADE	TARIFF POINTS		
	Group A	Group B	Group C
DISTINCTION	80	100	120
MERIT	52	65	80
PASS	26	35	40

Details of the subjects covered by each group can be found at www.ucas.com/students/ucas_tariff/ tarifftables

UCAS TARIFF TABLES

13

BTEC NATIONAL IN EARLY YEARS (NQF)					
GRADE	TARIFF POINTS	GRADE	TARIFF POINTS	GRADE	TARIFF POINTS
Theory				Practical	
Diploma		Certificate		D	120
DDD	320	DD	200	M	80
DDM	280	DM	160	P	40
DMM	240	MM	120		
MMM	220	MP	80		
MMP	160	PP	40		
MPP	120				
PPP	80				

Points apply to the following qualifications only: BTEC National Diploma in Early Years (100/1279/5); BTEC National Certificate in Early Years (100/1280/1)

14

BTEC NATIONALS (NQF)					
GRADE	TARIFF POINTS	GRADE	TARIFF POINTS	GRADE	TARIFF POINTS
Diploma		Certificate		Award	
DDD	360	DD	240	D	120
DDM	320	DM	200	M	80
DMM	280	MM	160	P	40
MMM	240	MP	120		
MMP	200	PP	80		
MPP	160				
PPP	120				

15

BTEC QUALIFICATIONS (QCF) (SUITE OF QUALIFICATIONS KNOWN AS NATIONALS)					
EXTENDED DIPLOMA	DIPLOMA	90 CREDIT DIPLOMA	SUBSIDIARY DIPLOMA	CERTIFICATE	TARIFF POINTS
D*D*D*					420
D*D*D					400
D*DD					380
DDD					360
DDM					320
DMM	D*D*				280
	D*D				260
MMM	DD				240
		D*D*			210
MMP	DM	D*D			200
		DD			180
MPP	MM	DM			160
			D*		140
PPP	MP	MM	D		120
		MP			100
	PP		M		80
			D*		70
		PP		D	60
			P	M	40
				P	20

16

BTEC SPECIALIST (QCF)			
GRADE	TARIFF POINTS		
	Diploma	Certificate	Award
DISTINCTION	120	60	20
MERIT	80	40	13
PASS	40	20	7

UCAS TARIFF TABLES

17

CACHE LEVEL 3 AWARD, CERTIFICATE AND DIPLOMA IN CHILD CARE & EDUCATION

AWARD		CERTIFICATE		DIPLOMA	
GRADE	TARIFF POINTS	GRADE	TARIFF POINTS	GRADE	TARIFF POINTS
A	30	A	110	A	360
B	25	B	90	B	300
C	20	C	70	C	240
D	15	D	55	D	180
E	10	E	35	E	120

18

CACHE LEVEL 3 EXTENDED DIPLOMA FOR THE CHILDREN AND YOUNG PEOPLE'S WORKFORCE (QCF)

GRADE	TARIFF POINTS
A*	420
A	340
B	290
C	240
D	140
E	80

19

CAMBRIDGE ESOL EXAMINATIONS

GRADE	TARIFF POINTS
Certificate of Proficiency in English	
A	140
B	110
C	70
Certificate in Advanced English	
A	70

20

CAMBRIDGE PRE-U

GRADE	TARIFF POINTS	GRADE	TARIFF POINTS	GRADE	TARIFF POINTS
Principal Subject		Global Perspectives and Research		Short Course	
D1	TBC	D1	TBC	D1	TBC
D2	145	D2	140	D2	TBC
D3	130	D3	126	D3	60
M1	115	M1	112	M1	53
M2	101	M2	98	M2	46
M3	87	M3	84	M3	39
P1	73	P1	70	P1	32
P2	59	P2	56	P2	26
P3	46	P3	42	P3	20

21

CERTIFICATE OF PERSONAL EFFECTIVENESS (COPE)

GRADE	TARIFF POINTS
PASS	70

Points are awarded for the Certificate of Personal Effectiveness (CoPE) awarded by ASDAN and CCEA

22

CISI INTRODUCTION TO SECURITIES AND INVESTMENT

GRADE	TARIFF POINTS
PASS WITH DISTINCTION	60
PASS WITH MERIT	40
PASS	20

23

CITY AND GUILDS LAND BASED SERVICES LEVEL 3 QUALIFICATIONS

GRADE	TARIFF POINTS			
	EXTENDED DIPLOMA	DIPLOMA	SUBSIDIARY DIPLOMA	CERTIFICATE
DISTINCTION*	420	280	140	70
DISTINCTION	360	240	120	60
MERIT	240	160	80	40
PASS	120	80	40	20

24

GRADED DANCE AND VOCATIONAL GRADED DANCE

GRADE	TARIFF POINTS	GRADE	TARIFF POINTS	GRADE	TARIFF POINTS
Graded Dance					
Grade 8		Grade 7		Grade 6	
DISTINCTION	65	DISTINCTION	55	DISTINCTION	40
MERIT	55	MERIT	45	MERIT	35
PASS	45	PASS	35	PASS	30
Vocational Graded Dance					
Advanced Foundation		Intermediate			
DISTINCTION	70	DISTINCTION	65		
MERIT	55	MERIT	50		
PASS	45	PASS	40		

25

DIPLOMA IN FASHION RETAIL

GRADE	TARIFF POINTS
DISTINCTION	160
MERIT	120
PASS	80

Applies to the NQF and QCF versions of the qualifications awarded by ABC Awards

UCAS TARIFF TABLES

26

DIPLOMA IN FOUNDATION STUDIES (ART & DESIGN AND ART, DESIGN & MEDIA)	
GRADE	TARIFF POINTS
DISTINCTION	285
MERIT	225
PASS	165

Awarded by ABC, Edexcel, UAL and WJEC

27

EDI LEVEL 3 CERTIFICATE IN ACCOUNTING, CERTIFICATE IN ACCOUNTING (IAS)	
GRADE	TARIFF POINTS
DISTINCTION	120
MERIT	90
PASS	70

28

ESSENTIAL SKILLS (NORTHERN IRELAND)	
GRADE	TARIFF POINTS
LEVEL 2	10

Only allocated at level 2 if studied as part of a wider composite qualification such as 14-19 Diploma or Welsh Baccalaureate

29

ESSENTIAL SKILLS WALES	
GRADE	TARIFF POINTS
LEVEL 4	30
LEVEL 3	20
LEVEL 2	10

Only allocated at level 2 if studied as part of a wider composite qualification such as 14-19 Diploma or Welsh Baccalaureate

30

EXTENDED PROJECT (STAND ALONE)	
GRADE	TARIFF POINTS
A*	70
A	60
B	50
C	40
D	30
E	20

Points for the Extended Project cannot be counted if taken as part of Progression/Advanced Diploma

31

FREE-STANDING MATHEMATICS	
GRADE	TARIFF POINTS
A	20
B	17
C	13
D	10
E	7

Covers free-standing Mathematics - Additional Maths, Using and Applying Statistics, Working with Algebraic and Graphical Techniques, Modelling with Calculus

32

FUNCTIONAL SKILLS	
GRADE	TARIFF POINTS
LEVEL 2	10

Only allocated if studied as part of a wider composite qualification such as 14-19 Diploma or Welsh Baccalaureate

33

GCE AND VCE									
GRADE	TARIFF POINTS	GRADE	TARIFF POINTS	GRADE	TARIFF POINTS	GRADE	TARIFF POINTS	GRADE	TARIFF POINTS
GCE & AVCE Double Award		GCE A level with additional AS (9 units)		GCE A level & AVCE		GCE AS Double Award		GCE AS & AS VCE	
A*A*	280	A*A	200	A*	140	AA	120	A	60
A*A	260	AA	180	A	120	AB	110	B	50
AA	240	AB	170	B	100	BB	100	C	40
AB	220	BB	150	C	80	BC	90	D	30
BB	200	BC	140	D	60	CC	80	E	20
BC	180	CC	120	E	40	CD	70		
CC	160	CD	110			DD	60		
CD	140	DD	90			DE	50		
DD	120	DE	80			EE	40		
DE	100	EE	60						
EE	80								

34

HONG KONG DIPLOMA OF SECONDARY EDUCATION					
GRADE	TARIFF POINTS	GRADE	TARIFF POINTS	GRADE	TARIFF POINTS
All subjects except mathematics		Mathematics compulsory component		Mathematics optional components	
5**	No value	5**	No value	5**	No value
5*	130	5*	60	5*	70
5	120	5	45	5	60
4	80	4	35	4	50
3	40	3	25	3	40

No value for 5** pending receipt of candidate evidence (post 2012)

UCAS TARIFF TABLES

35

IFS SCHOOL OF FINANCE (NQF & QCF)			
GRADE	TARIFF POINTS	GRADE	TARIFF POINTS
Certificate in Financial Studies (CeFS)		Diploma in Financial Studies (DipFS)	
A	60	A	120
B	50	B	100
C	40	C	80
D	30	D	60
E	20	E	40

Applicants with the ifs Diploma cannot also count points allocated to the ifs Certificate. Completion of both qualifications will result in a maximum of 120 UCAS Tariff points

36

LEVEL 3 CERTIFICATE / DIPLOMA FOR iMEDIA USERS (iMEDIA)	
GRADE	TARIFF POINTS
DIPLOMA	66
CERTIFICATE	40

Awarded by OCR

37

INTERNATIONAL BACCALAUREATE (IB) DIPLOMA			
GRADE	TARIFF POINTS	GRADE	TARIFF POINTS
45	720	34	479
44	698	33	457
43	676	32	435
42	654	31	413
41	632	30	392
40	611	29	370
39	589	28	348
38	567	27	326
37	545	26	304
36	523	25	282
35	501	24	260

38

INTERNATIONAL BACCALAUREATE (IB) CERTIFICATE					
GRADE	TARIFF POINTS	GRADE	TARIFF POINTS	GRADE	TARIFF POINTS
Higher Level		Standard Level		Core	
7	130	7	70	3	120
6	110	6	59	2	80
5	80	5	43	1	40
4	50	4	27	0	10
3	20	3	11		

39

IRISH LEAVING CERTIFICATE			
GRADE	TARIFF POINTS	GRADE	TARIFF POINTS
Higher		Ordinary	
A1	90	A1	39
A2	77	A2	26
B1	71	B1	20
B2	64	B2	14
B3	58	B3	7
C1	52		
C2	45		
C3	39		
D1	33		
D2	26		
D3	20		

40

IT PROFESSIONALS (iPRO)	
GRADE	TARIFF POINTS
DIPLOMA	100
CERTIFICATE	80

Awarded by OCR

41

KEY SKILLS	
GRADE	TARIFF POINTS
LEVEL 4	30
LEVEL 3	20
LEVEL 2	10

Only allocated at level 2 if studied as part of a wider composite qualification such as 14-19 Diploma or Welsh Baccalaureate

UCAS TARIFF TABLES

42

MUSIC EXAMINATIONS					
GRADE	TARIFF POINTS	GRADE	TARIFF POINTS	GRADE	TARIFF POINTS
Practical					
Grade 8		Grade 7		Grade 6	
DISTINCTION	75	DISTINCTION	60	DISTINCTION	45
MERIT	70	MERIT	55	MERIT	40
PASS	55	PASS	40	PASS	25
Theory					
Grade 8		Grade 7		Grade 6	
DISTINCTION	30	DISTINCTION	20	DISTINCTION	15
MERIT	25	MERIT	15	MERIT	10
PASS	20	PASS	10	PASS	5

Points shown are for the ABRSM, LCMM/University of West London, Rockschool and Trinity Guildhall/Trinity College London Advanced Level music examinations

43

OCR LEVEL 3 CERTIFICATE IN MATHEMATICS FOR ENGINEERING	
GRADE	TARIFF POINTS
A*	TBC
A	90
B	75
C	60
D	45
E	30

44

OCR LEVEL 3 CERTIFICATE FOR YOUNG ENTERPRISE	
GRADE	TARIFF POINTS
DISTINCTION	40
MERIT	30
PASS	20

45

OCR NATIONALS					
GRADE	TARIFF POINTS	GRADE	TARIFF POINTS	GRADE	TARIFF POINTS
National Extended Diploma		National Diploma		National Certificate	
D1	360	D	240	D	120
D2/M1	320	M1	200	M	80
M2	280	M2/P1	160	P	40
M3	240	P2	120		
P1	200	P3	80		
P2	160				
P3	120				

46

PRINCIPAL LEARNING WALES	
GRADE	TARIFF POINTS
A*	210
A	180
B	150
C	120
D	90
E	60

47

PROGRESSION DIPLOMA	
GRADE	TARIFF POINTS
A*	350
A	300
B	250
C	200
D	150
E	100

Advanced Diploma = Progression Diploma plus Additional & Specialist Learning (ASL). Please see the appropriate qualification to calculate the ASL score

48

GRADE	ROCKSCHOOL MUSIC PRACTITIONERS QUALIFICATIONS				
	TARIFF POINTS				
	Extended Diploma	Diploma	Subsidiary Diploma	Extended Certificate	Certificate
DISTINCTION	240	180	120	60	30
MERIT	160	120	80	40	20
PASS	80	60	40	20	10

49

SCOTTISH QUALIFICATIONS							
GRADE	TARIFF POINTS	GRADE	TARIFF POINTS	GRADE	TARIFF POINTS	GROUP	TARIFF POINTS
Advanced Higher		Higher		Scottish Interdisciplinary Project		Scottish National Certificates	
A	130	A	80	A	65	C	125
B	110	B	65	B	55	B	100
C	90	C	50	C	45	A	75
D	72	D	36				
Ungraded Higher		NPA PC Passport					
PASS	45	PASS	45				
		Core Skills					
		HIGHER	20				

Details of the subjects covered by each Scottish National Certificate can be found at www.ucas.com/students/ucas_tariff/tarifftables

50

SPEECH AND DRAMA EXAMINATIONS							
GRADE	TARIFF POINTS	GRADE	TARIFF POINTS	GRADE	TARIFF POINTS	GRADE	TARIFF POINTS
PCertLAM		Grade 8		Grade 7		Grade 6	
DISTINCTION	90	DISTINCTION	65	DISTINCTION	55	DISTINCTION	40
MERIT	80	MERIT	60	MERIT	50	MERIT	35
PASS	60	PASS	45	PASS	35	PASS	20

Details of the Speech and Drama Qualifications covered by the Tariff can be found at www.ucas.com/students/ucas_tariff/tarifftables

51

SPORTS LEADERS UK	
GRADE	TARIFF POINTS
PASS	30

These points are awarded to Higher Sports Leader Award and Level 3 Certificate in Higher Sports Leadership (QCF)

52

WELSH BACCALAUREATE ADVANCED DIPLOMA (CORE)	
GRADE	TARIFF POINTS
PASS	120

These points are awarded only when a candidate achieves the Welsh Baccalaureate Advanced Diploma

Results

4

Step 4 – Results

You should arrange your holidays so that you are at home when your exam results are published because, if there are any issues to discuss, admissions tutors will want to speak to you in person.

We receive many exam results direct from the exam boards – check the list at **www.ucas.com**.

If your qualification is listed, we send your results to the universities and colleges that you have accepted as your firm and insurance choices. If your qualification is not listed, you must send your exam results to the universities and colleges where you are holding offers.

After you have received your exam results check Track to find out if you have a place on your chosen course.

If you have met all the conditions for your firm choice, the university or college will confirm that you have a place. Occasionally, they may still confirm you have a place even if you have not quite met all the offer conditions; or they may offer you a place on a similar course.

If you have not met the conditions of your firm choice and the university or college has not confirmed your place, but you have met all the conditions of your insurance offer, your insurance university or college will confirm that you have a place.

When a university or college tells us that you have a place, we send you confirmation by letter.

RE-MARKED EXAMS

If you ask for any of your exams to be re-marked, you must tell the universities and colleges where you're holding offers. If a university or college cannot confirm your place based on the initial results, you should ask them if they would be able to reconsider their decision after the re-mark. They are under no obligation to reconsider their position even if your re-mark results in higher grades. Don't forget that re-marks may also result in lower grades.

The exam boards tell us about any re-marks that result in grade changes. We then send the revised grades to the universities and colleges where you're holding offers. As soon as you know about any grade changes, you should also tell these universities and colleges.

'CASHING IN' A LEVEL RESULTS

If you have taken A levels, your school or college must certificate or 'cash in' all your unit scores before the exam board can award final grades. If when you collect your A level results you have to add up your unit scores to find out your final grades, this means your school or college has not 'cashed in' your results.

We only receive cashed in results from the exam boards, so if your school or college has not cashed in your results, you must ask them to send a 'cash in' request to the exam board. You also need to tell the universities and colleges where you're holding offers that there'll be a delay in receiving your results and call us to find out when your results have been received.

When we receive your 'cashed in' results from the exam board we send them straight away to the universities and colleges where you're holding offers.

WHAT IF YOU DON'T HAVE A PLACE?

If you have not met the conditions of either your firm or insurance choice, and your chosen universities or colleges have not confirmed your place, you are eligible for Clearing. In Clearing you can apply for any courses that still have vacancies (but remember that admissions tutors will still be reading your original personal statement). Clearing operates from mid-July to late September 2013 (page 112).

BETTER RESULTS THAN EXPECTED?

If you obtain exam results that meet and exceed the conditions of the offer for your firm choice, you can for a short period use a process called Adjustment to look for an alternative place, whilst still keeping your original firm choice. See page 113 for information about Adjustment.

Next steps

5

Step 5 – Next steps

You might find yourself with different exam results than you were expecting, or you may change your mind about what you want to do. If so, there may be other options open to you.

CLEARING

Clearing is a service that helps people without a place find suitable course vacancies. It runs from mid-July until the end of September, but most people use it after the exam results are published in August.

You could consider related or alternative subjects or perhaps combining your original choice of subject with another. Your teachers or careers adviser, or the universities and colleges themselves, can provide useful guidance.

Course vacancies are listed at **www.ucas.com** and in the national media following the publication of exam results in August. **Once you have your exam results**, if you're in Clearing you need to look at the vacancy listings and then contact any university or college you are interested in.

Talk to the institutions; don't be afraid to call them. Make sure you have your Personal ID and Clearing Number ready and prepare notes on what you will say to them about:

- why you want to study the course
- why you want to study at their university or college
- any relevant employment or activities you have done that relate to the course
- your grades.

Accepting an offer – you can contact as many universities and colleges as you like through Clearing, and you may informally be offered more than one place. If this happens, you will need to decide which offer you want to accept. If you're offered a place you want to be formally considered for, you enter the course details in Track, and the university or college will then let you know if they're accepting you.

ADJUSTMENT

If you receive better results than expected, and meet and exceed the conditions of your conditional firm choice, you have the opportunity to reconsider what and where you want to study. This process is called Adjustment.

Adjustment runs from A level results day on 15 August 2013 until the end of August. Your individual Adjustment period starts on A level results day or when your conditional firm choice changes to unconditional firm, whichever is the later. You then have a maximum of five calendar days to register and secure an alternative course, if you decide you want to do this. If you want to try to find an alternative course you must register in Track to use Adjustment, so universities and colleges can view your application.

There are no vacancy listings for Adjustment, so you'll need to talk to the institutions. When you contact a university or college make it clear that you are applying through Adjustment, not Clearing. If they want to consider you they will ask for your Personal ID, so they can view your application.

If you don't find an alternative place then you remain accepted at your original firm choice.

Adjustment is entirely optional; remember that nothing really beats the careful research you carried out to find the right courses before you made your UCAS application. Talk to a careers adviser at your school, college or local careers office, as they can help you decide if registering to use Adjustment is right for you.

More information about Adjustment and Clearing is available at **www.ucas.com**. You can also view UCAStv video guides on how to use Adjustment and Clearing at **www.ucas.tv**.

IF YOU ARE STILL WITHOUT A PLACE TO STUDY

If you haven't found a suitable place, or changed your mind about what you want to do, there are lots of other options. Ask for advice from your school, college or careers office. Here are some suggestions you might want to consider:

- studying a part-time course (there's a part-time course search at **www.ucas.com** from July until September)
- studying a foundation degree
- re-sit your exams
- getting some work experience
- studying in another country
- reapplying next year to university or college through UCAS
- taking a gap year
- doing an apprenticeship (you'll find a vacancy search on the National Apprenticeship Service (NAS) website at **www.apprenticeships.org.uk**)
- finding a job
- starting a business.

More advice and links to other organisations can be found on the UCAS website at **www.ucas.com/students/nextsteps/advice**.

6

Starting university
or college

Step 6 – Starting university or college

Congratulations! Now that you have confirmed your place at university or college you will need to finalise your plans on how to get there, where to live and how to finance it. Make lists of things to do with deadlines and start contacting people whose help you call on. Will you travel independently or call on your parents or relatives to help with transport? If you are keeping a car at uni, have you checked out parking facilities and told your insurance company?

Make sure you have everything organised, including travel arrangements, essential documents and paperwork, books and equipment required for the course. The university will send you joining information – contact the Admissions Office or the Students' Union if you have questions about anything to do with starting your course.

Freshers week will help you settle in and make friends, but don't forget you are there to study. You may find the teaching methods rather alien at first, but remember there are plenty of sources of help, including your tutors, other students or student mentors, and the students' union.

Where to live – unless you are planning to live at home, your university or college will usually be able to provide you with guidance on finding somewhere to live. The earlier you contact them the better your chance of finding a suitable range of options, from hall to private landlords. Find out what facilities are available at the different types of accommodation options, and check whether it fits within your budget. Check what you need to bring with you and what is supplied. Don't leave it all to the last minute – especially things like arranging a bank account, checking what proof of identity you might need, gathering together a few essentials like a mug and supplies of coffee, insurance cover, TV licence etc.

Student finance – you will need to budget for living costs, accommodation, travel and books (and tuition fees if you are paying them up front). Learn about budgeting by visiting **www.ucas.com** where you will find further links to useful resources to help you manage your money. Remember that if you do get into financial difficulties the welfare office at the university will help you change tack and manage better in future, but it is always better to live within your means from the outset, and if you need help, find it before the situation gets stressful.

Useful contacts

CONNECTING WITH UCAS

You can follow UCAS on Twitter at **www.twitter.com/ ucas_online**, and ask a question or see what others are asking on Facebook at **www.facebook.com/ ucasonline**. You can also watch videos of UCAS advisers answering frequently asked questions on YouTube at **www.youtube.com/ucasonline**.

There are many UCAStv video guides to help with your journey into higher education, such as *How to choose your courses*, *Attending events*, *Open days* and *How to apply*. These can all be viewed at **www.ucas.tv** or in the relevant section of **www.ucas.com**.

If you need to speak to UCAS, please contact us on 0871 468 0 468 or 0044 871 468 0 468 from outside the UK. Calls from BT landlines within the UK will cost no more than 9p per minute. The cost of calls from mobiles and other networks may vary.

If you have hearing difficulties, you can call the Text Relay service on 18001 0871 468 0 468 (outside the UK 0044 151 494 1260). Calls are charged at normal rates.

CAREERS ADVICE

The Directgov Careers Helpline for Young People is for you if you live in England, are aged 13 to 19 and want advice on getting to where you want to be in life.

Careers advisers can give you information, advice and practical help with all sorts of things, like choosing subjects at school or mapping out your future career options. They can help you with anything that might be affecting you at school, college, work or in your personal or family life.

Contact a careers adviser at **www.direct.gov.uk/en/youngpeople/index.htm**.

Skills Development Scotland provides a starting point for anyone looking for careers information, advice or guidance.
www.myworldofwork.co.uk.

Careers Wales – Wales' national all-age careers guidance service.
www.careerswales.com
or **www.gyrfacymru.com**.

Northern Ireland Careers Service website for the new, all-age careers guidance service in Northern Ireland.
www.nidirect.gov.uk/careers.

If you're not sure what job you want or you need help to decide which course to do, give learndirect a call on 0800 101 901 or visit
www.learndirect.co.uk.

GENERAL HIGHER EDUCATION ADVICE

National Union of Students (NUS) is the national voice of students, helping them to campaign, get cheap student discounts and provide advice on living student life to the full – **www.nus.org.uk**.

STUDENTS WITH DISABILITIES

If you have a disability or specific learning difficulty, you are strongly encouraged to make early direct contact with individual institutions before submitting your application. Most universities and colleges have disability coordinators or advisers. You can find their contact details and further advice on the Disability Rights UK website – **www.disabilityalliance.org**.

There is financial help for students with disabilities, known as Disabled Students' Allowances (DSAs). More information is available on the Directgov website at **www.direct.gov.uk/disabledstudents**.

YEAR OUT

For useful information on taking a year out, see **www.gap-year.com**.

The Year Out Group website is packed with information and guidance for young people and their parents and advisers – **www.yearoutgroup.org**.

Essential reading

UCAS has brought together the best books and resources you need to make the important decisions regarding entry to higher education. With guidance on choosing courses, finding the right institution, information about student finance, admissions tests, gap years and lots more, you can find the most trusted guides at **www.ucasbooks.com**.

The publications listed on the following pages and many others are available through **www.ucasbooks.com** or from UCAS Publication Services unless otherwise stated.

UCAS PUBLICATION SERVICES

UCAS Publication Services
PO Box 130, Cheltenham, Gloucestershire GL52 3ZF

f: 01242 544 806
e: publicationservices@ucas.ac.uk
// **www.ucasbooks.com**

ENTIRE RESEARCH AND APPLICATION PROCESS EXPLAINED

The UCAS Guide to getting into University and College

This guide contains advice and up-to-date information about the entire research and application process, and brings together the expertise of UCAS staff, along with insights and tips from well known universities including Oxford and Cambridge, and students who are involved with or have experienced the process first-hand.

The book clearly sets out the information you need in an easy-to-read format, with myth busters, tips from students, checklists and much more; this book will be a companion for applicants throughout their entire journey into higher education.
Published by UCAS
Price £11.99
Publication date January 2011

NEED HELP COMPLETING YOUR APPLICATION?

How to Complete your UCAS Application 2013
A must for anyone applying through UCAS. Contains advice on the preparation needed, a step-by-step guide to filling out the UCAS application, information on the UCAS process and useful tips for completing the personal statement.
Published by Trotman
Price £12.99
Publication date May 2012

Insider's Guide to Applying to University
Full of honest insights, this is a thorough guide to the application process. It reveals advice from careers advisers and current students, guidance on making sense of university information and choosing courses. Also includes tips for the personal statement, interviews, admissions tests, UCAS Extra and Clearing.
Published by Trotman
Price £12.99
Publication date June 2011

How to Write a Winning UCAS Personal Statement
The personal statement is your chance to stand out from the crowd. Based on information from admissions tutors, this book will help you sell yourself. It includes specific guidance for over 30 popular subjects, common mistakes to avoid, information on what admissions tutors look for, and much more.
Published by Trotman
Price £12.99
Publication date March 2010

CHOOSING COURSES

Progression Series 2013 entry
The 'UCAS guide to getting into...' titles are designed to help you access good quality, useful information on some of the most competitive subject areas. The books cover advice on applying through UCAS, routes to qualifications, course details, job prospects, case studies and career advice.

New for 2013: information on the pros and cons of league tables and how to read them.

The UCAS Guide to getting into...
Art and Design
Economics, Finance and Accountancy
Engineering and Mathematics
Journalism, Broadcasting, Media Production and
  Performing Arts
Law
Medicine, Dentistry and Optometry
Nursing, Healthcare and Social Work
Psychology
Sports Science and Physiotherapy
Teaching and Education
Published by UCAS
Price £15.99 each
Publication date June 2012

UCAS Parent Guide
Free of charge.
Order online at www.ucas.com/parents.
Publication date February 2012

Open Days 2012

Attending open days, taster courses and higher education conventions is an important part of the application process. This publication makes planning attendance at these events quick and easy.

Published annually by UCAS.

Price £3.50

Publication date January 2012

Heap 2013: University Degree Course Offers

An independent, reliable guide to selecting university degree courses in the UK.

The guide lists degree courses available at universities and colleges throughout the UK and the grades, UCAS points or equivalent that you need to achieve to get on to each course listed.

Published by Trotman

Price £32.99

Publication date May 2012

ESSENTIAL READING

Choosing Your Degree Course & University

With so many universities and courses to choose from, it is not an easy decision for students embarking on their journey to higher education. This guide will offer expert guidance on the questions students need to ask when considering the opportunities available.

Published by Trotman

Price £24.99

Publication date April 2012

Degree Course Descriptions

Providing details of the nature of degree courses, the descriptions in this book are written by heads of departments and senior lecturers at major universities. Each description contains an overview of the course area, details of course structures, career opportunities and more.

Published by COA

Price £12.99

Publication date September 2011

CHOOSING WHERE TO STUDY

The Virgin Guide to British Universities

An insider's guide to choosing a university or college. Written by students and using independent statistics, this guide evaluates what you get from a higher education institution.

Published by Virgin

Price £15.99

Publication date May 2011

Times Good University Guide 2013

How do you find the best university for the subject you wish to study? You need a guide that evaluates the quality of what is available, giving facts, figures and comparative assessments of universities. The rankings provide hard data, analysed, interpreted and presented by a team of experts.

Published by Harper Collins

Price £16.99

Publication date June 2012

A Parent's Guide to Graduate Jobs

A must-have guide for any parent who is worried about their child's job prospects when they graduate.

In this guide, the graduate careers guru, Paul Redmond, advises parents how to help their son or daughter:

- increase their employability
- boost their earning potential
- acquire essential work skills
- use their own contacts to get them ahead
- gain the right work experience.

Published by Trotman
Price £12.99
Publication date January 2012

Which Uni?

One person's perfect uni might be hell for someone else. Picking the right one will give you the best chance of future happiness, academic success and brighter job prospects. This guide is packed with tables from a variety of sources, rating universities on everything from the quality of teaching to the make-up of the student population and much more.

Published by Trotman
Price £14.99
Publication date September 2012

Getting into the UK's Best Universities and Courses

This book is for those who set their goals high and dream of studying on a highly regarded course at a good university. It provides information on selecting the best courses for a subject, the application and personal statement, interviews, results day, timescales for applications and much more.

Published by Trotman
Price £12.99
Publication date June 2011

FINANCIAL INFORMATION

Student Finance - e-book

All students need to know about tuition fees, loans, grants, bursaries and much more. Covering all forms of income and expenditure, this comprehensive guide is produced in association with UCAS and offers great value for money.

Published by Constable Robinson
Price £4.99
Publication date May 2012

CAREERS PLANNING

A-Z of Careers and Jobs

It is vital to be well informed about career decisions and this guide will help you make the right choice. It provides full details of the wide range of opportunities on the market, the personal qualities and skills needed for each job, entry qualifications and training, realistic salary expectations and useful contact details.

Published by Kogan Page
Price £16.99
Publication date March 2012

The Careers Directory

An indispensable resource for anyone seeking careers information, covering over 350 careers. It presents up-to-date information in an innovative double-page format. Ideal for students in years 10 to 13 who are considering their futures and for other careers professionals.

Published by COA
Price £14.99
Publication date September 2011

Careers with a Science Degree

Over 100 jobs and areas of work for graduates of biological, chemical and physical sciences are described in this guide.

Whether you have yet to choose your degree subject and want to know where the various choices could lead, or are struggling for ideas about what to do with your science degree, this book will guide and inspire you. The title includes: nature of the work and potential employers, qualifications required for entry, including personal qualities and skills; training routes and opportunities for career development and postgraduate study options.
Published by Lifetime Publishing
Price £12.99
Publication date September 2010

Careers with an Arts and Humanities Degree

Covers careers and graduate opportunities related to these degrees.

The book describes over 100 jobs and areas of work suitable for graduates from a range of disciplines including: English and modern languages, history and geography, music and the fine arts. The guide highlights: graduate opportunities, training routes, postgraduate study options and entry requirements.
Published by Lifetime Publishing
Price £12.99
Publication date September 2010

'Getting into...' guides

Clear and concise guides to help applicants secure places. They include qualifications required, advice on applying, tests, interviews and case studies. The guides give an honest view and discuss current issues and careers.

Getting into Oxford and Cambridge - publication date: April 2011
Getting into Veterinary School - publication date: February 2011
Published by Trotman
Price £12.99 each

DEFERRING ENTRY

Gap Years: The Essential Guide

The essential book for all young people planning a gap year before continuing with their education. This up-to-date guide provides essential information on specialist gap year programmes, as well as the vast range of jobs and voluntary opportunities available to young people around the world.
Published by Crimson Publishing
Price £9.99
Publication date April 2012

Gap Year Guidebook 2012

This thorough and easy-to-use guide contains everything you need to know before taking a gap year. It includes real-life traveller tips, hundreds of contact details, realistic advice on everything from preparing, learning and working abroad, coping with coming home and much more.
Published by John Catt Education
Price £14.99
Publication date November 2011

Summer Jobs Worldwide 2012

This unique and specialist guide contains over 40,000 jobs for all ages. No other book includes such a variety and wealth of summer work opportunities in Britain and aboard. Anything from horse trainer in Iceland, to a guide for nature walks in Peru, to a yoga centre helper in Greece, to an animal keeper for London Zoo, can be found.
Published by Crimson Publishing
Price £14.99
Publication date November 2011

Please note all publications incur a postage and packing charge. All information was correct at the time of printing.

For a full list of publications, please visit **www.ucasbooks.com**.

Courses

Courses

Keen to get started on your sports science and physiotherapy career? This section contains details of the various degree courses available at UK institutions.

EXPLAINING THE LIST OF COURSES

The list of courses has been divided into subject categories (see over for a list of subjects). We list the universities and colleges by their UCAS institution codes. Within each institution, courses are listed first by award type (such as BA, BSc, FdA, HND, MA and many others), then alphabetically by course title.

You might find some courses showing an award type '(Mod)', which indicates a combined degree that might be modular in design. A small number of courses have award type '(FYr)'. This indicates a 12-month foundation course, after which students can choose to apply for a degree course. In either case, you should contact the university or college for further details.

Generally speaking, when a course comprises two or more subjects, the word used to connect the subjects indicates the make-up of the award: 'Subject A and Subject B' is a joint award, where both subjects carry equal weight; 'Subject A with Subject B' is a major/minor award, where Subject A accounts for at least 60% of your study. If the title shows 'Subject A/Subject B', it may indicate that students can decide on the weighting of the subjects at the end of the first year. You should check with the university or college for full details.

Each entry shows the UCAS course code and the duration of the course. Where known, the entry contains details of the minimum qualification requirements for the course, as supplied to UCAS by the universities and colleges. Bear in mind that possessing the minimum qualifications does not guarantee acceptance to the course: there may be far more applicants than places. You may be asked to attend an interview, present a portfolio or sit an admissions test.

Courses with entry requirements that require applicants to disclose information about spent and unspent convictions and may require a Criminal Records Bureau (CRB) check, are marked '**CRB Check:** Required'.

Before applying for any course, you are advised to contact the university or college to check any changes in entry requirements and to see if any new courses have come on stream since the lists were approved for publication. To make this easy, each institution's entry starts with their address, email, phone and fax details, as well as their website address.

LIST OF SUBJECT CATEGORIES

The list of courses in this section has been divided into the following subject categories

SPORTS SCIENCE

A20 THE UNIVERSITY OF ABERDEEN
UNIVERSITY OFFICE
KING'S COLLEGE
ABERDEEN AB24 3FX
t: +44 (0) 1224 273504 f: +44 (0) 1224 272034
e: sras@abdn.ac.uk
// www.abdn.ac.uk/sras

C600 BSc Sports and Exercise Science
Duration: 4FT Hon
Entry Requirements: *GCE:* BBB. *SQAH:* BBBB. *SQAAH:* BCC. *IB:* 28.

C602 MSci Sports and Exercise Science with Industrial Placement
Duration: 5FT Hon
Entry Requirements: *GCE:* ABB. *SQAH:* AABB. *IB:* 32.

A30 UNIVERSITY OF ABERTAY DUNDEE
BELL STREET
DUNDEE DD1 1HG
t: 01382 308080 f: 01382 308081
e: sro@abertay.ac.uk
// www.abertay.ac.uk

CN62 BA Sport and Management
Duration: 4FT Hon   CRB Check: Required
Entry Requirements: *GCE:* DDD. *SQAH:* BBC. *IB:* 26. Interview required.

C600 BSc Sport & Exercise
Duration: 4FT Hon   CRB Check: Required
Entry Requirements: *GCE:* DDD. *SQAH:* ABB. *IB:* 26. Interview required.

CB64 BSc Sport & Exercise Nutrition
Duration: 4FT Hon   CRB Check: Required
Entry Requirements: *GCE:* DDD. *SQAH:* ABB. *IB:* 26. Interview required.

CC68 BSc Sport and Psychology
Duration: 4FT Hon   CRB Check: Required
Entry Requirements: *GCE:* DDD. *SQAH:* BBB. *IB:* 26. Interview required.

A40 ABERYSTWYTH UNIVERSITY
ABERYSTWYTH UNIVERSITY, WELCOME CENTRE
PENGLAIS CAMPUS
ABERYSTWYTH
CEREDIGION SY23 3FB
t: 01970 622021 f: 01970 627410
e: ug-admissions@aber.ac.uk
// www.aber.ac.uk

C600 BSc Sport and Exercise Science
Duration: 3FT Hon
Entry Requirements: *GCE:* 280. *IB:* 28.

A44 ACCRINGTON & ROSSENDALE COLLEGE
BROAD OAK ROAD,
ACCRINGTON,
LANCASHIRE, BB5 2AW.
t: 01254 389933 f: 01254 354001
e: info@accross.ac.uk
// www.accrosshighereducation.co.uk/

C602 FdSc Sports and Exercise Science
Duration: 2FT Fdg
Entry Requirements: Interview required.

A60 ANGLIA RUSKIN UNIVERSITY
BISHOP HALL LANE
CHELMSFORD
ESSEX CM1 1SQ
t: 0845 271 3333 f: 01245 251789
e: answers@anglia.ac.uk
// www.anglia.ac.uk

C600 BSc Sports Science
Duration: 3FT Hon
Entry Requirements: *GCE:* 200. *SQAH:* BCCC. *SQAAH:* CC. *IB:* 24. *OCR ND:* M1 *OCR NED:* P1

CX6C BSc (Hons) Sports Coaching and Physical Education (with Foundation Year)
Duration: 4FT Hon
Entry Requirements: Contact the institution for details.

C601 BSc(Hons) Sports Science (with Foundation Year)
Duration: 4FT Hon
Entry Requirements: Contact the institution for details.

B06 BANGOR UNIVERSITY
BANGOR UNIVERSITY
BANGOR
GWYNEDD LL57 2DG
t: 01248 388484 f: 01248 370451
e: admissions@bangor.ac.uk
// www.bangor.ac.uk

QC56 BA Cymraeg/Physical Education
Duration: 3FT Hon
Entry Requirements: *GCE:* 260-280. *IB:* 28.

CQ65 BA Cymraeg/Sports Science
Duration: 3FT Hon
Entry Requirements: *GCE:* 260-280. *IB:* 28.

CQ63 BA English Language and Physical Education
Duration: 3FT Hon
Entry Requirements: *GCE:* 260. *IB:* 28.

QC36 BA English Language and Sports Science
Duration: 3FT Hon
Entry Requirements: *GCE:* 260-280. *IB:* 28.

CR63 BA Italian/Physical Education (4 years)
Duration: 4FT Hon
Entry Requirements: *GCE:* 260-280. *IB:* 28.

CR6H BA Italian/Sports Science (4 years)
Duration: 4FT Hon
Entry Requirements: *GCE:* 260-280. *IB:* 28.

RC16 BA Physical Education/French (4 years)
Duration: 4FT Hon
Entry Requirements: *GCE:* 260-280. *IB:* 28.

RC26 BA Physical Education/German (4 years)
Duration: 4FT Hon
Entry Requirements: *GCE:* 260-280. *IB:* 28.

QC16 BA Physical Education/Linguistics
Duration: 3FT Hon
Entry Requirements: *GCE:* 260-280. *IB:* 28.

CR64 BA Physical Education/Spanish (4 years)
Duration: 4FT Hon
Entry Requirements: *GCE:* 260-280. *IB:* 28.

CR6K BA Spanish/Sports Science (4 years)
Duration: 4FT Hon
Entry Requirements: *GCE:* 260-280. *IB:* 28.

CR61 BA Sports Science/French (4 years)
Duration: 4FT Hon
Entry Requirements: *GCE:* 260-280. *IB:* 28.

CR62 BA Sports Science/German (4 years)
Duration: 4FT Hon
Entry Requirements: *GCE:* 260-280. *IB:* 28.

CQ61 BA Sports Science/Linguistics
Duration: 3FT Hon
Entry Requirements: *GCE:* 260-280. *IB:* 28.

RC1P BSc Physical Education/French
Duration: 4FT Hon
Entry Requirements: *GCE:* 260-280. *IB:* 28.

RC2P BSc Physical Education/German
Duration: 4FT Hon
Entry Requirements: *GCE:* 260-280. *IB:* 28.

RC3P BSc Physical Education/Italian
Duration: 4FT Hon
Entry Requirements: *GCE:* 260-280. *IB:* 28.

RC4P BSc Physical Education/Spanish
Duration: 4FT Hon
Entry Requirements: *GCE:* 260-280. *IB:* 28.

C602 BSc Sport Science (Outdoor Activities)
Duration: 3FT Hon
Entry Requirements: *GCE:* 260-300. *IB:* 28.

CX6H BSc Sport Science (Physical Education)
Duration: 3FT Hon
Entry Requirements: *GCE:* 260-300. *IB:* 28.

C6CV BSc Sport Science with Psychology
Duration: 3FT Hon
Entry Requirements: *GCE:* 260-300. *IB:* 28.

CQ6M BSc Sport Science/Cymraeg
Duration: 3FT Hon
Entry Requirements: *GCE:* 260-280. *IB:* 28.

CR6C BSc Sport Science/French
Duration: 4FT Hon
Entry Requirements: *GCE:* 260-280. *IB:* 28.

CR6F BSc Sport Science/German
Duration: 4FT Hon
Entry Requirements: *GCE:* 260-280. *IB:* 28.

BC6J BSc Sport Science/Italian
Duration: 4FT Hon
Entry Requirements: *GCE:* 260-280. *IB:* 28.

CQ6C BSc Sport Science/Linguistics
Duration: 3FT Hon
Entry Requirements: *GCE:* 260-280. *IB:* 28.

CR6L BSc Sport Science/Spanish
Duration: 4FT Hon
Entry Requirements: *GCE:* 260-280. *IB:* 28.

C680 BSc Sport and Exercise Psychology
Duration: 3FT Hon
Entry Requirements: Contact the institution for details.

C651 BSc Sport, Health & Physical Education
Duration: 3FT Hon
Entry Requirements: *GCE:* 260-300. *IB:* 28.

CB69 BSc Sport, Health and Exercise Sciences
Duration: 3FT Hon
Entry Requirements: *GCE:* 260-300. *IB:* 28.

C600 BSc Sports Science
Duration: 3FT Hon
Entry Requirements: *GCE:* 260-280. *IB:* 28.

26NC HND Sports Science (Outdoor Recreation)
Duration: 2FT HND
Entry Requirements: *GCE:* 60-100. *IB:* 24.

B16 UNIVERSITY OF BATH
CLAVERTON DOWN
BATH BA2 7AY
t: 01225 383019 f: 01225 386366
e: admissions@bath.ac.uk
// www.bath.ac.uk

BC17 BSc Sport and Exercise Science
Duration: 3FT Hon
Entry Requirements: *GCE:* AAA. *SQAAH:* AAA. *IB:* 36.

BCC7 BSc Sport and Exercise Science (with study abroad/industry/combined)
Duration: 4SW Hon
Entry Requirements: *GCE:* AAA. *SQAAH:* AAA. *IB:* 36.

C600 FdSc Sport (Health & Fitness)
Duration: 2FT Fdg
Entry Requirements: *GCE:* 80.

B22 UNIVERSITY OF BEDFORDSHIRE
PARK SQUARE
LUTON
BEDS LU1 3JU
t: 0844 8482234 f: 01582 489323
e: admissions@beds.ac.uk
// www.beds.ac.uk

CNP2 BA Sport Management
Duration: 3FT Hon
Entry Requirements: *Foundation:* Pass. *GCE:* 200. *SQAH:* BCC. *SQAAH:* BCC. *IB:* 24. *OCR ND:* M1 *OCR NED:* P1

CX69 BA Sport and Community Leadership
Duration: 3FT Hon
Entry Requirements: *GCE:* 200.

C601 BA Sport and Physical Education
Duration: 3FT Hon
Entry Requirements: *GCE:* 240. *IB:* 26. *OCR ND:* D *OCR NED:* M3

CX61 BSc Sport Science and Coaching
Duration: 3FT Hon
Entry Requirements: *GCE:* 200.

C600 BSc Sport and Exercise Science
Duration: 3FT Hon
Entry Requirements: *Foundation:* Pass. *GCE:* 240. *SQAH:* BBBB-BBBC. *SQAAH:* BCC. *IB:* 24. *OCR ND:* D *OCR NED:* M3

C613 BSc Sports Science and Personal Training
Duration: 3FT Hon
Entry Requirements: *GCE:* 200.

B32 THE UNIVERSITY OF BIRMINGHAM
EDGBASTON
BIRMINGHAM B15 2TT
t: 0121 415 8900 f: 0121 414 7159
e: admissions@bham.ac.uk
// www.birmingham.ac.uk

C6L4 BA Sport, Physical Education and Coaching Science
Duration: 3FT Hon   CRB Check: Required
Entry Requirements: *GCE:* ABB. *SQAH:* AABBB. *SQAAH:* AB.

GC17 BSc Mathematics and Sports Science
Duration: 3FT Hon
Entry Requirements: *GCE:* AAA-AAB. *SQAH:* AAAAB-AAABB. *SQAAH:* AA.

CF62 BSc Sports and Materials Science
Duration: 3FT Hon
Entry Requirements: *GCE:* AAB. *SQAH:* AAABB-AABBB. *SQAAH:* AA.

B35 UNIVERSITY COLLEGE BIRMINGHAM
SUMMER ROW
BIRMINGHAM B3 1JB
t: 0121 604 1040 f: 0121 604 1166
e: admissions@ucb.ac.uk
// www.ucb.ac.uk

C600 BSc Sports Therapy
Duration: 3FT Hon   CRB Check: Required
Entry Requirements: *GCE:* 220. *IB:* 24.

C602 FdSc Sports Therapy
Duration: 2FT Fdg   CRB Check: Required
Entry Requirements: *GCE:* 120.

B37 BISHOP BURTON COLLEGE
BISHOP BURTON
BEVERLEY
EAST YORKSHIRE HU17 8QG
t: 01964 553000 f: 01964 553101
e: enquiries@bishopburton.ac.uk
// www.bishopburton.ac.uk

DC46 BSc Equine Sports Coaching
Duration: 1FT Hon
Entry Requirements: Contact the institution for details.

DC4Q BSc Equine Sports Coaching
Duration: 3FT Hon
Entry Requirements: *GCE:* 140. Interview required.

CD6K BSc Equine Sports Performance
Duration: 3FT Hon
Entry Requirements: *GCE:* 140. *IB:* 24. Interview required.

CD6L BSc Equine Sports Performance
Duration: 1FT Hon
Entry Requirements: Contact the institution for details.

CX61 BSc Sport Coaching Development and Fitness
Duration: 3FT Hon
Entry Requirements: *GCE:* 140. Interview required.

DC4P FdSc Equine Sports Coaching
Duration: 2FT Fdg
Entry Requirements: *GCE:* 80-120. Interview required.

DCK6 FdSc Equine Sports Coaching (with foundation year)
Duration: 3FT Fdg
Entry Requirements: Contact the institution for details.

CD64 FdSc Equine Sports Performance
Duration: 2FT Fdg
Entry Requirements: *GCE:* 80. Interview required.

DCL6 FdSc Equine Sports Performance (with foundation year)
Duration: 3FT Fdg
Entry Requirements: Contact the institution for details.

XC16 FdSc Sport Coaching Development and Fitness
Duration: 2FT Fdg
Entry Requirements: *GCE:* 80. Interview required.

B38 BISHOP GROSSETESTE UNIVERSITY COLLEGE LINCOLN
BISHOP GROSSETESTE UNIVERSITY COLLEGE
LINCOLN LN1 3DY
t: 01522 583658 f: 01522 530243
e: admissions@bishopg.ac.uk
// www.bishopg.ac.uk/courses

CX63 BA Education Studies and Sport
Duration: 3FT Hon   CRB Check: Required
Entry Requirements: *GCE:* 220.

X3C6 BA Education Studies with Sport
Duration: 3FT Hon   CRB Check: Required
Entry Requirements: Contact the institution for details.

CC86 BA Psychology and Sport
Duration: 3FT Hon   CRB Check: Required
Entry Requirements: Contact the institution for details.

CG6C BSc Sport and Mathematics
Duration: 3FT Hon   CRB Check: Required
Entry Requirements: Contact the institution for details.

B40 BLACKBURN COLLEGE
FEILDEN STREET
BLACKBURN BB2 1LH
t: 01254 292594 f: 01254 679647
e: he-admissions@blackburn.ac.uk
// www.blackburn.ac.uk

BC96 FdA Health and Personal Training
Duration: 2FT Fdg
Entry Requirements: *GCE:* 80.

CX61 FdA Sports Coaching
Duration: 2FT Fdg
Entry Requirements: *GCE:* 120.

C601 FdA Sports Development
Duration: 2FT Fdg
Entry Requirements: *GCE:* 120.

B41 BLACKPOOL AND THE FYLDE COLLEGE AN ASSOCIATE COLLEGE OF LANCASTER UNIVERSITY
ASHFIELD ROAD
BISPHAM
BLACKPOOL
LANCS FY2 0HB
t: 01253 504346 f: 01253 504198
e: admissions@blackpool.ac.uk
// www.blackpool.ac.uk

C601 BA Sports Studies and Development (Top Up)
Duration: 1FT Hon
Entry Requirements: Contact the institution for details.

XC16 BSc Sports Coaching (Top-Up)
Duration: 1FT Hon
Entry Requirements: Contact the institution for details.

C600 FdA Sports Studies and Development
Duration: 2FT Fdg
Entry Requirements: *GCE:* 80-360.

CX6C FdSc Sports Coaching
Duration: 2FT Fdg
Entry Requirements: *GCE:* 80-360.

B44 UNIVERSITY OF BOLTON
DEANE ROAD
BOLTON BL3 5AB
t: 01204 903903 f: 01204 399074
e: enquiries@bolton.ac.uk
// www.bolton.ac.uk

C601 BA Sport Development
Duration: 3FT Hon
Entry Requirements: *GCE:* 240. Interview required.

C606 BA Sport Development & Coaching
Duration: 3FT Hon   CRB Check: Required
Entry Requirements: *GCE:* 240. Interview required.

C603 BSc Sport & Exercise Science
Duration: 3FT Hon
Entry Requirements: *GCE:* 240. Interview required.

C602 BSc Sports Rehabilitation
Duration: 3FT Hon   CRB Check: Required
Entry Requirements: *GCE:* 240. Interview required.

C600 BSc Sports Science & Coaching
Duration: 3FT Hon   CRB Check: Required
Entry Requirements: *GCE:* 240. Interview required.

C605 FdSc Sports Science & Coaching
Duration: 2FT Fdg   CRB Check: Required
Entry Requirements: Contact the institution for details.

B50 BOURNEMOUTH UNIVERSITY
TALBOT CAMPUS
FERN BARROW
POOLE
DORSET BH12 5BB
t: 01202 524111
// www.bournemouth.ac.uk

CB69 BSc Exercise Science (Health and Rehabilitation)
Duration: 3FT Hon
Entry Requirements: *GCE:* 300. *IB:* 31. *BTEC Dip:* DM. *BTEC ExtDip:* DDM. Interview required.

C600 BSc Sport Development & Coaching Sciences
Duration: 4SW Hon
Entry Requirements: *GCE:* 320. *IB:* 32. *BTEC SubDip:* D. *BTEC Dip:* DD. *BTEC ExtDip:* DDM.

CX61 FdSc Sports Development and Coaching
Duration: 2FT Fdg
Entry Requirements: *GCE:* 120. Interview required.

B60 BRADFORD COLLEGE: AN ASSOCIATE COLLEGE OF LEEDS METROPOLITAN UNIVERSITY
GREAT HORTON ROAD
BRADFORD
WEST YORKSHIRE BD7 1AY
t: 01274 433008 f: 01274 431652
e: heregistry@bradfordcollege.ac.uk
// www.bradfordcollege.ac.uk/ university-centre

CN6F FdSc Health-Related Exercise and Fitness
Duration: 2FT Fdg   CRB Check: Required
Entry Requirements: Interview required.

CX6C FdSc Sports Coaching
Duration: 2FT Fdg   CRB Check: Required
Entry Requirements: Interview required.

B70 BRIDGWATER COLLEGE
BATH ROAD
BRIDGWATER
SOMERSET TA6 4PZ
t: 01278 455464 f: 01278 444363
e: enquiries@bridgwater.ac.uk
// www.bridgwater.ac.uk

106C HND Sport and Exercise Sciences (Sports Science)
Duration: 2FT HND
Entry Requirements: *GCE:* 120. *IB:* 24.

B72 UNIVERSITY OF BRIGHTON
MITHRAS HOUSE 211
LEWES ROAD
BRIGHTON BN2 4AT
t: 01273 644644 f: 01273 642607
e: admissions@brighton.ac.uk
// www.brighton.ac.uk

X1C6 BA Physical Education with QTS (Secondary) (4 years)
Duration: 4FT Hon
Entry Requirements: *GCE:* AAB. *IB:* 36. Interview required.

CXP1 BA Sport Coaching and Development (Top-Up)
Duration: 1FT Hon
Entry Requirements: HND required.

C603 BA Sport Studies
Duration: 3FT Hon
Entry Requirements: *GCE:* BBB. *IB:* 28.

CX6C BSc Sport Coaching
Duration: 3FT Hon
Entry Requirements: *GCE:* ABB. *IB:* 32.

C600 BSc Sport and Exercise Science
Duration: 3FT Hon
Entry Requirements: *GCE:* ABB. *IB:* 32.

C602 BSc Sport and Fitness (Top-Up)
Duration: 1FT Hon
Entry Requirements: HND required.

CJ69 BSc Sports Product Design with Professional Experience
Duration: 4SW Hon
Entry Requirements: *GCE:* BBB. *IB:* 34. Interview required.
Portfolio required.

B79 BRISTOL FILTON COLLEGE
FILTON AVENUE
BRISTOL BS34 7AT
t: 0117 909 2255 f: 0117 931 2233
e: info@filton.ac.uk
// www.filton.ac.uk

006C HND Sport & Exercise Science
Duration: 2FT HND
Entry Requirements: *GCE:* 160. Interview required.

B80 UNIVERSITY OF THE WEST OF ENGLAND, BRISTOL
FRENCHAY CAMPUS
COLDHARBOUR LANE
BRISTOL BS16 1QY
t: +44 (0)117 32 83333 f: +44 (0)117 32 82810
e: admissions@uwe.ac.uk
// www.uwe.ac.uk

NCF6 BA Sports Business Management
Duration: 3FT Hon
Entry Requirements: *GCE:* 280.

DC46 BSc Equestrian Sports Science
Duration: 3FT Hon
Entry Requirements: *GCE:* 280.

C600 BSc Sports Coaching
Duration: 3FT Hon
Entry Requirements: *GCE:* 320.

C603 BSc Sports Studies (Top-up)
Duration: 1FT Hon
Entry Requirements: HND required.

BC96 BSc Sports Therapy and Rehabilitation
Duration: 3FT Hon   CRB Check: Required
Entry Requirements: *GCE:* 340. Interview required.

C608 BSc (Hons) Sports Science
Duration: 3FT/4SW Hon
Entry Requirements: *GCE:* 300.

NC26 FdA Sports Business Management
Duration: 2FT Fdg
Entry Requirements: *GCE:* 160.

C607 FdSc Sport Performance
Duration: 2FT Fdg
Entry Requirements: *GCE:* 160.

C602 FdSc Sports Coaching
Duration: 2FT Fdg
Entry Requirements: *GCE:* 160.

B84 BRUNEL UNIVERSITY
UXBRIDGE
MIDDLESEX UB8 3PH
t: 01895 265265 f: 01895 269790
e: admissions@brunel.ac.uk
// www.brunel.ac.uk

C6N1 BSc Business Studies and Sport Sciences
Duration: 3FT Hon
Entry Requirements: *GCE:* ABB. *SQAAH:* ABB. *IB:* 33. *BTEC Dip:* D*D. *BTEC ExtDip:* D*DD. *OCR ND:* D *OCR NED:* D1

NC1P BSc Business Studies and Sport Sciences (4 year Thick SW)
Duration: 4SW Hon
Entry Requirements: *GCE:* ABB. *SQAAH:* ABB. *IB:* 33. *BTEC Dip:* D*D. *BTEC ExtDip:* D*DD. *OCR ND:* D *OCR NED:* D1

C600 BSc Sport Sciences
Duration: 3FT Hon
Entry Requirements: *GCE:* ABB. *SQAAH:* ABB. *IB:* 33. *BTEC Dip:* DD. *BTEC ExtDip:* D*DD. *OCR ND:* D *OCR NED:* D2

C602 BSc Sport Sciences (4 year Thick SW)
Duration: 4SW Hon
Entry Requirements: *GCE:* ABB. *SQAAH:* ABB. *IB:* 33. *BTEC Dip:* DD. *BTEC ExtDip:* D*DD. *OCR ND:* D *OCR NED:* D2

C603 BSc Sport Sciences (Coaching)
Duration: 3FT Hon
Entry Requirements: *GCE:* ABB. *SQAAH:* ABB. *IB:* 33. *BTEC Dip:* DD. *BTEC ExtDip:* D*DD. *OCR ND:* D *OCR NED:* D2

CX61 BSc Sport Sciences (Coaching) 4 year Thick SW
Duration: 4SW Hon
Entry Requirements: *GCE:* ABB. *SQAAH:* ABB. *IB:* 33. *BTEC Dip:* DD. *BTEC ExtDip:* D*DD. *OCR ND:* D *OCR NED:* D2

C604 BSc Sport Sciences (Human Performance)
Duration: 3FT Hon
Entry Requirements: *GCE:* ABB. *SQAAH:* ABB. *IB:* 33. *BTEC Dip:* DD. *BTEC ExtDip:* D*DD. *OCR ND:* D *OCR NED:* D2

C605 BSc Sport Sciences (Human Performance) 4 year Thick SW
Duration: 4SW Hon
Entry Requirements: *GCE:* ABB. *SQAAH:* ABB. *IB:* 33. *BTEC Dip:* DD. *BTEC ExtDip:* D*DD. *OCR ND:* D *OCR NED:* D2

CN68 BSc Sport Sciences (Management of Sport Development)
Duration: 3FT Hon
Entry Requirements: *GCE:* ABB. *SQAAH:* ABB. *IB:* 33. *BTEC Dip:* DD. *BTEC ExtDip:* D*DD. *OCR ND:* D *OCR NED:* D2

CN6V BSc Sport Sciences (Management of Sport Development) 4 year Thick SW
Duration: 4SW Hon
Entry Requirements: *GCE:* ABB. *SQAAH:* ABB. *IB:* 33. *BTEC Dip:* DD. *BTEC ExtDip:* D*DD. *OCR ND:* D *OCR NED:* D2

CX63 BSc Sport Sciences (Physical Education & Youth Sport)
Duration: 3FT Hon
Entry Requirements: *GCE:* ABB. *SQAAH:* ABB. *IB:* 33. *BTEC Dip:* DD. *BTEC ExtDip:* D*DD. *OCR ND:* D *OCR NED:* D2

CX6H BSc Sport Sciences (Physical Education and Youth Sport) 4 year Thick SW
Duration: 4SW Hon
Entry Requirements: *GCE:* ABB. *SQAAH:* ABB. *IB:* 33. *BTEC Dip:* DD. *BTEC ExtDip:* D*DD. *OCR ND:* D *OCR NED:* D2

B94 BUCKINGHAMSHIRE NEW UNIVERSITY
QUEEN ALEXANDRA ROAD
HIGH WYCOMBE
BUCKINGHAMSHIRE HP11 2JZ
t: 0800 0565 660 f: 01494 605 023
e: admissions@bucks.ac.uk
// bucks.ac.uk

WC56 BA Dance and Fitness
Duration: 3FT Hon
Entry Requirements: *GCE:* 200-240. *IB:* 24. *OCR ND:* M1 *OCR NED:* M3 Interview required.

CX6C BSc Sports Science and Coaching Studies
Duration: 3FT Hon
Entry Requirements: *GCE:* 200-240. *IB:* 24. *OCR ND:* M1 *OCR NED:* M3

CX61 FdSc Sports Coaching and Performance
Duration: 2FT Fdg
Entry Requirements: *GCE:* 100-140. *IB:* 24. *OCR ND:* P2 *OCR NED:* P3 Interview required.

C10 CANTERBURY CHRIST CHURCH UNIVERSITY
NORTH HOLMES ROAD
CANTERBURY
KENT CT1 1QU
t: 01227 782900 f: 01227 782888
e: admissions@canterbury.ac.uk
// www.canterbury.ac.uk

MC96 BA Applied Criminology and Sport & Exercise Science
Duration: 3FT Hon
Entry Requirements: *GCE:* 240. *IB:* 24.

GC56 BA Business Computing and Sport & Exercise Science
Duration: 3FT Hon
Entry Requirements: *GCE:* 240. *IB:* 24.

G5C6 BA Business Computing with Sport & Exercise Science
Duration: 3FT Hon
Entry Requirements: *GCE:* 240. *IB:* 24.

QC36 BA English Language & Communication and Sport & Exercise Science
Duration: 3FT Hon
Entry Requirements: *GCE:* 240. *IB:* 24.

Q3CP BA English Language & Communication with Sport & Exercise Science
Duration: 3FT Hon
Entry Requirements: *GCE:* 240. *IB:* 24.

NC1P BA Entrepreneurship and Sport & Exercise Science
Duration: 3FT Hon
Entry Requirements: *GCE:* 240. *IB:* 24.

N1CQ BA Entrepreneurship with Sport Science
Duration: 3FT Hon
Entry Requirements: *GCE:* 240. *IB:* 24.

GCL6 BA Internet Computing and Sport & Exercise Science
Duration: 3FT Hon
Entry Requirements: *GCE:* 240. *IB:* 24.

G4CQ BA Internet Computing with Sport & Exercise Science
Duration: 3FT Hon
Entry Requirements: *GCE:* 240. *IB:* 24.

XC36 BA Physical Education and Sport & Exercise Science
Duration: 3FT Hon   CRB Check: Required
Entry Requirements: *GCE:* 260. *IB:* 24. Interview required.

C6G5 BA Sport & Exercise Science with Business Computing
Duration: 3FT Hon
Entry Requirements: *GCE:* 240. *IB:* 24.

C6QH BA Sport & Exercise Science with English Language & Communication
Duration: 3FT Hon
Entry Requirements: *GCE:* 240. *IB:* 24.

C6ND BA Sport & Exercise Science with Entrepreneurship
Duration: 3FT Hon
Entry Requirements: *GCE:* 240. *IB:* 24.

C6GL BA Sport & Exercise Science with Internet Computing
Duration: 3FT Hon
Entry Requirements: *GCE:* 240. *IB:* 24.

C6NM BA Sport & Exercise Science with Marketing 'International Only'
Duration: 4FT Hon
Entry Requirements: Interview required.

CT67 BA/BSc American Studies and Sport & Exercise Science
Duration: 3FT Hon
Entry Requirements: *GCE:* 240. *IB:* 24.

TCR6 BA/BSc American Studies and Sport & Exercise Science (With a Year in USA)
Duration: 4FT Hon
Entry Requirements: Contact the institution for details.

T7C6 BA/BSc American Studies with Sport & Exercise Science
Duration: 3FT Hon
Entry Requirements: *GCE:* 240. *IB:* 24.

TRC6 BA/BSc American Studies with Sport & Exercise Science (With a Year in USA)
Duration: 4FT Hon
Entry Requirements: Contact the institution for details.

M9C6 BA/BSc Applied Criminology with Sport & Exercise Science
Duration: 3FT Hon
Entry Requirements: *GCE:* 240. *IB:* 24.

GC46 BA/BSc Digital Media and Sport & Exercise Science
Duration: 3FT Hon
Entry Requirements: *GCE:* 240. *IB:* 24.

CX63 BA/BSc Early Childhood Studies and Sport & Exercise Science
Duration: 3FT Hon   CRB Check: Required
Entry Requirements: *GCE:* 240. *IB:* 24.

X3C6 BA/BSc Early Childhood Studies with Sport & Exercise Science
Duration: 3FT Hon   CRB Check: Required
Entry Requirements: *GCE:* 240. *IB:* 24.

CQ63 BA/BSc English Literature and Sport & Exercise Science
Duration: 3FT Hon
Entry Requirements: *GCE:* 240. *IB:* 24.

Q3C6 BA/BSc English Literature with Sport & Exercise Science
Duration: 3FT Hon
Entry Requirements: *GCE:* 240. *IB:* 24.

WC16 BA/BSc Fine & Applied Arts and Sport & Exercise Science
Duration: 3FT Hon
Entry Requirements: *GCE:* 240. *IB:* 24.

W1C6 BA/BSc Fine & Applied Arts with Sport & Exercise Science
Duration: 3FT Hon
Entry Requirements: *GCE:* 240. *IB:* 24.

CR61 BA/BSc French and Sport & Exercise Science
Duration: 3FT Hon
Entry Requirements: *GCE:* 240. *IB:* 24.

R1C6 BA/BSc French with Sport & Exercise Science
Duration: 3FT Hon
Entry Requirements: Contact the institution for details.

LC76 BA/BSc Geography and Sport & Exercise Science
Duration: 3FT Hon
Entry Requirements: *GCE:* 240. *IB:* 24.

L7C6 BA/BSc Geography with Sport & Exercise Science
Duration: 3FT Hon
Entry Requirements: *GCE:* 240. *IB:* 24.

CV61 BA/BSc History and Sport & Exercise Science
Duration: 3FT Hon
Entry Requirements: *GCE:* 240. *IB:* 24.

V1C6 BA/BSc History with Sport & Exercise Science
Duration: 3FT Hon
Entry Requirements: *GCE:* 240. *IB:* 24.

MC26 BA/BSc Legal Studies and Sport & Exercise Science
Duration: 3FT Hon
Entry Requirements: *GCE:* 240. *IB:* 24.

M2C6 BA/BSc Legal Studies with Sport & Exercise Science
Duration: 3FT Hon
Entry Requirements: *GCE:* 240. *IB:* 24.

XC3P BA/BSc Physical Education and Sport & Exercise Science 'Int only'
Duration: 4FT Hon
Entry Requirements: Interview required.

CC86 BA/BSc Psychology and Sport & Exercise Science
Duration: 3FT Hon
Entry Requirements: *GCE:* 260. *IB:* 24.

C8C6 BA/BSc Psychology with Sport & Exercise Science
Duration: 3FT Hon
Entry Requirements: *GCE:* 260. *IB:* 24.

CL63 BA/BSc Sociology & Social Science and Sport & Exercise Science
Duration: 3FT Hon
Entry Requirements: *GCE:* 240. *IB:* 24.

L3C6 BA/BSc Sociology & Social Science with Sport & Exercise Science
Duration: 3FT Hon
Entry Requirements: *GCE:* 240. *IB:* 24.

NC86 BA/BSc Sport & Exercise Science and Tourism & Leisure Studies
Duration: 3FT Hon
Entry Requirements: *GCE:* 240. *IB:* 24.

CPT7 BA/BSc Sport & Exercise Science with American Studies (With a Year in USA)
Duration: 4FT Hon
Entry Requirements: Contact the institution for details.

C6M2 BA/BSc Sport & Exercise Science with Legal Studies
Duration: 3FT Hon
Entry Requirements: *GCE:* 240. *IB:* 24.

C6N8 BA/BSc Sport & Exercise Science with Tourism & Leisure Studies
Duration: 3FT Hon
Entry Requirements: *GCE:* 240. *IB:* 24.

N8C6 BA/BSc Tourism & Leisure Studies with Sport & Exercise Science
Duration: 3FT Hon
Entry Requirements: *GCE:* 240. *IB:* 24.

C604 BSc Applied Health and Fitness
Duration: 3FT Hon
Entry Requirements: Contact the institution for details.

CC16 BSc Biosciences and Sport & Exercise Science
Duration: 3FT Hon
Entry Requirements: *GCE:* 240. *IB:* 24.

CC1P BSc Biosciences and Sport & Exercise Science (with Foundation Year)
Duration: 4FT Hon
Entry Requirements: Contact the institution for details.

NC16 BSc Business Studies and Sport & Exercise Science
Duration: 3FT Hon
Entry Requirements: *GCE:* 240. *IB:* 24.

N1C6 BSc Business Studies with Sport & Exercise Science
Duration: 3FT Hon
Entry Requirements: *GCE:* 240. *IB:* 24.

N1CP BSc Business Studies with Sport & Exercise Science 'International Only'
Duration: 4FT Hon
Entry Requirements: Interview required.

GCK6 BSc Computing and Sport & Exercise Science
Duration: 3FT Hon
Entry Requirements: *GCE:* 240. *IB:* 24.

G4CP BSc Computing with Sport & Exercise Science
Duration: 3FT Hon
Entry Requirements: *GCE:* 240. *IB:* 24.

CN65 BSc Marketing and Sport & Exercise Science
Duration: 3FT Hon
Entry Requirements: *GCE:* 240. *IB:* 24.

N5C6 BSc Marketing with Sport & Exercise Science
Duration: 3FT Hon
Entry Requirements: *GCE:* 240. *IB:* 24.

C600 BSc Sport & Exercise Science
Duration: 3FT Hon
Entry Requirements: *GCE:* 240. *IB:* 24.

C603 BSc Sport & Exercise Science 'International Only'
Duration: 4FT Hon
Entry Requirements: Interview required.

C6GK BSc Sport & Exercise Science with Computing
Duration: 3FT Hon
Entry Requirements: *GCE:* 240. *IB:* 24.

C6L3 BSc.BA Sport & Exercise Science with Sociology & Social Science
Duration: 3FT Hon
Entry Requirements: *GCE:* 240. *IB:* 24.

C1C6 BSc/BA Biosciences with Sport & Exercise Science
Duration: 3FT Hon
Entry Requirements: *GCE:* 240. *IB:* 24.

C1CP BSc/BA Biosciences with Sport & Exercise Science (with Foundation Year)
Duration: 4FT Hon
Entry Requirements: Contact the institution for details.

G4C6 BSc/BA Digital Media with Sport & Exercise Science
Duration: 3FT Hon
Entry Requirements: *GCE:* 240. *IB:* 24.

C6T7 BSc/BA Sport & Exercise Science with American Studies
Duration: 3FT Hon
Entry Requirements: *GCE:* 240. *IB:* 24.

C6M9 BSc/BA Sport & Exercise Science with Applied Criminology
Duration: 3FT Hon
Entry Requirements: *GCE:* 240. *IB:* 24.

C6C1 BSc/BA Sport & Exercise Science with Biosciences
Duration: 3FT Hon
Entry Requirements: *GCE:* 240. *IB:* 24.

C6N1 BSc/BA Sport & Exercise Science with Business Studies
Duration: 3FT Hon
Entry Requirements: *GCE:* 240. *IB:* 24.

C6G4 BSc/BA Sport & Exercise Science with Digital Media
Duration: 3FT Hon
Entry Requirements: *GCE:* 240. *IB:* 24.

C6X3 BSc/BA Sport & Exercise Science with Early Childhood Studies
Duration: 3FT Hon   CRB Check: Required
Entry Requirements: *GCE:* 240. *IB:* 24.

C6Q3 BSc/BA Sport & Exercise Science with English Literature
Duration: 3FT Hon
Entry Requirements: *GCE:* 240. *IB:* 24.

C6W1 BSc/BA Sport & Exercise Science with Fine & Applied Arts
Duration: 3FT Hon
Entry Requirements: *GCE:* 240. *IB:* 24.

C6R1 BSc/BA Sport & Exercise Science with French
Duration: 3FT Hon
Entry Requirements: *GCE:* 240. *IB:* 24.

C6L7 BSc/BA Sport & Exercise Science with Geography
Duration: 3FT Hon
Entry Requirements: *GCE:* 240. *IB:* 24.

C6V1 BSc/BA Sport & Exercise Science with History
Duration: 3FT Hon
Entry Requirements: *GCE:* 240. *IB:* 24.

C6N5 BSc/BA Sport & Exercise Science with Marketing
Duration: 3FT Hon
Entry Requirements: *GCE:* 240. *IB:* 24.

C6C8 BSc/BA Sport & Exercise Science with Psychology
Duration: 3FT Hon
Entry Requirements: *GCE:* 260. *IB:* 24.

C20 CARDIFF METROPOLITAN UNIVERSITY (UWIC)
ADMISSIONS UNIT
LLANDAFF CAMPUS
WESTERN AVENUE
CARDIFF CF5 2YB
t: 029 2041 6070 f: 029 2041 6286
e: admissions@cardiffmet.ac.uk
// www.cardiffmet.ac.uk

C605 BSc Sport & Exercise Science (Intercalated)
Duration: 1FT Hon
Entry Requirements: Interview required.

CB6K BSc Sport Biomedicine & Nutrition (4 yrs inc Foundation)
Duration: 4FT Hon
Entry Requirements: *Foundation:* Pass. *GCE:* 80. *IB:* 24. *BTEC Dip:* PP. *BTEC ExtDip:* PPP. *OCR ND:* P3 *OCR NED:* P3

CB64 BSc Sport Biomedicine and Nutrition (3 years)
Duration: 3FT Hon
Entry Requirements: *GCE:* 240. *IB:* 24. *BTEC Dip:* DD. *BTEC ExtDip:* MMM. *OCR ND:* D *OCR NED:* M3

C603 BSc Sport Coaching
Duration: 3FT Hon
Entry Requirements: *GCE:* 300. *IB:* 25. *BTEC ExtDip:* DDM. *OCR NED:* M1

C607 BSc Sport Conditioning, Rehabilitation and Massage
Duration: 3FT Hon
Entry Requirements: *GCE:* 320. *IB:* 26. *BTEC ExtDip:* DDM.

C602 BSc Sport Development
Duration: 3FT Hon
Entry Requirements: *GCE:* 300. *IB:* 25. *BTEC ExtDip:* DDM. *OCR NED:* M1

CN62 BSc Sport Management
Duration: 3FT Hon
Entry Requirements: *GCE:* 300. *IB:* 25. *BTEC ExtDip:* DDM. *OCR NED:* M1

C600 BSc Sport and Exercise Science
Duration: 3FT Hon
Entry Requirements: *GCE:* 340. *IB:* 28. *BTEC ExtDip:* DDD. *OCR NED:* D1

C604 BSc Sport and Physical Education
Duration: 3FT Hon
Entry Requirements: *GCE:* 320. *IB:* 26. *BTEC ExtDip:* DDM.

106C HND Sport Development and Coaching
Duration: 2FT HND
Entry Requirements: Interview required.

C22 COLEG SIR GAR / CARMARTHENSHIRE COLLEGE
SANDY ROAD
LLANELLI
CARMARTHENSHIRE SA15 4DN
t: 01554 748000 f: 01554 748170
e: admissions@colegsirgar.ac.uk
// www.colegsirgar.ac.uk

CX6C BSc Sports Coaching and Performance
Duration: 1FT Hon
Entry Requirements: Contact the institution for details.

C30 UNIVERSITY OF CENTRAL LANCASHIRE
PRESTON
LANCS PR1 2HE
t: 01772 201201 f: 01772 894954
e: uadmissions@uclan.ac.uk
// www.uclan.ac.uk

C615 BA Adventure Sports Coaching
Duration: 3FT Hon
Entry Requirements: *GCE:* 240-280. *SQAH:* AABB-BBBC. *IB:* 28.
OCR ND: D

C616 BA Exercise and Fitness Management (Top-Up)
Duration: 1FT Hon
Entry Requirements: HND required.

CX6D BA Sport (Coaching) (Top-up)
Duration: 1FT Hon
Entry Requirements: HND required.

C613 BA Sport (Development) Top-up
Duration: 1FT Hon
Entry Requirements: HND required.

C606 BA Sport (Studies) (Top-up)
Duration: 1FT Hon
Entry Requirements: HND required.

CX69 BA Sports Coaching
Duration: 3FT/4SW Hon
Entry Requirements: *GCE:* 240-280. *SQAH:* AAAC-BBBB. *IB:* 28.
OCR ND: D *OCR NED:* M2

CXQ1 BA Sports Coaching (Blended Learning, Top-Up)
Duration: 1FT Hon
Entry Requirements: Contact the institution for details.

CL65 BA Sports Development
Duration: 3FT/4SW Hon
Entry Requirements: *GCE:* 240-280. *SQAH:* AABB-BBBC. *IB:* 28.
OCR ND: D

C602 BA Sports Studies
Duration: 3FT/4SW Hon
Entry Requirements: *GCE:* 240-280. *SQAH:* AABB-BBBC. *IB:* 28.
OCR ND: D

B4C6 BSc Nutrition & Exercise Sciences (Human Nutrition)
Duration: 3FT Hon
Entry Requirements: Contact the institution for details.

B4C1 BSc Nutrition & Exercise Sciences (Personal Fitness Training)
Duration: 3FT Hon
Entry Requirements: Contact the institution for details.

B4C0 BSc Nutrition and Exercise Sciences
Duration: 3FT Hon
Entry Requirements: Contact the institution for details.

CB61 BSc Sport & Exercise Physiology (Top-up)
Duration: 1FT Hon
Entry Requirements: HND required.

C600 BSc Sport Science
Duration: 3FT Hon
Entry Requirements: *Foundation:* Distinction. *GCE:* 260-300.
SQAH: BBBBC-BBCCC. *IB:* 30. *OCR NED:* M2

CB63 BSc Sports Therapy
Duration: 3FT Hon   CRB Check: Required
Entry Requirements: *GCE:* 280. *IB:* 30. *OCR ND:* D *OCR NED:* M2
Interview required.

CB69 BSc Strength and Conditioning
Duration: 3FT Hon
Entry Requirements: *GCE:* 260. *OCR ND:* D *OCR NED:* M2

BC96 FdA Health & Personal Training
Duration: 2FT Fdg
Entry Requirements: *GCE:* 80.

CX6X FdA Sports Coaching
Duration: 2FT Fdg
Entry Requirements: *GCE:* 80-200. *IB:* 24.

C612 FdA Sports Development
Duration: 2FT Fdg
Entry Requirements: *GCE:* 120.

C604 FdSc Sport and Exercise Science
Duration: 2FT Fdg
Entry Requirements: *GCE:* 160.

C603 FdSc Sports & Exercise Science
Duration: 2FT Fdg
Entry Requirements: *GCE:* 120.

C55 UNIVERSITY OF CHESTER
PARKGATE ROAD
CHESTER CH1 4BJ
t: 01244 511000 f: 01244 511300
e: enquiries@chester.ac.uk
// www.chester.ac.uk

NCM6 BA Advertising and Sport Development
Duration: 3FT Hon
Entry Requirements: *GCE:* 240-280. *SQAH:* BBBB. *IB:* 26.

CN62 BA Business Management and Sport Development
Duration: 3FT Hon
Entry Requirements: *GCE:* 240-280. *SQAH:* BBBB. *IB:* 26.

WC66 BA Digital Photography and Sport Development
Duration: 3FT Hon
Entry Requirements: *GCE:* 240-280. *SQAH:* BBBB. *IB:* 26.

XC36 BA Education Studies and Sport & Exercise Sciences
Duration: 3FT Hon
Entry Requirements: *Foundation:* Pass. *GCE:* 260-300. *SQAH:* BBBB. *IB:* 28.

QC36 BA English and Sport & Exercise Sciences
Duration: 3FT Hon
Entry Requirements: *Foundation:* Merit. *GCE:* 260-300. *SQAH:* BBBB. *IB:* 28.

NC86 BA Events Management and Sport Development
Duration: 3FT Hon
Entry Requirements: *GCE:* 240-280. *SQAH:* BBBB. *IB:* 26.

PC3Q BA Film Studies and Sport Development
Duration: 3FT Hon
Entry Requirements: *GCE:* 240-280. *SQAH:* BBBB. *IB:* 26.

VC16 BA History and Sport & Exercise Sciences
Duration: 3FT Hon
Entry Requirements: *GCE:* 260-300. *SQAH:* BBBB. *IB:* 28.

PC56 BA Journalism and Sport Development
Duration: 3FT Hon
Entry Requirements: *GCE:* 240-280. *SQAH:* BBBB. *IB:* 26.

PC2P BA Marketing & Public Relations and Sport Development
Duration: 3FT Hon
Entry Requirements: *GCE:* 240-280. *SQAH:* BBBB. *IB:* 26.

CR61 BA Sport & Exercise Sciences and French
Duration: 4FT Hon
Entry Requirements: *GCE:* 260-300. *SQAH:* BBBB. *IB:* 28.

CR62 BA Sport & Exercise Sciences and German
Duration: 4FT Hon
Entry Requirements: *GCE:* 260-300. *SQAH:* BBBB. *IB:* 26.

CR64 BA Sport & Exercise Sciences and Spanish
Duration: 4FT Hon
Entry Requirements: *GCE:* 260-300. *SQAH:* BBBB. *IB:* 28.

C602 BA Sport Development
Duration: 3FT Hon
Entry Requirements: *GCE:* 240-280. *SQAH:* BBBB. *IB:* 26.

CPP3 BA Sport Development and Commercial Music Production
Duration: 3FT Hon
Entry Requirements: *Foundation:* Pass. *GCE:* 260-300. *SQAH:* BBBB. *IB:* 28.

CPPH BA Sport Development and Media Studies
Duration: 3FT Hon
Entry Requirements: *GCE:* 240-280. *SQAH:* BBBB. *IB:* 26.

CPQ3 BA Sport Development and Radio Production
Duration: 3FT Hon
Entry Requirements: *Foundation:* Pass. *GCE:* 260-300. *SQAH:* BBBB. *IB:* 28.

CP6J BA Sport Development and TV Production
Duration: 3FT Hon
Entry Requirements: *Foundation:* Pass. *GCE:* 260-300. *SQAH:* BBBB. *IB:* 28.

CC16 BSc Biology and Sport & Exercise Sciences
Duration: 3FT Hon
Entry Requirements: *GCE:* 260-300. *SQAH:* BBBB. *IB:* 28.

FC86 BSc Geography and Sport & Exercise Sciences
Duration: 3FT Hon
Entry Requirements: *GCE:* 260-300. *SQAH:* BBBB. *IB:* 28.

GC16 BSc Mathematics and Sport & Exercise Sciences
Duration: 3FT Hon
Entry Requirements: *GCE:* 260-300. *SQAH:* BBBB. *IB:* 28.

C600 BSc Sport & Exercise Sciences
Duration: 3FT Hon
Entry Requirements: *Foundation:* Pass. *GCE:* 260-300. *SQAH:* BBBB. *IB:* 28.

CC68 BSc Sport & Exercise Sciences and Psychology
Duration: 3FT Hon
Entry Requirements: *Foundation:* Pass. *GCE:* 260-300. *SQAH:* BBBB. *IB:* 28.

CX6C BSc Sports Coaching (Level 6 Top-Up only)
Duration: 1FT Hon   CRB Check: Required
Entry Requirements: Contact the institution for details.

CX61 FdSc Sports Coaching
Duration: 2FT Fdg   CRB Check: Required
Entry Requirements: *GCE:* 160-200. *SQAH:* CCCC. *IB:* 24.

C58 UNIVERSITY OF CHICHESTER
BISHOP OTTER CAMPUS
COLLEGE LANE
CHICHESTER
WEST SUSSEX PO19 6PE
t: 01243 816002 f: 01243 816161
e: admissions@chi.ac.uk
// www.chiuni.ac.uk

CX63 BA Physical Education and Sports Coaching
Duration: 3FT Hon   CRB Check: Required
Entry Requirements: *GCE:* BCC. *SQAH:* BBBCC. *SQAAH:* BCC. *IB:* 30. *BTEC Dip:* DD. Interview required.

C603 BA Sport Development
Duration: 3FT Hon
Entry Requirements: *GCE:* 260. *SQAAH:* CCC. *IB:* 30. *BTEC Dip:* DM. *BTEC ExtDip:* DMM.

NC26 BA Sport and Fitness Management
Duration: 3FT Hon
Entry Requirements: *GCE:* BCD-CCC. *SQAAH:* CCC. *IB:* 30. *BTEC Dip:* DM. *BTEC ExtDip:* DMM.

CX6C BSc Community Sports Coaching
Duration: 1FT Hon   CRB Check: Required
Entry Requirements: Interview required.

C604 BSc Sport & Exercise Science
Duration: 3FT Hon
Entry Requirements: *GCE:* BCD-CCC. *SQAH:* CCC. *IB:* 30. *BTEC Dip:* DD. *BTEC ExtDip:* DMM.

C602 BSc Sports Coaching Science
Duration: 3FT Hon   CRB Check: Required
Entry Requirements: *GCE:* BCD-CCC. *SQAH:* CCC. *IB:* 30. *BTEC Dip:* DM. *BTEC ExtDip:* DMM.

CB69 BSc Sports Therapy
Duration: 3FT Hon
Entry Requirements: *GCE:* 300. *SQAAH:* BBB. *IB:* 32. *BTEC Dip:* DD. *BTEC ExtDip:* DDD.

CX61 FdSc Community Sports Coaching
Duration: 2FT Fdg   CRB Check: Required
Entry Requirements: *GCE:* 80. *IB:* 28. Interview required.

C78 CORNWALL COLLEGE
POOL
REDRUTH
CORNWALL TR15 3RD
t: 01209 616161 f: 01209 611612
e: he.admissions@cornwall.ac.uk
// www.cornwall.ac.uk

C600 BSc Sports Performance and Coaching (top up)
Duration: 1FT Hon
Entry Requirements: Interview required.

CF67 FdSc Marine Sports Science
Duration: 2FT Fdg   CRB Check: Required
Entry Requirements: *GCE:* 80-120. Interview required.

CB69 FdSc Sport, Health & Fitness
Duration: 2FT Fdg   CRB Check: Required
Entry Requirements: *GCE:* 120. *IB:* 24. Interview required. Portfolio required.

CF68 FdSc Surf Science and Technology
Duration: 2FT Fdg
Entry Requirements: Interview required.

C85 COVENTRY UNIVERSITY
THE STUDENT CENTRE
COVENTRY UNIVERSITY
1 GULSON RD
COVENTRY CV1 2JH
t: 024 7615 2222 f: 024 7615 2223
e: studentenquiries@coventry.ac.uk
// www.coventry.ac.uk

C600 BSc Sport and Exercise Science
Duration: 3FT/4SW Hon
Entry Requirements: *GCE:* CCC. *SQAH:* CCCCC. *IB:* 27. *BTEC ExtDip:* MMM. *OCR NED:* M3

BC96 BSc Sports Therapy
Duration: 3FT Hon
Entry Requirements: *GCE:* BCC. *SQAH:* BCCCC. *IB:* 28. *BTEC ExtDip:* DMM. *OCR NED:* M2

C99 UNIVERSITY OF CUMBRIA
FUSEHILL STREET
CARLISLE
CUMBRIA CA1 2HH
t: 01228 616234 f: 01228 616235
// www.cumbria.ac.uk

C604 BA Coaching and Sport Development
Duration: 3FT Hon   CRB Check: Required
Entry Requirements: *Foundation:* Distinction. *GCE:* 240. *IB:* 28. *OCR ND:* D

XCC6 BA Physical Education
Duration: 3FT Hon   CRB Check: Required
Entry Requirements: *Foundation:* Pass. *GCE:* 240. *IB:* 32.

C601 BA Sport, Physical Activity and Health Development
Duration: 3FT Hon   CRB Check: Required
Entry Requirements: *Foundation:* Distinction. *GCE:* 240. *IB:* 28. *OCR ND:* D

CB69 BSc Sport Rehabilitation
Duration: 3FT Hon
Entry Requirements: *GCE:* 240.

C600 BSc Sport and Exercise Science
Duration: 3FT Hon
Entry Requirements: *Foundation:* Distinction. *GCE:* 240. *IB:* 28. *OCR ND:* D

CX61 DipHE Coaching and Sport Development
Duration: 2FT Dip   CRB Check: Required
Entry Requirements: *Foundation:* Pass. *GCE:* 80. *IB:* 24.

XC36 DipHE Physical Education
Duration: 2FT Dip
Entry Requirements: Contact the institution for details.

C609 DipHE Sport and Exercise Science
Duration: 2FT Dip   CRB Check: Required
Entry Requirements: *Foundation:* Pass. *GCE:* 80. *IB:* 24.

C607 DipHE Sport, Physical Activity and Health Development
Duration: 2FT Dip   CRB Check: Required
Entry Requirements: *Foundation:* Pass. *GCE:* 80. *IB:* 24.

CX6D FdA Sport Coaching and Development
Duration: 2FT Fdg
Entry Requirements: *GCE:* 80.

CB63 FdSc Sports Massage Therapy
Duration: 2FT Fdg
Entry Requirements: Contact the institution for details.

D22 DEARNE VALLEY COLLEGE
MANVERS PARK
WATH-UPON-DEARNE
ROTHERHAM S63 7EW
t: 01709 513101 f: 01709 513110
e: learn@dearne-coll.ac.uk
// www.dearne-coll.ac.uk

C600 FdSc Sports Coaching (Performance & Participation)
Duration: 2FT Fdg
Entry Requirements: *GCE:* 160. Interview required.

D39 UNIVERSITY OF DERBY
KEDLESTON ROAD
DERBY DE22 1GB
t: 01332 591167 f: 01332 597724
e: askadmissions@derby.ac.uk
// www.derby.ac.uk

TC76 BA American Studies and Sport & Exercise Studies
Duration: 3FT Hon
Entry Requirements: *Foundation:* Distinction. *GCE:* 260-300. *IB:* 28. *BTEC Dip:* D*D*. *BTEC ExtDip:* DMM. *OCR NED:* M2

MC26 BA Applied Criminology and Sport & Exercise Studies
Duration: 3FT Hon
Entry Requirements: *Foundation:* Distinction. *GCE:* 260-300. *IB:* 28. *BTEC Dip:* D*D*. *BTEC ExtDip:* DMM. *OCR NED:* M2

WC56 BA Dance & Movement Studies and Sport & Exercise Studies
Duration: 3FT Hon
Entry Requirements: *Foundation:* Distinction. *GCE:* 260-300. *IB:* 28. *BTEC Dip:* D*D*. *BTEC ExtDip:* DMM. *OCR NED:* M2

PC36 BA Film & Television Studies and Sport & Exercise Studies
Duration: 3FT Hon
Entry Requirements: *Foundation:* Distinction. *GCE:* 260-300. *IB:* 28. *BTEC Dip:* D*D*. *BTEC ExtDip:* DMM. *OCR NED:* M2

PCJ6 BA Media Studies and Sport & Exercise Studies
Duration: 3FT Hon
Entry Requirements: *Foundation:* Distinction. *GCE:* 260-300. *IB:* 28. *BTEC Dip:* D*D*. *BTEC ExtDip:* DMM. *OCR NED:* M2

WC36 BA Popular Music Production and Sport & Exercise Studies
Duration: 3FT Hon
Entry Requirements: *Foundation:* Distinction. *GCE:* 260-300. *IB:* 28. *BTEC Dip:* D*D*. *BTEC ExtDip:* DMM. *OCR NED:* M2

C600 BA Sport & Exercise Studies
Duration: 3FT Hon
Entry Requirements: *GCE:* 260. *IB:* 28. *BTEC Dip:* D*D*. *BTEC ExtDip:* DMM. *OCR NED:* M2

CX63 BA Sport & Exercise Studies and Education Studies
Duration: 3FT Hon
Entry Requirements: *Foundation:* Distinction. *GCE:* 260-300. *IB:* 28. *BTEC Dip:* D*D*. *BTEC ExtDip:* DMM. *OCR NED:* M2

CQ63 BA Sport & Exercise Studies and English
Duration: 3FT Hon
Entry Requirements: *Foundation:* Distinction. *GCE:* 260-300. *IB:* 28. *BTEC Dip:* D*D*. *BTEC ExtDip:* DMM. *OCR NED:* M2

CF66 BA Sport & Exercise Studies and Geology
Duration: 3FT Hon
Entry Requirements: *Foundation:* Distinction. *GCE:* 260-300. *IB:* 28. *BTEC Dip:* D*D*. *BTEC ExtDip:* DMM. *OCR NED:* M2

CN66 BA Sport & Exercise Studies and Human Resource Management
Duration: 3FT Hon
Entry Requirements: *Foundation:* Distinction. *GCE:* 260-300. *IB:* 28. *BTEC Dip:* D*D*. *BTEC ExtDip:* DMM. *OCR NED:* M2

CM61 BA Sport & Exercise Studies and Law
Duration: 3FT Hon
Entry Requirements: *Foundation:* Distinction. *GCE:* 260-300. *IB:* 28. *BTEC Dip:* D*D*. *BTEC ExtDip:* DMM. *OCR NED:* M2

CN6N BA Sport & Exercise Studies and Marketing
Duration: 3FT Hon
Entry Requirements: *Foundation:* Distinction. *GCE:* 260-300. *IB:* 28. *BTEC Dip:* D*D*. *BTEC ExtDip:* DMM. *OCR NED:* M2

C611 BA Sports Massage & Exercise Therapy and Sports Development
Duration: 3FT Hon
Entry Requirements: *Foundation:* Distinction. *GCE:* 260-280. *IB:* 28. *BTEC Dip:* D*D*. *BTEC ExtDip:* DMM. *OCR NED:* M2

LC76 BA/BSc Geography and Sport & Exercise Studies
Duration: 3FT Hon
Entry Requirements: *Foundation:* Distinction. *GCE:* 260-300. *IB:* 28. *BTEC Dip:* D*D*. *BTEC ExtDip:* DMM. *OCR NED:* M2

CX6C BA/BSc Sports Coaching and Sports Development
Duration: 3FT Hon
Entry Requirements: *Foundation:* Distinction. *GCE:* 260-280. *IB:* 28. *BTEC Dip:* D*D*. *BTEC ExtDip:* DMM. *OCR NED:* M2

CC6W BA/BSc Sports Coaching and Sports Psychology
Duration: 3FT Hon
Entry Requirements: *Foundation:* Distinction. *GCE:* 260-280. *IB:* 28. *BTEC Dip:* D*D*. *BTEC ExtDip:* DMM. *OCR NED:* M2

CCPW BA/BSc Sports Development and Sports Psychology
Duration: 3FT Hon
Entry Requirements: *Foundation:* Distinction. *GCE:* 260-280. *IB:* 28. *BTEC Dip:* D*D*. *BTEC ExtDip:* DMM. *OCR NED:* M2

CC69 BA/BSc Sports Massage & Exercise Therapies and Sports Coaching
Duration: 3FT Hon
Entry Requirements: *Foundation:* Distinction. *GCE:* 260-280. *IB:* 28. *BTEC Dip:* D*D*. *BTEC ExtDip:* DMM. *OCR NED:* M2

CCQ8 BA/BSc Sports Massage & Exercise Therapy and Sports Psychology
Duration: 3FT Hon
Entry Requirements: *Foundation:* Distinction. *GCE:* 260-280. *IB:* 28. *BTEC Dip:* D*D*. *BTEC ExtDip:* DMM. *OCR NED:* M2

C603 BSc Sport & Exercise Science
Duration: 3FT Hon
Entry Requirements: *GCE:* 280. *IB:* 28. *BTEC Dip:* D*D*. *BTEC ExtDip:* DMM. *OCR NED:* M2

CC61 BSc Sport & Exercise Studies and Biology
Duration: 3FT Hon
Entry Requirements: *Foundation:* Distinction. *GCE:* 260-300. *IB:* 28. *BTEC Dip:* D*D*. *BTEC ExtDip:* DMM. *OCR NED:* M2

CN6F BSc Sport & Exercise Studies and Business Management
Duration: 3FT Hon
Entry Requirements: *Foundation:* Distinction. *GCE:* 260-300. *IB:* 28. *BTEC Dip:* D*D*. *BTEC ExtDip:* DMM. *OCR NED:* M2

CG61 BSc Sport & Exercise Studies and Mathematics
Duration: 3FT Hon
Entry Requirements: *Foundation:* Distinction. *GCE:* 260-300. *IB:* 28. *BTEC Dip:* D*D*. *BTEC ExtDip:* DMM. *OCR NED:* M2

CX61 FdA Sports Coaching
Duration: 2FT Fdg
Entry Requirements: *Foundation:* Pass. *GCE:* 160. *IB:* 26. *BTEC Dip:* D*D*. *BTEC ExtDip:* DMM. *OCR ND:* M2 *OCR NED:* P2

D52 DONCASTER COLLEGE
THE HUB
CHAPPELL DRIVE
SOUTH YORKSHIRE DN1 2RF
t: 01302 553610
e: he@don.ac.uk
// www.don.ac.uk

C600 BSc Sport, Exercise and Health Sciences (Top Up)
Duration: 1FT Hon
Entry Requirements: Contact the institution for details.

C601 FdSc Sport, Exercise and Health Sciences
Duration: 2FT Fdg
Entry Requirements: Contact the institution for details.

006C HND Sport and Exercise Sciences (Sport Studies)
Duration: 2FT HND
Entry Requirements: *GCE:* 80.

D55 DUCHY COLLEGE
STOKE CLIMSLAND
CALLINGTON
CORNWALL PL17 8PB
t: 01579 372327 f: 01579 372200
e: uni@duchy.ac.uk
// www.duchy.ac.uk

CN68 FdSc Adventure Sports Coaching
Duration: 2FT Fdg
Entry Requirements: *GCE:* 100-120.

CX61 FdSc Sports Development & Coaching
Duration: 2FT Fdg
Entry Requirements: *GCE:* 100-120.

NC26 FdSc Tournament Golf
Duration: 2FT Fdg
Entry Requirements: *GCE:* 100-120.

D58 DUDLEY COLLEGE OF TECHNOLOGY
THE BROADWAY
DUDLEY DY1 4AS
t: 01384 363277/6 f: 01384 363311
e: admissions@dudleycol.ac.uk
// www.dudleycol.ac.uk

C600 HND Sports Science
Duration: 2FT HND
Entry Requirements: Contact the institution for details.

D65 UNIVERSITY OF DUNDEE
NETHERGATE
DUNDEE DD1 4HN
t: 01382 383838 f: 01382 388150
e: contactus@dundee.ac.uk
// www.dundee.ac.uk/admissions/undergraduate/

CB69 BSc Sports Biomedicine
Duration: 4FT Hon
Entry Requirements: *GCE:* AAB. *SQAH:* ABBB. *IB:* 30.

D86 DURHAM UNIVERSITY
DURHAM UNIVERSITY
UNIVERSITY OFFICE
DURHAM DH1 3HP
t: 0191 334 2000 f: 0191 334 6055
e: admissions@durham.ac.uk
// www.durham.ac.uk

C603 BA Sport, Exercise and Physical Activity
Duration: 3FT Hon
Entry Requirements: *GCE:* AAB. *SQAH:* AAB. *SQAAH:* AAABB. *IB:* 36.

C604 BA Sport, Exercise and Physical Activity with Foundation
Duration: 4FT Hon
Entry Requirements: Contact the institution for details.

E14 UNIVERSITY OF EAST ANGLIA
NORWICH NR4 7TJ
t: 01603 591515 f: 01603 591523
e: admissions@uea.ac.uk
// www.uea.ac.uk

XC16 BA Physical Education
Duration: 3FT Hon   CRB Check: Required
Entry Requirements: *GCE:* ABB. *SQAH:* AAABB. *SQAAH:* ABB. *IB:* 32. *BTEC SubDip:* D. *BTEC Dip:* DM. *BTEC ExtDip:* DDM. *OCR ND:* D *OCR NED:* D2

E28 UNIVERSITY OF EAST LONDON
DOCKLANDS CAMPUS
UNIVERSITY WAY
LONDON E16 2RD
t: 020 8223 3333 f: 020 8223 2978
e: study@uel.ac.uk
// www.uel.ac.uk

X3C6 BA Early Childhood Studies with Sports Development
Duration: 3FT Hon
Entry Requirements: *GCE:* 240. *IB:* 24.

N5C6 BA Marketing with Sports Development
Duration: 3FT Hon
Entry Requirements: *GCE:* 240. *IB:* 24.

W3C6 BA Music Culture with Sports Development
Duration: 3FT Hon
Entry Requirements: *GCE:* 240. *IB:* 24.

C8C6 BA Psychosocial Studies with Sports Development
Duration: 3FT Hon
Entry Requirements: *GCE:* 240. *IB:* 24.

W4CP BA Theatre Studies with Sports & Exercise Science
Duration: 3FT Hon
Entry Requirements: *GCE:* 240. *IB:* 24. Interview required.

L5C6 BA Youth & Community Work with Sports Development
Duration: 3FT Hon
Entry Requirements: *GCE:* 240. *IB:* 24.

C6L6 BA/BSc Sports & Exercise Science/Cultural Studies
Duration: 3FT Hon
Entry Requirements: *GCE:* 240. *IB:* 24.

CP65 BA/BSc Sports Coaching/Journalism Studies
Duration: 3FT Hon
Entry Requirements: *GCE:* 240. *IB:* 24.

C7C6 BSc Biochemistry with Sports & Exercise Science
Duration: 3FT Hon
Entry Requirements: *GCE:* 240. *IB:* 24.

CP6M BSc Fitness & Health and Sport Journalism
Duration: 3FT Hon
Entry Requirements: *GCE:* 280.

C6P5 BSc Fitness & Health with Sport Journalism
Duration: 3FT Hon
Entry Requirements: *GCE:* 280. *IB:* 24.

B9C6 BSc Health Promotion with Sports Development
Duration: 3FT Hon
Entry Requirements: *GCE:* 240. *IB:* 24.

B1C6 BSc Human Biology with Sports Coaching
Duration: 3FT Hon
Entry Requirements: *GCE:* 240. *IB:* 24.

C600 BSc Sport and Exercise Science
Duration: 3FT Hon
Entry Requirements: *GCE:* 240. *IB:* 24.

CI61 BSc Sport and Exercise Science and Computing
Duration: 3FT Hon
Entry Requirements: *GCE:* 240. *IB:* 24.

CP6N BSc Sports & Exercise Science and Sport Journalism
Duration: 3FT Hon
Entry Requirements: *GCE:* 240. *IB:* 24.

CX63 BSc Sports & Exercise Science with Education Studies
Duration: 3FT Hon
Entry Requirements: *GCE:* 240. *IB:* 24.

C6BC BSc Sports & Exercise Science with Human Biology
Duration: 3FT Hon
Entry Requirements: *GCE:* 240. *IB:* 24.

C6N5 BSc Sports & Exercise Science with Marketing
Duration: 3FT Hon
Entry Requirements: *GCE:* 240. *IB:* 24.

C6CV BSc Sports & Exercise Science with Psychology
Duration: 3FT Hon
Entry Requirements: *GCE:* 240. *IB:* 24.

C6PM BSc Sports & Exercise Science with Sport Journalism
Duration: 3FT Hon
Entry Requirements: *GCE:* 280. *IB:* 24.

C602 BSc Sports Coaching
Duration: 3FT Hon
Entry Requirements: *GCE:* 240. *IB:* 24.

C6B9 BSc Sports Coaching with Clinical Science
Duration: 3FT Hon
Entry Requirements: *GCE:* 240. *IB:* 24.

C6C8 BSc Sports Coaching with Psychology
Duration: 3FT Hon
Entry Requirements: *GCE:* 240. *IB:* 24.

CPP5 BSc Sports Development and Sport Journalism
Duration: 3FT Hon
Entry Requirements: *GCE:* 280. *IB:* 24.

C6N2 BSc Sports Development with Business Management
Duration: 3FT Hon
Entry Requirements: *GCE:* 240. *IB:* 24.

C6N8 BSc Sports Development with Events Management
Duration: 3FT Hon
Entry Requirements: *GCE:* 240. *IB:* 24.

C6B1 BSc Sports Development with Human Biology
Duration: 3FT Hon
Entry Requirements: *GCE:* 240. *IB:* 24.

C6NM BSc Sports Development with Marketing
Duration: 3FT Hon
Entry Requirements: *GCE:* 240. *IB:* 24.

C9C8 BSc Sports Development with Psychology
Duration: 3FT Hon
Entry Requirements: *GCE:* 240. *IB:* 24.

C6CW BSc Sports Development with Psychosocial Studies
Duration: 3FT Hon
Entry Requirements: *GCE:* 240. *IB:* 24.

C6BY BSc Sports Development with Public Health
Duration: 3FT Hon
Entry Requirements: *GCE:* 240. *IB:* 24.

C6PN BSc Sports Development with Sport Journalism
Duration: 3FT Hon
Entry Requirements: *GCE:* 280. *IB:* 24.

C6L9 BSc Sports Development with Third World Development
Duration: 3FT Hon
Entry Requirements: *GCE:* 240. *IB:* 24.

C6L5 BSc Sports Development with Youth & Community Work
Duration: 3FT Hon
Entry Requirements: *GCE:* 240. *IB:* 24.

C6B2 BSc Sports Development/Toxicology
Duration: 3FT Hon
Entry Requirements: *GCE:* 240. *IB:* 24.

E29 EAST RIDING COLLEGE
LONGCROFT HALL
GALLOWS LANE
BEVERLEY
EAST YORKSHIRE HU17 7DT
t: 0845 120 0037
e: info@eastridingcollege.ac.uk
// www.eastridingcollege.ac.uk/

C600 FdSc Sport, Exercise and Health Sciences
Duration: 2FT Fdg
Entry Requirements: Contact the institution for details.

E30 EASTON COLLEGE
EASTON
NORWICH
NORFOLK NR9 5DX
t: 01603 731232 f: 01603 741438
e: info@easton.ac.uk
// www.easton.ac.uk

C600 FdSc Sports Coaching
Duration: 2FT Fdg
Entry Requirements: Interview required.

E42 EDGE HILL UNIVERSITY
ORMSKIRK
LANCASHIRE L39 4QP
t: 01695 657000 f: 01695 584355
e: study@edgehill.ac.uk
// www.edgehill.ac.uk

C604 BA Sport Development
Duration: 3FT Deg   CRB Check: Required
Entry Requirements: *GCE:* 280. *IB:* 26. *OCR ND:* D *OCR NED:* M2

C603 BA Sports Studies
Duration: 3FT Hon
Entry Requirements: *GCE:* 280. *IB:* 26. *OCR ND:* D *OCR NED:* M2

C605 BSc Coach Education
Duration: 3FT Hon   CRB Check: Required
Entry Requirements: *GCE:* 280. *IB:* 26. *OCR ND:* D *OCR NED:* M2

C602 BSc Sport and Exercise Science
Duration: 3FT Hon
Entry Requirements: *GCE:* 280. *IB:* 26. *OCR ND:* D *OCR NED:* M2

CB63 BSc Sports Therapy
Duration: 3FT Hon   CRB Check: Required
Entry Requirements: *GCE:* 300. *IB:* 26. *OCR ND:* D *OCR NED:* M1

E56 THE UNIVERSITY OF EDINBURGH
STUDENT RECRUITMENT & ADMISSIONS
57 GEORGE SQUARE
EDINBURGH EH8 9JU
t: 0131 650 4360 f: 0131 651 1236
e: sra.enquiries@ed.ac.uk
// www.ed.ac.uk/studying/undergraduate/

XC16 BEd Physical Education (4 years)
Duration: 4FT Hon   CRB Check: Required
Entry Requirements: *GCE:* BBB. *SQAH:* BBBB. *IB:* 34. Interview required.

C610 BSc Applied Sport Science
Duration: 4FT Hon
Entry Requirements: *GCE:* BBC. *SQAH:* BBBB. *IB:* 33.

E59 EDINBURGH NAPIER UNIVERSITY
CRAIGLOCKHART CAMPUS
EDINBURGH EH14 1DJ
t: +44 (0)8452 60 60 40 f: 0131 455 6464
e: info@napier.ac.uk
// www.napier.ac.uk

CB69 BSc Sport & Exercise Science (Sports Coaching top up)
Duration: 1FT Ord
Entry Requirements: Contact the institution for details.

CX61 BSc Sport & Exercise Science (Sports Coaching)
Duration: 3FT/4FT Ord/Hon
Entry Requirements: *GCE:* 260.

C603 BSc Sport & Exercise Science (Sports Injuries top up)
Duration: 1FT Ord
Entry Requirements: HND required.

C601 BSc Sport & Exercise Science (top-up)
Duration: 1FT Ord
Entry Requirements: Contact the institution for details.

C600 BSc Sport and Exercise Science
Duration: 3FT/4FT Ord/Hon
Entry Requirements: *GCE:* 260.

CB61 BSc Sport and Exercise Science (Exercise Physiology)
Duration: 3FT/4FT Ord/Hon
Entry Requirements: *GCE:* 260.

CC68 BSc Sport and Exercise Science (Sport Psychology)
Duration: 3FT/4FT Ord/Hon
Entry Requirements: *GCE:* 260.

CB6X BSc Sport and Exercise Science (Sports Injuries)
Duration: 3FT/4FT Ord/Hon
Entry Requirements: *GCE:* 260.

E70 THE UNIVERSITY OF ESSEX
WIVENHOE PARK
COLCHESTER
ESSEX CO4 3SQ
t: 01206 873666 f: 01206 874477
e: admit@essex.ac.uk
// www.essex.ac.uk

C600 BSc Sports & Exercise Science
Duration: 3FT Hon
Entry Requirements: *GCE:* BBB. *SQAH:* AABB. *IB:* 32. *OCR ND:* D

CP00 BSc Sports and Exercise Science (Including Foundation Year)
Duration: 4FT Hon
Entry Requirements: *GCE:* 180. *IB:* 24.

C602 BSc Sports and Exercise Science (Including Year Abroad)
Duration: 4FT Hon
Entry Requirements: *GCE:* BBB. *SQAH:* AABB. *IB:* 32. *OCR ND:* D

E81 EXETER COLLEGE
HELE ROAD
EXETER
DEVON EX4 4JS
t: 0845 111 6000
e: info@exe-coll.ac.uk
// www.exe-coll.ac.uk/he

C600 FdSc Coaching and Fitness
Duration: 2FT Fdg
Entry Requirements: *GCE:* 160.

BC36 FdSc Sports Therapy
Duration: 2FT Fdg
Entry Requirements: *GCE:* 160.

E84 UNIVERSITY OF EXETER
LAVER BUILDING
NORTH PARK ROAD
EXETER
DEVON EX4 4QE
t: 01392 723044 f: 01392 722479
e: admissions@exeter.ac.uk
// www.exeter.ac.uk

C602 BSc Exercise and Sport Sciences
Duration: 3FT Hon
Entry Requirements: *GCE:* AAB-ABB. *SQAH:* AAABB-AABBB. *SQAAH:* ABB-BBB.

C8C6 BSc Psychology with Sport & Exercise Science
Duration: 3FT Hon
Entry Requirements: *GCE:* AAA-AAB. *SQAH:* AAAAB-AAABB. *SQAAH:* AAB-ABB. *BTEC ExtDip:* DDM.

F66 FARNBOROUGH COLLEGE OF TECHNOLOGY
BOUNDARY ROAD
FARNBOROUGH
HAMPSHIRE GU14 6SB
t: 01252 407028 f: 01252 407041
e: admissions@farn-ct.ac.uk
// www.farn-ct.ac.uk

C601 BSc Sport Science (Exercise and Health Management)
Duration: 3FT Hon
Entry Requirements: *GCE:* 200. Interview required.

C600 FdSc Sport Performance and Personal Training
Duration: 2FT Fdg
Entry Requirements: *GCE:* 160.

G14 UNIVERSITY OF GLAMORGAN, CARDIFF AND PONTYPRIDD
ENQUIRIES AND ADMISSIONS UNIT
PONTYPRIDD CF37 1DL
t: 08456 434030 f: 01443 654050
e: enquiries@glam.ac.uk
// www.glam.ac.uk

CP00 BA Sports Development
Duration: 4SW Hon
Entry Requirements: *GCE:* BBC. *IB:* 25. *BTEC SubDip:* M. *BTEC Dip:* D*D*. *BTEC ExtDip:* DMM. *OCR NED:* M2

C600 BSc Sport and Exercise Science
Duration: 3FT Hon   CRB Check: Required
Entry Requirements: *GCE:* BBC. *IB:* 28. *BTEC Dip:* D*D*. *BTEC ExtDip:* DMM.

CX6D BSc Sports Coaching and Performance (Top-up)
Duration: 1FT Hon   CRB Check: Required
Entry Requirements: Contact the institution for details.

C605 BSc Sports Science and Rugby
Duration: 3FT Hon   CRB Check: Required
Entry Requirements: *GCE:* BBC. *IB:* 28. *BTEC Dip:* D*D*. *BTEC ExtDip:* DMM.

C604 BSc Sports Studies
Duration: 3FT Hon   CRB Check: Required
Entry Requirements: *GCE:* BBC. *IB:* 28. *BTEC Dip:* D*D*. *BTEC ExtDip:* DMM.

CX69 FdSc Football Coaching and Performance
Duration: 2FT Fdg   CRB Check: Required
Entry Requirements: *GCE:* DDE. *IB:* 24. *BTEC Dip:* MM. *BTEC ExtDip:* MPP.

CX61 FdSc Rugby Coaching & Performance
Duration: 2FT Fdg   CRB Check: Required
Entry Requirements: *GCE:* 100-140. *IB:* 24. *BTEC Dip:* MM. *BTEC ExtDip:* MPP.

G28 UNIVERSITY OF GLASGOW
71 SOUTHPARK AVENUE
UNIVERSITY OF GLASGOW
GLASGOW G12 8QQ
t: 0141 330 6062 f: 0141 330 2961
e: student.recruitment@glasgow.ac.uk
// www.glasgow.ac.uk

BC16 BSc Physiology and Sports Science
Duration: 4FT Hon
Entry Requirements: *GCE:* ABB. *SQAH:* AAAB-BBBB. *IB:* 32.

BC46 BSc Physiology, Sports Science and Nutrition
Duration: 4FT Hon
Entry Requirements: *GCE:* ABB. *SQAH:* AAAB-BBBB. *IB:* 32.

CB69 BSc Sports Medicine
Duration: 4FT Hon
Entry Requirements: *GCE:* ABB. *SQAH:* AAAB-BBBB. *IB:* 32.

C600 BSc Sports Science
Duration: 3FT Ord
Entry Requirements: *GCE:* ABB. *SQAH:* AAAB-BBBB. *IB:* 32.

G50 THE UNIVERSITY OF GLOUCESTERSHIRE
PARK CAMPUS
THE PARK
CHELTENHAM GL50 2RH
t: 01242 714501 f: 01242 714869
e: admissions@glos.ac.uk
// www.glos.ac.uk

C605 BSc Applied Sport and Exercise Studies
Duration: 1FT Hon   CRB Check: Required
Entry Requirements: Contact the institution for details.

C60A BSc Sport Fitness and Physical Activity
Duration: 3FT Hon
Entry Requirements: Contact the institution for details.

C602 BSc Sport Science
Duration: 2FT Hon   CRB Check: Required
Entry Requirements: Contact the institution for details.

C603 BSc Sport Science
Duration: 3FT Hon   CRB Check: Required
Entry Requirements: *GCE:* 280-300.

C600 BSc Sport and Exercise Sciences
Duration: 3FT Hon   CRB Check: Required
Entry Requirements: *GCE:* 280-300.

XC16 BSc Sports Coaching and Sports Development
Duration: 3FT Hon   CRB Check: Required
Entry Requirements: *GCE:* 280-300.

C601 BSc Sports Development
Duration: 3FT Hon   CRB Check: Required
Entry Requirements: *GCE:* 280-300.

XW35 BSc Sports Education and Dance
Duration: 3FT Hon
Entry Requirements: Contact the institution for details.

XCD6 BSc Sports Education and Sport Science
Duration: 3FT Hon   CRB Check: Required
Entry Requirements: *GCE:* 280-300.

XCC6 BSc Sports Education and Sports Development
Duration: 3FT Hon   CRB Check: Required
Entry Requirements: *GCE:* 280-300.

C611 BSc Sports Strength and Conditioning
Duration: 3FT Hon   CRB Check: Required
Entry Requirements: *GCE:* 280-300.

C606 BSc Sports Therapy
Duration: 3FT Hon   CRB Check: Required
Entry Requirements: *GCE:* 280-300.

C607 FdSc Sports (Development)
Duration: 2FT Fdg   CRB Check: Required
Entry Requirements: *GCE:* 120.

G53 GLYNDWR UNIVERSITY
PLAS COCH
MOLD ROAD
WREXHAM LL11 2AW
t: 01978 293439 f: 01978 290008
e: sid@glyndwr.ac.uk
// www.glyndwr.ac.uk

C610 BSc Sport Coaching
Duration: 3FT Hon
Entry Requirements: Interview required.

C606 BSc Sport and Exercise Sciences
Duration: 3FT Hon
Entry Requirements: Interview required.

G70 UNIVERSITY OF GREENWICH
GREENWICH CAMPUS
OLD ROYAL NAVAL COLLEGE
PARK ROW
LONDON SE10 9LS
t: 020 8331 9000 f: 020 8331 8145
e: courseinfo@gre.ac.uk
// www.gre.ac.uk

C600 BSc Sports Science
Duration: 3FT Hon
Entry Requirements: *GCE:* 300. *IB:* 24.

C6X1 BSc Sports Science with Coaching
Duration: 3FT Hon
Entry Requirements: *GCE:* 300. *IB:* 24.

C690 BSc Sports Science with Professional Football Coaching
Duration: 3FT Hon
Entry Requirements: *GCE:* 300. *IB:* 24.

C604 FdSc Sports Science
Duration: 2FT Fdg
Entry Requirements: Contact the institution for details.

C605 FdSc Sports Studies
Duration: 2FT Fdg
Entry Requirements: *GCE:* 100. *IB:* 24.

G80 GRIMSBY INSTITUTE OF FURTHER AND HIGHER EDUCATION
NUNS CORNER
GRIMSBY
NE LINCOLNSHIRE DN34 5BQ
t: 0800 328 3631
e: headmissions@grimsby.ac.uk
// www.grimsby.ac.uk

XC16 BSc Sports Coaching (Top-Up)
Duration: 1FT Hon
Entry Requirements: Interview required. HND required.

CX61 FdA Sports Coaching (Performance and Participation)
Duration: 2FT Fdg
Entry Requirements: *OCR ND:* P2 Interview required.

BC96 FdSc Health Related Exercise and Fitness
Duration: 2FT Fdg
Entry Requirements: *GCE:* 120. Interview required. HND required.

H36 UNIVERSITY OF HERTFORDSHIRE
UNIVERSITY ADMISSIONS SERVICE
COLLEGE LANE
HATFIELD
HERTS AL10 9AB
t: 01707 284800
// www.herts.ac.uk

N1C6 BSc Business/Sports Studies
Duration: 3FT/4SW Hon
Entry Requirements: *GCE:* 300.

G4C6 BSc Computing/Sports Studies
Duration: 3FT/4SW Hon
Entry Requirements: *GCE:* 280.

L1C6 BSc Economics/Sports Studies
Duration: 3FT/4SW Hon
Entry Requirements: *GCE:* 280.

F9C6 BSc Environmental Studies/Sports Studies
Duration: 3FT/4SW Hon
Entry Requirements: *GCE:* 280.

RC86 BSc European Studies/Sports Studies
Duration: 3FT/4SW Hon
Entry Requirements: *GCE:* 280.

B9C6 BSc Health Studies/Sports Studies
Duration: 3FT/4SW Hon
Entry Requirements: *GCE:* 280.

B1C6 BSc Human Biology/Sports Studies
Duration: 3FT/4SW Hon
Entry Requirements: *GCE:* 280. *IB:* 25.

L7C6 BSc Human Geography/Sports Studies
Duration: 3FT/4SW Hon
Entry Requirements: *GCE:* 280.

P5C6 BSc Journalism & Media Cultures/Sports Studies
Duration: 3FT/4SW Hon
Entry Requirements: *GCE:* 300.

V5C6 BSc Philosophy/Sports Studies
Duration: 3FT/4SW Hon
Entry Requirements: *GCE:* 300.

C8C6 BSc Psychology/Sports Studies
Duration: 3FT/4SW Hon
Entry Requirements: *GCE:* 320.

C600 BSc Sport & Exercise Science
Duration: 3FT/4SW Hon CRB Check: Required
Entry Requirements: *GCE:* 300.

C602 BSc Sports Studies
Duration: 3FT/4SW Hon
Entry Requirements: *GCE:* 280.

C6N1 BSc Sports Studies/Business
Duration: 3FT/4SW Hon
Entry Requirements: *GCE:* 300.

C6G4 BSc Sports Studies/Computing
Duration: 3FT/4SW Hon
Entry Requirements: *GCE:* 280.

C6L1 BSc Sports Studies/Economics
Duration: 3FT/4SW Hon
Entry Requirements: *GCE:* 280.

C6F9 BSc Sports Studies/Environmental Studies
Duration: 3FT/4SW Hon
Entry Requirements: *GCE:* 280.

C6R8 BSc Sports Studies/European Studies
Duration: 3FT/4SW Hon
Entry Requirements: *GCE:* 280.

C6R1 BSc Sports Studies/French
Duration: 3FT/4SW Hon
Entry Requirements: *GCE:* 280.

C6B9 BSc Sports Studies/Health Studies
Duration: 3FT/4SW Hon
Entry Requirements: *GCE:* 280.

C6B1 BSc Sports Studies/Human Biology
Duration: 3FT/4SW Hon
Entry Requirements: *GCE:* 280.

C6L7 BSc Sports Studies/Human Geography
Duration: 3FT/4SW Hon
Entry Requirements: *GCE:* 280.

C6P5 BSc Sports Studies/Journalism & Media Cultures
Duration: 3FT/4SW Hon
Entry Requirements: *GCE:* 300.

C6V5 BSc Sports Studies/Philosophy
Duration: 3FT/4SW Hon
Entry Requirements: *GCE:* 300.

C6C8 BSc Sports Studies/Psychology
Duration: 3FT/4SW Hon
Entry Requirements: *GCE:* 320.

C6R4 BSc Sports Studies/Spanish
Duration: 3FT/4SW Hon
Entry Requirements: *GCE:* 280.

CB63 BSc Sports Therapy
Duration: 3FT/4SW Hon   CRB Check: Required
Entry Requirements: *GCE:* 300. Interview required.

C601 FdSc Sports Studies
Duration: 2FT Fdg
Entry Requirements: *GCE:* 120.

H49 UNIVERSITY OF THE HIGHLANDS AND ISLANDS
UHI EXECUTIVE OFFICE
NESS WALK
INVERNESS
SCOTLAND IV3 5SQ
t: 01463 279000 f: 01463 279001
e: info@uhi.ac.uk
// www.uhi.ac.uk

206C HNC Fitness, Health & Exercise
Duration: 1FT HNC
Entry Requirements: *GCE:* D. *SQAH:* CC.

16XC HNC Sports Coaching with Development of Sport
Duration: 1FT HNC
Entry Requirements: *GCE:* D. *SQAH:* CC.

1X6C HND Sports Coaching with Development of Sport
Duration: 2FT HND
Entry Requirements: *GCE:* C. *SQAH:* CC.

H54 HOPWOOD HALL COLLEGE
ROCHDALE ROAD
MIDDLETON
MANCHESTER M24 6XH
t: 0161 643 7560 f: 0161 643 2114
e: admissions@hopwood.ac.uk
// www.hopwood.ac.uk

C600 FdSc Sports Development
Duration: 2FT Fdg
Entry Requirements: Contact the institution for details.

H72 THE UNIVERSITY OF HULL
THE UNIVERSITY OF HULL
COTTINGHAM ROAD
HULL HU6 7RX
t: 01482 466100 f: 01482 442290
e: admissions@hull.ac.uk
// www.hull.ac.uk

C8C6 BSc Psychology with Sports Science
Duration: 3FT Hon
Entry Requirements: *GCE:* 280. *IB:* 32. *BTEC ExtDip:* DMM.

C601 BSc Sport and Exercise Science
Duration: 3FT Hon
Entry Requirements: *GCE:* 280. *IB:* 30. *BTEC ExtDip:* DDD.

CB69 BSc Sports Coaching and Performance
Duration: 3FT Hon   CRB Check: Required
Entry Requirements: *GCE:* 280. *IB:* 30. *BTEC ExtDip:* DDD.

C602 BSc Sports Rehabilitation
Duration: 3FT Hon   CRB Check: Required
Entry Requirements: *GCE:* 280. *IB:* 30. *BTEC ExtDip:* DDD.

H73 HULL COLLEGE
QUEEN'S GARDENS
HULL HU1 3DG
t: 01482 329943 f: 01482 598733
e: info@hull-college.ac.uk
// www.hull-college.ac.uk/higher-education

C600 FdA Sports Studies
Duration: 2FT Fdg   CRB Check: Required
Entry Requirements: *GCE:* 160. Interview required. Admissions Test required.

K24 THE UNIVERSITY OF KENT
RECRUITMENT & ADMISSIONS OFFICE
REGISTRY
UNIVERSITY OF KENT
CANTERBURY, KENT CT2 7NZ
t: 01227 827272 f: 01227 827077
e: information@kent.ac.uk
// www.kent.ac.uk

C601 BA Sport and Exercise Management
Duration: 3FT Hon
Entry Requirements: *GCE:* BBB. *SQAH:* ABBBB. *SQAAH:* BBB. *IB:* 33. *OCR ND:* D *OCR NED:* D2

C602 BSc Sport Science
Duration: 3FT Hon
Entry Requirements: *GCE:* ABB. *SQAH:* AABBB. *SQAAH:* ABB. *IB:* 33. *OCR ND:* D *OCR NED:* D2

C600 BSc Sport Therapy, Health and Fitness
Duration: 3FT Hon
Entry Requirements: *GCE:* ABB. *SQAH:* AABBB. *SQAAH:* ABB. *IB:* 33. *OCR ND:* D *OCR NED:* D2

C604 BSc Sport and Exercise for Health
Duration: 3FT Hon
Entry Requirements: *GCE:* BBB. *SQAH:* ABBBB. *SQAAH:* BBB. *IB:* 33. *OCR ND:* D *OCR NED:* M1

K84 KINGSTON UNIVERSITY
STUDENT INFORMATION & ADVICE CENTRE
COOPER HOUSE
40-46 SURBITON ROAD
KINGSTON UPON THAMES KT1 2HX
t: 0844 8552177 f: 020 8547 7080
e: aps@kingston.ac.uk
// www.kingston.ac.uk

C6N1 BSc Sport Science with Business
Duration: 4SW Hon
Entry Requirements: *GCE:* 220-280.

C6NC BSc Sport Science with Business
Duration: 3FT Hon
Entry Requirements: *GCE:* 220-280.

C6ND BSc Sport Science with Business (Foundation)
Duration: 4FT Hon
Entry Requirements: *GCE:* 60.

CX6C BSc Sports Analysis & Coaching
Duration: 3FT Hon
Entry Requirements: *GCE:* 220-280.

CX6D BSc Sports Analysis & Coaching (including foundation)
Duration: 4FT Hon
Entry Requirements: *GCE:* 60.

C600 BSc Sports Science
Duration: 3FT Hon
Entry Requirements: *GCE:* 220-280.

C601 BSc Sports Science
Duration: 4SW Hon
Entry Requirements: *GCE:* 220-280.

C608 BSc Sports Science (Foundation)
Duration: 4FT Hon
Entry Requirements: *GCE:* 60.

CX61 BSc/BA Sports Analysis & Coaching
Duration: 4SW Hon
Entry Requirements: *GCE:* 220-280.

L05 LAKES COLLEGE - WEST CUMBRIA
HALLWOOD ROAD
LILLYHALL
WORKINGTON CA14 4JN
t: 01946 839300 f: 01946 839302
e: student.services@lcwc.ac.uk
// www.lcwc.ac.uk

C601 HND Sport and Exercise Studies
Duration: 2FT HND
Entry Requirements: Contact the institution for details.

L21 LEEDS CITY COLLEGE
TECHNOLOGY CAMPUS
COOKRIDGE STREET
LEEDS LS2 8BL
t: 0113 216 2406 f: 0113 216 2401
e: helen.middleton@leedscitycollege.ac.uk
// www.leedscitycollege.ac.uk

CX6C BA Sports Coaching
Duration: 1FT Hon   CRB Check: Required
Entry Requirements: Contact the institution for details.

CX61 FdA Sports Coaching and Development
Duration: 2FT Fdg
Entry Requirements: GCE: E.

L23 UNIVERSITY OF LEEDS
THE UNIVERSITY OF LEEDS
WOODHOUSE LANE
LEEDS LS2 9JT
t: 0113 343 3999
e: admissions@leeds.ac.uk
// www.leeds.ac.uk

C601 BSc Sport and Exercise Sciences
Duration: 3FT Hon
Entry Requirements: GCE: AAB. SQAAH: AAB. BTEC ExtDip: DDD.
Interview required.

BC16 BSc Sports Science & Physiology
Duration: 3FT/4FT Hon
Entry Requirements: GCE: AAB. SQAAH: AAB. BTEC ExtDip: DDD.
Interview required.

L24 LEEDS TRINITY UNIVERSITY COLLEGE
BROWNBERRIE LANE
HORSFORTH
LEEDS LS18 5HD
t: 0113 283 7150 f: 0113 283 7222
e: enquiries@leedstrinity.ac.uk
// www.leedstrinity.ac.uk

CX61 BA Physical Education (Primary) and Sports Development
Duration: 3FT Hon   CRB Check: Required
Entry Requirements: GCE: 280. IB: 25. OCR ND: D OCR NED: M2

CX63 BA Sports Development and PE
Duration: 3FT Hon   CRB Check: Required
Entry Requirements: GCE: 280. IB: 25. OCR ND: D OCR NED: M2

CB64 BSc Sport, Health, Exercise and Nutrition
Duration: 3FT Hon
Entry Requirements: GCE: 280. IB: 25. OCR ND: D OCR NED: M2

L27 LEEDS METROPOLITAN UNIVERSITY
COURSE ENQUIRIES OFFICE
CITY CAMPUS
LEEDS LS1 3HE
t: 0113 81 23113 f: 0113 81 23129
// www.leedsmet.ac.uk

X3C6 BA Physical Education with Outdoor Education
Duration: 3FT Hon
Entry Requirements: GCE: 280. IB: 25.

C6X3 BA Sport & Exercise Science with Outdoor Education
Duration: 3FT Hon
Entry Requirements: GCE: 280. IB: 25.

CN6G BA Sport, Leisure & Culture
Duration: 3FT Hon
Entry Requirements: GCE: 240. IB: 24.

CX6D BA/BSc Sports Coaching
Duration: 3FT Hon   CRB Check: Required
Entry Requirements: GCE: 300. IB: 26.

C600 BSc Sport and Exercise Science
Duration: 3FT Hon
Entry Requirements: GCE: 280. IB: 26.

CB6X BSc Sports & Exercise Therapy
Duration: 3FT Hon   CRB Check: Required
Entry Requirements: GCE: 260.

C605 BSc Sports Performance
Duration: 1FT Hon
Entry Requirements: HND required.

C606 BSc Sports Studies (Top-up)
Duration: 1FT Hon
Entry Requirements: HND required.

C607 BSc Sports, Physical Activity & Health
Duration: 3FT Hon
Entry Requirements: *GCE:* 280. *IB:* 25.

L39 UNIVERSITY OF LINCOLN
ADMISSIONS
BRAYFORD POOL
LINCOLN LN6 7TS
t: 01522 886097 f: 01522 886146
e: admissions@lincoln.ac.uk
// www.lincoln.ac.uk

CD63 BSc Equine Sports Science
Duration: 3FT Hon
Entry Requirements: *GCE:* 260.

C600 BSc Sport & Exercise Science
Duration: 3FT Hon
Entry Requirements: *GCE:* 280.

C602 BSc Sport Development and Coaching
Duration: 3FT Hon
Entry Requirements: *GCE:* 280.

L42 LINCOLN COLLEGE
MONKS ROAD
LINCOLN LN2 5HQ
t: 01522 876000 f: 01522 876200
e: enquiries@lincolncollege.ac.uk
// www.lincolncollege.ac.uk

CX61 FdSc Sport Development and Coaching
Duration: 2FT Fdg
Entry Requirements: Contact the institution for details.

CB69 FdSc Sport Performance and Exercise Development
Duration: 2FT Hon
Entry Requirements: *GCE:* 120. Interview required.

C601 FdSc Sport and Exercise Development
Duration: 2FT Fdg
Entry Requirements: Contact the institution for details.

C600 FdSc Sport and Exercise Science
Duration: 2FT Fdg
Entry Requirements: Contact the institution for details.

L46 LIVERPOOL HOPE UNIVERSITY
HOPE PARK
LIVERPOOL L16 9JD
t: 0151 291 3331 f: 0151 291 3434
e: administration@hope.ac.uk
// www.hope.ac.uk

NC2Q BA Business Management and Sport Studies
Duration: 3FT Hon
Entry Requirements: *GCE:* 300-320. *IB:* 25.

CX63 BA Education and Sport Studies
Duration: 3FT Hon   CRB Check: Required
Entry Requirements: *GCE:* 300-320. *IB:* 25.

NC56 BA Marketing and Sport Studies
Duration: 3FT Hon
Entry Requirements: *GCE:* 300-320. *IB:* 25.

X1CP BA Primary Teaching with Sport Studies
Duration: 4FT Hon   CRB Check: Required
Entry Requirements: *GCE:* 300-320. *IB:* 25. Interview required. Admissions Test required.

GCKP BSc Computing and Sport Studies
Duration: 3FT Hon
Entry Requirements: *GCE:* 300-320.

FC68 BSc Geography and Sport & Exercise Science
Duration: 3FT Hon
Entry Requirements: *GCE:* 300-320. *IB:* 25.

FC86 BSc Geography and Sport Studies
Duration: 3FT Hon
Entry Requirements: *GCE:* 300-320. *IB:* 25.

LC65 BSc Health and Sport & Exercise Science
Duration: 3FT Hon
Entry Requirements: *GCE:* 300-320. *IB:* 25.

CBP9 BSc Health and Sport Studies
Duration: 3FT Hon
Entry Requirements: *GCE:* 300-320. *IB:* 25.

CC61 BSc Human Biology and Sport & Exercise Science
Duration: 3FT Hon
Entry Requirements: *GCE:* 300-320. *IB:* 25.

CB61 BSc Human Biology and Sport Studies
Duration: 3FT Hon
Entry Requirements: *GCE:* 300-320. *IB:* 25.

CC8P BSc Psychology and Sport & Exercise Science
Duration: 3FT Hon
Entry Requirements: *GCE:* 300-320. *IB:* 25.

CC86 BSc Psychology and Sport Studies
Duration: 3FT Hon
Entry Requirements: *GCE:* 300-320. *IB:* 25.

C604 BSc Sport & Exercise Science
Duration: 3FT Hon
Entry Requirements: *GCE:* 300-320. *IB:* 25.

C600 BSc Sport Studies
Duration: 3FT Hon
Entry Requirements: *GCE:* 300-320. *IB:* 25.

L51 LIVERPOOL JOHN MOORES UNIVERSITY
KINGSWAY HOUSE
HATTON GARDEN
LIVERPOOL L3 2AJ
t: 0151 231 5090 f: 0151 904 6368
e: courses@ljmu.ac.uk
// www.ljmu.ac.uk

XC16 BA Coaching Development
Duration: 3FT Hon CRB Check: Required
Entry Requirements: *GCE:* 280. Interview required.

XC36 BA Education Studies and Physical Education
Duration: 3FT Hon CRB Check: Required
Entry Requirements: *GCE:* 280. Interview required.

CXP3 BA Sport Development and Physical Education
Duration: 3FT Hon CRB Check: Required
Entry Requirements: *GCE:* 300. Interview required.

CXQ3 BSc Science and Football
Duration: 3FT Hon
Entry Requirements: *GCE:* 280-320. *IB:* 25.

C600 BSc Sport and Exercise Science
Duration: 3FT Hon
Entry Requirements: *GCE:* 280-320. *IB:* 25.

L53 COLEG LLANDRILLO CYMRU
LLANDUDNO ROAD
RHOS-ON-SEA
COLWYN BAY
NORTH WALES LL28 4HZ
t: 01492 542338/339 f: 01492 543052
e: degrees@llandrillo.ac.uk
// www.llandrillo.ac.uk

CX61 BA Sports Coaching
Duration: 1FT Hon CRB Check: Required
Entry Requirements: Interview required.

CX6C FdA Sports Coaching
Duration: 2FT Fdg CRB Check: Required
Entry Requirements: *GCE:* 160. *IB:* 24. Interview required.

L68 LONDON METROPOLITAN UNIVERSITY
166-220 HOLLOWAY ROAD
LONDON N7 8DB
t: 020 7133 4200
e: admissions@londonmet.ac.uk
// www.londonmet.ac.uk

C603 BSc Sports Science
Duration: 3FT Hon
Entry Requirements: *GCE:* 200. *IB:* 28.

CX63 BSc Sports Science and Physical Education
Duration: 3FT Hon
Entry Requirements: *GCE:* 220. *IB:* 28.

CB63 BSc Sports Therapy
Duration: 3FT Hon
Entry Requirements: *GCE:* 280. *IB:* 28.

CW65 BSc Sports and Dance Therapy
Duration: 3FT Hon
Entry Requirements: *GCE:* 240. *IB:* 28.

CX6D FdSc Football and Community Sports Coaching with Arsenal FC
Duration: 2FT Fdg
Entry Requirements: *GCE:* 160.

C605 FdSc Personal Training and Fitness Consultancy
Duration: 2FT Fdg
Entry Requirements: *GCE:* 160.

L75 LONDON SOUTH BANK UNIVERSITY
ADMISSIONS AND RECRUITMENT CENTRE
90 LONDON ROAD
LONDON SE1 6LN
t: 0800 923 8888 f: 020 7815 8273
e: course.enquiry@lsbu.ac.uk
// www.lsbu.ac.uk

C600 BSc Sport and Exercise Science
Duration: 3FT Hon
Entry Requirements: *GCE:* 200. *IB:* 24.

C602 BSc Sports and Exercise Science
Duration: 1.5FT Hon
Entry Requirements: Contact the institution for details.

L77 LOUGHBOROUGH COLLEGE
RADMOOR ROAD
LOUGHBOROUGH LE11 3BT
t: 0845 166 2950 f: 0845 833 2840
e: info@loucoll.ac.uk
// www.loucoll.ac.uk

N290 BA Sports Management
Duration: 1FT Hon
Entry Requirements: HND required.

CN68 BSc Applied Sports Science (Management)
Duration: 1FT Hon
Entry Requirements: HND required.

C601 BSc Applied Sports Science (top-up)
Duration: 1FT Hon
Entry Requirements: Contact the institution for details.

CX61 FdSc Sports Coaching
Duration: 2FT Fdg
Entry Requirements: *GCE:* 240-280.

C600 FdSc Sports Science
Duration: 2FT Fdg
Entry Requirements: *GCE:* 240-280.

N222 FdSc Sports Science, Sports Development and Management
Duration: 2FT Fdg
Entry Requirements: *GCE:* 240-280.

L79 LOUGHBOROUGH UNIVERSITY
LOUGHBOROUGH
LEICESTERSHIRE LE11 3TU
t: 01509 223522 f: 01509 223905
e: admissions@lboro.ac.uk
// www.lboro.ac.uk

QC36 BA English and Sports Science
Duration: 3FT Hon
Entry Requirements: *GCE:* AAB. *SQAAH:* AB-BB. *IB:* 34. *BTEC ExtDip:* DDM.

FC16 BSc Chemistry and Sports Science
Duration: 3FT Hon
Entry Requirements: *SQAH:* BBBCC. *SQAAH:* BC. *IB:* 32. *BTEC ExtDip:* DDM.

FCC6 BSc Chemistry and Sports Science
Duration: 4SW Hon
Entry Requirements: *SQAH:* BBBCC. *SQAAH:* BC. *IB:* 32. *BTEC ExtDip:* DDM.

FC86 BSc Geography and Sports Science
Duration: 3FT Hon
Entry Requirements: *GCE:* AAB. *SQAAH:* AA-AB.

CG61 BSc Mathematics and Sports Science
Duration: 3FT Hon
Entry Requirements: *GCE:* AAA-AAB. *SQAH:* ABB. *SQAAH:* AA. *IB:* 36.

GC16 BSc Mathematics and Sports Science
Duration: 4SW Hon
Entry Requirements: *GCE:* AAA-AAB. *SQAH:* ABB. *SQAAH:* AA. *IB:* 36.

CX63 BSc Sport and Exercise Science
Duration: 3FT Hon
Entry Requirements: *GCE:* AAA. *IB:* 36.

CF63 BSc Sports Science and Physics
Duration: 4SW Hon
Entry Requirements: *GCE:* AAB-ABB. *SQAH:* AB. *SQAAH:* AB. *IB:* 34.

FC36 BSc Sports Science and Physics
Duration: 3FT Hon
Entry Requirements: *GCE:* AAB-ABB. *SQAH:* AB. *SQAAH:* AB. *IB:* 34.

CN62 BSc Sports Science with Management
Duration: 3FT Hon
Entry Requirements: *GCE:* AAB. *IB:* 34.

CH67 BSc Sports Technology
Duration: 3FT Hon
Entry Requirements: *GCE:* ABB. *SQAAH:* AB. *IB:* 33.

HC76 BSc Sports Technology
Duration: 4SW Hon
Entry Requirements: *GCE:* ABB. *SQAAH:* AB. *IB:* 33.

M10 THE MANCHESTER COLLEGE
OPENSHAW CAMPUS
ASHTON OLD ROAD
OPENSHAW
MANCHESTER M11 2WH
t: 0800 068 8585 f: 0161 920 4103
e: enquiries@themanchestercollege.ac.uk
// www.themanchestercollege.ac.uk

C600 FdA Sport and Exercise Science
Duration: 2FT Fdg
Entry Requirements: Contact the institution for details.

CX61 FdA Sports Coaching
Duration: 2FT Fdg
Entry Requirements: *GCE:* 160. *BTEC ExtDip:* MPP.

M40 THE MANCHESTER METROPOLITAN UNIVERSITY
ADMISSIONS OFFICE
ALL SAINTS (GMS)
ALL SAINTS
MANCHESTER M15 6BH
t: 0161 247 2000
// www.mmu.ac.uk

NC1Q BA Business/Sport Development
Duration: 3FT Hon
Entry Requirements: *GCE:* 280. *IB:* 28. *BTEC Dip:* D*D*. *BTEC ExtDip:* DMM.

LC5P BA Childhood & Youth Studies/Sport Development
Duration: 3FT Hon
Entry Requirements: *GCE:* 280. *IB:* 28. *BTEC Dip:* D*D*. *BTEC ExtDip:* DMM.

LC3Q BA Coaching Studies/Crime Studies
Duration: 3FT Hon
Entry Requirements: *GCE:* 280. *IB:* 28. *BTEC Dip:* D*D*. *BTEC ExtDip:* DMM.

CXQ3 BA Coaching Studies/Education Studies
Duration: 3FT Hon
Entry Requirements: *GCE:* 280. *IB:* 28. *BTEC Dip:* D*D*. *BTEC ExtDip:* DMM.

C611 BA Coaching and Sport Development (Foundation)
Duration: 4FT Hon
Entry Requirements: *GCE:* 160. *IB:* 24. *BTEC Dip:* MM. *BTEC ExtDip:* MPP.

C610 BA Coaching and Sports Development
Duration: 3FT Hon
Entry Requirements: *GCE:* 280. *IB:* 28. *BTEC Dip:* D*D*. *BTEC ExtDip:* DMM.

LCHP BA Crime Studies/Sport Development
Duration: 3FT Hon
Entry Requirements: *GCE:* 280. *IB:* 28. *BTEC Dip:* D*D*. *BTEC ExtDip:* DMM.

WC46 BA Drama/Sport Development
Duration: 3FT Hon
Entry Requirements: *GCE:* 280. *IB:* 28. *BTEC Dip:* D*D*. *BTEC ExtDip:* DMM. Interview required.

NCM6 BA Marketing/Sport Development
Duration: 3FT Hon
Entry Requirements: *GCE:* 280. *IB:* 28. *BTEC Dip:* D*D*. *BTEC ExtDip:* DMM.

C608 BA Physical Education and Sport Pedagogy
Duration: 3FT Hon
Entry Requirements: *GCE:* 280. *IB:* 28. *BTEC Dip:* D*D*. *BTEC ExtDip:* DMM.

LCHQ BA Sociology/Sport Development
Duration: 3FT Hon
Entry Requirements: *GCE:* 280. *IB:* 28. *BTEC Dip:* D*D*. *BTEC ExtDip:* DMM.

NC16 BA/BSc Business/Outdoor Studies
Duration: 3FT Hon
Entry Requirements: *GCE:* 280. *IB:* 28. *BTEC Dip:* D*D*. *BTEC ExtDip:* DMM.

CN61 BA/BSc Business/Sport
Duration: 3FT Hon
Entry Requirements: *GCE:* 280. *IB:* 28. *BTEC Dip:* D*D*. *BTEC ExtDip:* DMM.

CXP3 BA/BSc Childhood & Youth Studies/Sport
Duration: 3FT Hon
Entry Requirements: *GCE:* 280. *IB:* 28. *BTEC Dip:* D*D*. *BTEC ExtDip:* DMM.

www.ucas.com

at the heart of connecting people to higher education

CX6C BA/BSc Coaching Studies/Outdoor Studies
Duration: 3FT Hon
Entry Requirements: *GCE:* 280. *IB:* 28. *BTEC Dip:* D*D*. *BTEC ExtDip:* DMM.

XC1P BA/BSc Coaching Studies/Sport
Duration: 3FT Hon
Entry Requirements: *GCE:* 280. *IB:* 28. *BTEC Dip:* D*D*. *BTEC ExtDip:* DMM.

WC3Q BA/BSc Creative Music Production/Outdoor Studies
Duration: 3FT Hon
Entry Requirements: *GCE:* 280. *IB:* 28. *BTEC Dip:* D*D*. *BTEC ExtDip:* DMM. Interview required.

WC8P BA/BSc Creative Writing/Outdoor Studies
Duration: 3FT Hon
Entry Requirements: *GCE:* 280. *IB:* 28. *BTEC Dip:* D*D*. *BTEC ExtDip:* DMM. Portfolio required.

CL6H BA/BSc Crime Studies/Outdoor Studies
Duration: 3FT Hon
Entry Requirements: *GCE:* 280. *IB:* 28. *BTEC Dip:* D*D*. *BTEC ExtDip:* DMM.

CW65 BA/BSc Dance/Sport
Duration: 3FT Hon
Entry Requirements: *GCE:* 280. *IB:* 28. *BTEC Dip:* D*D*. *BTEC ExtDip:* DMM. Interview required.

WCK6 BA/BSc Drama/Outdoor Studies
Duration: 3FT Hon
Entry Requirements: *GCE:* 280. *IB:* 28. *BTEC Dip:* D*D*. *BTEC ExtDip:* DMM. Interview required.

CW64 BA/BSc Drama/Sport
Duration: 3FT Hon
Entry Requirements: *GCE:* 280. *IB:* 28. *BTEC Dip:* D*D*. *BTEC ExtDip:* DMM. Interview required.

CX63 BA/BSc Education Studies/Sport
Duration: 3FT Hon
Entry Requirements: *GCE:* 280. *IB:* 28. *BTEC Dip:* D*D*. *BTEC ExtDip:* DMM.

QC36 BA/BSc English/Outdoor Studies
Duration: 3FT Hon
Entry Requirements: *GCE:* 280. *IB:* 28. *BTEC Dip:* D*D*. *BTEC ExtDip:* DMM.

CW66 BA/BSc Film & Television Studies/Sport
Duration: 3FT Hon
Entry Requirements: *GCE:* 280. *IB:* 28. *BTEC Dip:* D*D*. *BTEC ExtDip:* DMM.

NC36 BA/BSc Financial Management/Sport
Duration: 3FT Hon
Entry Requirements: *GCE:* 280. *IB:* 28. *BTEC Dip:* D*D*. *BTEC ExtDip:* DMM.

NC66 BA/BSc Human Resource Management/Outdoor Studies
Duration: 3FT Hon
Entry Requirements: *GCE:* 280. *IB:* 28. *BTEC Dip:* D*D*. *BTEC ExtDip:* DMM.

MC2P BA/BSc Legal Studies/Sport
Duration: 3FT Hon
Entry Requirements: *GCE:* 280. *IB:* 28. *BTEC Dip:* D*D*. *BTEC ExtDip:* DMM.

CV65 BA/BSc Philosophy/Sport
Duration: 3FT Hon
Entry Requirements: *GCE:* 280. *IB:* 28. *BTEC Dip:* D*D*. *BTEC ExtDip:* DMM.

C607 BA/BSc Sport/Sport Development
Duration: 3FT Hon
Entry Requirements: *GCE:* 280. *IB:* 28. *BTEC Dip:* D*D*. *BTEC ExtDip:* DMM.

C600 BSc Exercise and Sport Science
Duration: 3FT Hon
Entry Requirements: *GCE:* 280-300. *IB:* 28. *BTEC Dip:* D*D*. *BTEC ExtDip:* DMM.

C602 BSc Exercise and Sport Science (Foundation)
Duration: 4FT Hon
Entry Requirements: *GCE:* 160. *IB:* 24. *BTEC Dip:* MM. *BTEC ExtDip:* MPP.

C601 BSc Outdoor Studies
Duration: 3FT Hon
Entry Requirements: *GCE:* 280. *IB:* 28. *BTEC Dip:* D*D*. *BTEC ExtDip:* DMM.

C604 BSc Outdoor Studies (Foundation)
Duration: 4FT Hon
Entry Requirements: *GCE:* 160. *IB:* 24. *BTEC Dip:* MM. *BTEC ExtDip:* MPP.

LC36 BSc Outdoor Studies/Sport
Duration: 3FT Hon
Entry Requirements: *GCE:* 280. *IB:* 28. *BTEC Dip:* D*D*. *BTEC ExtDip:* DMM.

CC68 BSc Psychology/Sport
Duration: 3FT Hon
Entry Requirements: *GCE:* 280. *IB:* 28. *BTEC Dip:* D*D*. *BTEC ExtDip:* DMM.

M77 MID CHESHIRE COLLEGE
HARTFORD CAMPUS
NORTHWICH
CHESHIRE CW8 1LJ
t: 01606 74444 f: 01606 720700
e: eandrews@midchesh.ac.uk
// www.midchesh.ac.uk

XC16 FdA Sports Coaching & Physical Education
Duration: 2FT Fdg
Entry Requirements: *GCE:* 120-240.

M80 MIDDLESEX UNIVERSITY
MIDDLESEX UNIVERSITY
THE BURROUGHS
LONDON NW4 4BT
t: 020 8411 5555 f: 020 8411 5649
e: enquiries@mdx.ac.uk
// www.mdx.ac.uk

C604 BSc Sport and Exercise Rehabilitation
Duration: 3FT Hon
Entry Requirements: Contact the institution for details.

C615 BSc Sport and Exercise Science
Duration: 3FT Hon
Entry Requirements: *GCE:* 200-300. *IB:* 28.

CQ00 BSc Sport and Exercise Science (Sport Performance)
Duration: 3FT Hon
Entry Requirements: Contact the institution for details.

CQ01 BSc Sport and Exercise Science (Teaching & Coaching Sport)
Duration: 3FT Hon
Entry Requirements: Contact the institution for details.

C601 BSc Sports and Exercise Science with foundation year at Barnet College
Duration: 4FT Hon
Entry Requirements: Contact the institution for details.

C600 FdSc Coaching and Sports Development (Southgate and MDX)
Duration: 2FT Fdg
Entry Requirements: *GCE:* 100. Interview required.

M99 MYERSCOUGH COLLEGE
MYERSCOUGH HALL
BILSBORROW
PRESTON PR3 0RY
t: 01995 642222 f: 01995 642333
e: enquiries@myerscough.ac.uk
// www.myerscough.ac.uk

XC16 BA Golf Coaching and Performance (Top-up)
Duration: 1FT Hon
Entry Requirements: Interview required.

CN62 BSc Sportsturf Science and Management
Duration: 3FT Hon
Entry Requirements: *GCE:* AA-CCD. *SQAH:* AAAAA-CCCCC. *SQAAH:* AAA-CCC. *IB:* 24. *BTEC Dip:* DD. *BTEC ExtDip:* MMM. *OCR ND:* D *OCR NED:* M3 Interview required.

XC1P FdA Cricket Coaching
Duration: 2FT Fdg
Entry Requirements: *GCE:* A-C. *SQAH:* AA-CC. *SQAAH:* A-C. *IB:* 24. Interview required.

CX6C FdA Football Coaching
Duration: 2FT Fdg
Entry Requirements: *GCE:* A-C. *SQAH:* AA-CC. *SQAAH:* A-C. *IB:* 24. Interview required.

C602 FdA Health and Personal Training
Duration: 2FT Fdg
Entry Requirements: *GCE:* A-C. *SQAH:* AA-CC. *SQAAH:* A-C. *IB:* 24. Interview required.

CX6D FdA Rugby Coaching
Duration: 2FT Fdg
Entry Requirements: *GCE:* A-C. *SQAH:* AA-CC. *SQAAH:* A-C. *IB:* 24. Interview required.

CX61 FdA Sports Coaching
Duration: 2FT Fdg
Entry Requirements: *GCE:* A-C. *SQAH:* AA-CC. *SQAAH:* A-C. *IB:* 24. Interview required.

C601 FdSc Golf Performance
Duration: 2FT Fdg
Entry Requirements: *GCE:* A-C. *SQAH:* AA-CC. *SQAAH:* A-C. *IB:* 24. Interview required.

C600 FdSc Sport & Exercise Science
Duration: 2FT Fdg
Entry Requirements: *GCE:* A-C. *SQAH:* AA-CC. *SQAAH:* A-C. *IB:* 24. Interview required.

N13 NEATH PORT TALBOT COLLEGE
NEATH CAMPUS
DWR-Y-FELIN ROAD
NEATH
NEATH PORT TALBOT BOROUGH SA10 7RF
t: 01639 648000 f: 01639 648077
e: admissions@nptc.ac.uk
// www.nptc.ac.uk

CX61 FdA Sports Coaching and Performance
Duration: 2FT Fdg
Entry Requirements: Contact the institution for details.

N23 NEWCASTLE COLLEGE
STUDENT SERVICES
RYE HILL CAMPUS
SCOTSWOOD ROAD
NEWCASTLE UPON TYNE NE4 7SA
t: 0191 200 4110 f: 0191 200 4349
e: enquiries@ncl-coll.ac.uk
// www.newcastlecollege.co.uk

BC96 BSc Applied Health & Exercise Science (Top-up)
Duration: 1FT Hon   CRB Check: Required
Entry Requirements: Interview required.

CX6C BSc Applied Sports Coaching Science (Top-up)
Duration: 1FT Deg   CRB Check: Required
Entry Requirements: Contact the institution for details.

CB6X BSc Sports Therapy (Top-up)
Duration: 1FT Hon
Entry Requirements: Contact the institution for details.

CX6D CertHE Football Coaching
Duration: 1FT Cer
Entry Requirements: GCE: 100-120. OCR ND: P2 OCR NED: P3
Interview required.

CN62 FdA Applied Sport Management and Development
Duration: 2FT Fdg
Entry Requirements: GCE: 160-200. OCR ND: P1 OCR NED: P2
Interview required.

C606 FdSc Applied Health and Exercise Science
Duration: 2FT Fdg
Entry Requirements: GCE: 160-200. OCR ND: P1 OCR NED: P2
Interview required.

CX61 FdSc Applied Sports Coaching Science
Duration: 2FT Fdg
Entry Requirements: GCE: 160-200. OCR ND: P1 OCR NED: P2
Interview required.

CB69 FdSc Sports Training and Rehabilitation
Duration: 2FT Fdg
Entry Requirements: GCE: 160-200. OCR ND: P1 OCR NED: P2
Interview required.

N28 NEW COLLEGE DURHAM
FRAMWELLGATE MOOR CAMPUS
DURHAM DH1 5ES
t: 0191 375 4210/4211 f: 0191 375 4222
e: admissions@newdur.ac.uk
// www.newcollegedurham.ac.uk

C601 FdSc Applied Sports and Exercise Science
Duration: 2FT Fdg   CRB Check: Required
Entry Requirements: Contact the institution for details.

C600 FdSc Sport and Exercise Studies
Duration: 2FT Fdg
Entry Requirements: GCE: 40.

N36 NEWMAN UNIVERSITY COLLEGE, BIRMINGHAM
GENNERS LANE
BARTLEY GREEN
BIRMINGHAM B32 3NT
t: 0121 476 1181 f: 0121 476 1196
e: Admissions@newman.ac.uk
// www.newman.ac.uk

WC46 BA Drama and Sports Studies
Duration: 3FT Hon
Entry Requirements: Foundation: Distinction. GCE: 260. IB: 24.
BTEC ExtDip: DMM. OCR ND: M2 OCR NED: M2

X3C6 BA Education Studies with Sport Studies
Duration: 3FT Hon
Entry Requirements: Foundation: Distinction. GCE: 260. IB: 24.
BTEC ExtDip: DMM. OCR ND: M2 OCR NED: M2

Q3C6 BA English with Sports Studies
Duration: 3FT Hon
Entry Requirements: Foundation: Distinction. GCE: 260. IB: 24.
BTEC ExtDip: DMM. OCR ND: M2 OCR NED: M2

NC26 BA Management & Business and Sports Studies
Duration: 3FT Hon
Entry Requirements: Foundation: Distinction. GCE: 260. IB: 24.
BTEC ExtDip: DMM. OCR ND: M2 OCR NED: M2

N2C6 BA Management & Business with Sports Studies
Duration: 3FT Hon
Entry Requirements: *Foundation:* Distinction. *GCE:* 260. *IB:* 24. *BTEC ExtDip:* DMM. *OCR ND:* M2 *OCR NED:* M2

CX83 BA Sports Studies and Applied Psychology
Duration: 3FT Hon
Entry Requirements: *Foundation:* Distinction. *GCE:* 260. *IB:* 24. *BTEC ExtDip:* DMM. *OCR ND:* M2 *OCR NED:* M2

CW61 BA Sports Studies and Art & Design
Duration: 3FT Hon
Entry Requirements: *Foundation:* Distinction. *GCE:* 260. *IB:* 24. *BTEC ExtDip:* DMM. *OCR ND:* M2 *OCR NED:* M2

CB69 BA Sports Studies and Counselling Studies
Duration: 3FT Hon
Entry Requirements: *Foundation:* Distinction. *GCE:* 260. *IB:* 24. *BTEC ExtDip:* DMM. *OCR ND:* M2 *OCR NED:* M2

CV65 BA Sports Studies and Philosophy, Religion & Ethics
Duration: 3FT Hon
Entry Requirements: *Foundation:* Distinction. *GCE:* 260. *IB:* 24. *BTEC ExtDip:* DMM. *OCR ND:* M2 *OCR NED:* M2

C6W1 BA Sports Studies with Art & Design
Duration: 3FT Hon
Entry Requirements: *Foundation:* Distinction. *GCE:* 280. *IB:* 25. *BTEC ExtDip:* DMM. *OCR ND:* M2 *OCR NED:* M2

C6B9 BA Sports Studies with Counselling Studies
Duration: 3FT Hon
Entry Requirements: *Foundation:* Distinction. *GCE:* 280. *IB:* 25. *BTEC ExtDip:* DMM. *OCR ND:* M2 *OCR NED:* M2

C6W8 BA Sports Studies with Creative Writing
Duration: 3FT Hon
Entry Requirements: *Foundation:* Distinction. *GCE:* 280. *IB:* 25. *BTEC ExtDip:* DMM. *OCR ND:* M2 *OCR NED:* M2

C6W4 BA Sports Studies with Drama
Duration: 3FT Hon
Entry Requirements: *Foundation:* Distinction. *GCE:* 280. *IB:* 25. *BTEC ExtDip:* DMM. *OCR ND:* M2 *OCR NED:* M2

C6XH BA Sports Studies with Education Studies
Duration: 3FT Hon
Entry Requirements: *Foundation:* Distinction. *GCE:* 280. *IB:* 25. *BTEC ExtDip:* DMM. *OCR ND:* M2 *OCR NED:* M2

C6Q3 BA Sports Studies with English Literature
Duration: 3FT Hon
Entry Requirements: *Foundation:* Distinction. *GCE:* 280. *IB:* 25. *BTEC ExtDip:* DMM. *OCR ND:* M2 *OCR NED:* M2

C6N2 BA Sports Studies with Management & Business
Duration: 3FT Hon
Entry Requirements: *Foundation:* Distinction. *GCE:* 280. *IB:* 25. *BTEC ExtDip:* DMM. *OCR ND:* M2 *OCR NED:* M2

C6V5 BA Sports Studies with Philosophy & Theology
Duration: 3FT Hon
Entry Requirements: *Foundation:* Distinction. *GCE:* 280. *IB:* 25. *BTEC ExtDip:* DMM. *OCR ND:* M2 *OCR NED:* M2

C6VM BA Sports Studies with Philosophy, Religion & Ethics
Duration: 3FT Hon
Entry Requirements: *Foundation:* Distinction. *GCE:* 280. *IB:* 25. *BTEC ExtDip:* DMM. *OCR ND:* M2 *OCR NED:* M2

V6C6 BA Theology with Sports Studies
Duration: 3FT Hon
Entry Requirements: *Foundation:* Distinction. *GCE:* 260. *IB:* 24. *BTEC ExtDip:* DMM. *OCR ND:* M2 *OCR NED:* M2

LC56 BA Working with Children Young People & Families and Sports Studies
Duration: 3FT Hon
Entry Requirements: *Foundation:* Distinction. *GCE:* 260. *IB:* 24. *BTEC ExtDip:* DMM. *OCR ND:* M2 *OCR NED:* M2

L5C6 BA Working with Children Young People & Families with Sports Studies
Duration: 3FT Hon
Entry Requirements: *Foundation:* Distinction. *GCE:* 260. *IB:* 24. *BTEC ExtDip:* DMM. *OCR ND:* M2 *OCR NED:* M2

GC56 BSc IT and Sports Studies
Duration: 3FT Hon
Entry Requirements: *Foundation:* Distinction. *GCE:* 260. *IB:* 24. *BTEC ExtDip:* DMM. *OCR ND:* M2 *OCR NED:* M2

G5C6 BSc IT with Sport Studies
Duration: 3FT Hon
Entry Requirements: *Foundation:* Distinction. *GCE:* 260. *IB:* 24. *BTEC ExtDip:* DMM. *OCR ND:* M2 *OCR NED:* M2

C8C6 BSc Psychology with Sports Studies
Duration: 3FT Hon
Entry Requirements: *Foundation:* Distinction. *GCE:* 280. *IB:* 25. *BTEC ExtDip:* DMM. *OCR ND:* M2 *OCR NED:* M2

C601 BSc Sports Science
Duration: 3FT Hon
Entry Requirements: Contact the institution for details.

C600 BSc Sports Studies
Duration: 3FT Hon
Entry Requirements: *Foundation:* Distinction. *GCE:* 280. *IB:* 25.
BTEC ExtDip: DMM. *OCR ND:* M2 *OCR NED:* M2

C6C8 BSc Sports Studies with Applied Psychology
Duration: 3FT Hon
Entry Requirements: *Foundation:* Distinction. *GCE:* 280. *IB:* 25.
BTEC ExtDip: DMM. *OCR ND:* M2 *OCR NED:* M2

C6G5 BSc Sports Studies with IT
Duration: 3FT Hon
Entry Requirements: *Foundation:* Distinction. *GCE:* 280. *IB:* 25.
BTEC ExtDip: DMM. *OCR ND:* M2 *OCR NED:* M2

N37 UNIVERSITY OF WALES, NEWPORT
ADMISSIONS
LODGE ROAD
CAERLEON
NEWPORT NP18 3QT
t: 01633 432030 f: 01633 432850
e: admissions@newport.ac.uk
// www.newport.ac.uk

CM62 BA/BSc Sport and Youth Justice
Duration: 3FT Hon **CRB Check:** Required
Entry Requirements: *GCE:* 240. *IB:* 24. Interview required.

CX6C BSc Sports Coaching
Duration: 3FT Hon **CRB Check:** Required
Entry Requirements: *GCE:* 240. *IB:* 24.

C600 BSc Sports Studies
Duration: 3FT Hon **CRB Check:** Required
Entry Requirements: *GCE:* 240. *IB:* 24. Interview required.

C6C8 BSc Sports Studies with Psychology
Duration: 3FT Hon **CRB Check:** Required
Entry Requirements: *GCE:* 240. *IB:* 24. Interview required.

N38 UNIVERSITY OF NORTHAMPTON
PARK CAMPUS
BOUGHTON GREEN ROAD
NORTHAMPTON NN2 7AL
t: 0800 358 2232 f: 01604 722083
e: admissions@northampton.ac.uk
// www.northampton.ac.uk

N4C6 BA Accounting/Sport Studies
Duration: 3FT Hon
Entry Requirements: *GCE:* 260-280. *SQAH:* AAA-BBBB. *IB:* 24.
BTEC Dip: DD. *BTEC ExtDip:* DMM. *OCR ND:* D *OCR NED:* M2

N1CP BA Business Entrepreneurship/Sport Studies
Duration: 3FT Hon
Entry Requirements: *GCE:* 260-280. *SQAH:* AAA-BBBB. *IB:* 24.
BTEC Dip: DD. *BTEC ExtDip:* DMM. *OCR ND:* D *OCR NED:* M2

N1C6 BA Business/Sport Studies
Duration: 3FT Hon
Entry Requirements: *GCE:* 260-280. *SQAH:* AAA-BBBB. *IB:* 24.
BTEC Dip: DD. *BTEC ExtDip:* DMM. *OCR ND:* D *OCR NED:* M2

W8C6 BA Creative Writing/Sport Studies
Duration: 3FT Hon
Entry Requirements: *GCE:* 260-280. *SQAH:* AAA-BBBB. *IB:* 24.
BTEC Dip: DD. *BTEC ExtDip:* DMM. *OCR ND:* D *OCR NED:* M2

M9C6 BA Criminology/Sport Studies
Duration: 3FT Hon
Entry Requirements: *GCE:* 260-280. *SQAH:* AAA-BBBB. *IB:* 24.
BTEC Dip: DD. *BTEC ExtDip:* DMM. *OCR ND:* D *OCR NED:* M2

W5C6 BA Dance/Sport Studies
Duration: 3FT Hon
Entry Requirements: *GCE:* 260-280. *SQAH:* AAA-BBBB. *IB:* 24.
BTEC Dip: DD. *BTEC ExtDip:* DMM. *OCR ND:* D *OCR NED:* M2
Interview required.

W4C6 BA Drama/Sport Studies
Duration: 3FT Hon
Entry Requirements: *GCE:* 260-280. *SQAH:* AAA-BBBB. *IB:* 24.
BTEC Dip: DD. *BTEC ExtDip:* DMM. *OCR ND:* D *OCR NED:* M2
Interview required.

L1C6 BA Economics/Sport Studies
Duration: 3FT Hon
Entry Requirements: *GCE:* 260-280. *SQAH:* AAA-BBBB. *IB:* 24.
BTEC Dip: DD. *BTEC ExtDip:* DMM. *OCR ND:* D *OCR NED:* M2

X3C6 BA Education Studies/Sport Studies
Duration: 3FT Hon
Entry Requirements: *GCE:* 260-280. *SQAH:* AAA-BBBB. *IB:* 24.
BTEC Dip: DD. *BTEC ExtDip:* DMM. *OCR ND:* D *OCR NED:* M2

N8C6 BA Events Management/Sport Studies
Duration: 3FT Hon
Entry Requirements: *GCE:* 260-280. *SQAH:* AAA-BBBB. *IB:* 24.
BTEC Dip: DD. *BTEC ExtDip:* DMM. *OCR ND:* D *OCR NED:* M2

W6C6 BA Film & Television Studies/Sport Studies
Duration: 3FT Hon
Entry Requirements: *GCE:* 260-280. *SQAH:* AAA-BBBB. *IB:* 24.
BTEC Dip: DD. *BTEC ExtDip:* DMM. *OCR ND:* D *OCR NED:* M2

W1C6 BA Fine Art Painting & Drawing/Sport Studies
Duration: 3FT Hon
Entry Requirements: *GCE:* 260-280. *SQAH:* AAA-BBBB. *IB:* 24.
BTEC Dip: DD. *BTEC ExtDip:* DMM. *OCR ND:* D *OCR NED:* M2

R1C6 BA French/Sport Studies
Duration: 3FT Hon
Entry Requirements: *GCE:* 260-280. *SQAH:* AAA-BBBB. *IB:* 24.
BTEC Dip: DD. *BTEC ExtDip:* DMM. *OCR ND:* D *OCR NED:* M2

L4C6 BA Health Studies/Sport Studies
Duration: 3FT Hon
Entry Requirements: *GCE:* 260-280. *SQAH:* AAA-BBBB. *IB:* 24.
BTEC Dip: DD. *BTEC ExtDip:* DMM. *OCR ND:* D *OCR NED:* M2

V1C6 BA History/Sport Studies
Duration: 3FT Hon
Entry Requirements: *GCE:* 260-280. *SQAH:* AAA-BBBB. *IB:* 24.
BTEC Dip: DD. *BTEC ExtDip:* DMM. *OCR ND:* D *OCR NED:* M2

L7C6 BA Human Geography/Sport Studies
Duration: 3FT Hon
Entry Requirements: *GCE:* 260-280. *SQAH:* AAA-BBBB. *IB:* 24.
BTEC Dip: DD. *BTEC ExtDip:* DMM. *OCR ND:* D *OCR NED:* M2

N6C6 BA Human Resource Management/Sport Studies
Duration: 3FT Hon
Entry Requirements: *GCE:* 260-280. *SQAH:* AAA-BBBB. *IB:* 24.
BTEC Dip: DD. *BTEC ExtDip:* DMM. *OCR ND:* D *OCR NED:* M2

P5C6 BA Journalism/Sport Studies
Duration: 3FT Hon
Entry Requirements: *GCE:* 260-280. *SQAH:* AAA-BBBB. *IB:* 24.
BTEC Dip: DD. *BTEC ExtDip:* DMM. *OCR ND:* D *OCR NED:* M2

N2C6 BA Management/Sport Studies
Duration: 3FT Hon
Entry Requirements: *GCE:* 260-280. *SQAH:* AAA-BBBB. *IB:* 24.
BTEC Dip: DD. *BTEC ExtDip:* DMM. *OCR ND:* D *OCR NED:* M2

L2C6 BA Politics/Sport Studies
Duration: 3FT Hon
Entry Requirements: *GCE:* 260-280. *SQAH:* AAA-BBBB. *IB:* 24.
BTEC Dip: DD. *BTEC ExtDip:* DMM. *OCR ND:* D *OCR NED:* M2

W3C6 BA Popular Music/Sport Studies
Duration: 3FT Hon
Entry Requirements: *GCE:* 260-280. *SQAH:* AAA-BBBB. *IB:* 24.
BTEC Dip: DD. *BTEC ExtDip:* DMM. *OCR ND:* D *OCR NED:* M2

C8C6 BA Psychology/Sport Studies
Duration: 3FT Hon
Entry Requirements: *GCE:* 260-280. *SQAH:* AAA-BBBB. *IB:* 24.
BTEC Dip: DD. *BTEC ExtDip:* DMM. *OCR ND:* D *OCR NED:* M2

L5C6 BA Social Care/Sport Studies
Duration: 3FT Hon
Entry Requirements: *GCE:* 260-280. *SQAH:* AAA-BBBB. *IB:* 24.
BTEC Dip: DD. *BTEC ExtDip:* DMM. *OCR ND:* D *OCR NED:* M2

L3C6 BA Sociology/Sport Studies
Duration: 3FT Hon
Entry Requirements: *GCE:* 260-280. *SQAH:* AAA-BBBB. *IB:* 24.
BTEC Dip: DD. *BTEC ExtDip:* DMM. *OCR ND:* D *OCR NED:* M2

C602 BA Sport Development
Duration: 3FT Hon
Entry Requirements: *GCE:* 260-280. *SQAH:* AAA-BBBB. *IB:* 24.
BTEC Dip: DD. *BTEC ExtDip:* DMM. *OCR ND:* D *OCR NED:* M2

C6NG BA Sport Studies with Applied Management
Duration: 3FT Hon
Entry Requirements: *GCE:* 260-280. *SQAH:* AAA-BBBB. *IB:* 24.
BTEC Dip: DD. *BTEC ExtDip:* DMM. *OCR ND:* D *OCR NED:* M2

C6N4 BA Sport Studies/Accounting
Duration: 3FT Hon
Entry Requirements: *GCE:* 260-280. *SQAH:* AAA-BBBB. *IB:* 24.
BTEC Dip: DD. *BTEC ExtDip:* DMM. *OCR ND:* D *OCR NED:* M2

C6N1 BA Sport Studies/Business
Duration: 3FT Hon
Entry Requirements: *GCE:* 260-280. *SQAH:* AAA-BBBB. *IB:* 24.
BTEC Dip: DD. *BTEC ExtDip:* DMM. *OCR ND:* D *OCR NED:* M2

C6NF BA Sport Studies/Business Entrepreneurship
Duration: 3FT Hon
Entry Requirements: *GCE:* 260-280. *SQAH:* AAA-BBBB. *IB:* 24.
BTEC Dip: DD. *BTEC ExtDip:* DMM. *OCR ND:* D *OCR NED:* M2

C6W8 BA Sport Studies/Creative Writing
Duration: 3FT Hon
Entry Requirements: *GCE:* 260-280. *SQAH:* AAA-BBBB. *IB:* 24.
BTEC Dip: DD. *BTEC ExtDip:* DMM. *OCR ND:* D *OCR NED:* M2

C6M9 BA Sport Studies/Criminology
Duration: 3FT Hon
Entry Requirements: *GCE:* 260-280. *SQAH:* AAA-BBBB. *IB:* 24. *BTEC Dip:* DD. *BTEC ExtDip:* DMM. *OCR ND:* D *OCR NED:* M2

C6W5 BA Sport Studies/Dance
Duration: 3FT Hon
Entry Requirements: *GCE:* 260-280. *SQAH:* AAA-BBBB. *IB:* 24. *BTEC Dip:* DD. *BTEC ExtDip:* DMM. *OCR ND:* D *OCR NED:* M2
Interview required.

C6W4 BA Sport Studies/Drama
Duration: 3FT Hon
Entry Requirements: *GCE:* 260-280. *SQAH:* AAA-BBBB. *IB:* 24. *BTEC Dip:* DD. *BTEC ExtDip:* DMM. *OCR ND:* D *OCR NED:* M2
Interview required.

C6L1 BA Sport Studies/Economics
Duration: 3FT Hon
Entry Requirements: *GCE:* 260-280. *SQAH:* AAA-BBBB. *IB:* 24. *BTEC Dip:* DD. *BTEC ExtDip:* DMM. *OCR ND:* D *OCR NED:* M2

C6X3 BA Sport Studies/Education Studies
Duration: 3FT Hon
Entry Requirements: *GCE:* 260-280. *SQAH:* AAA-BBBB. *IB:* 24. *BTEC Dip:* DD. *BTEC ExtDip:* DMM. *OCR ND:* D *OCR NED:* M2

C6N8 BA Sport Studies/Events Management
Duration: 3FT Hon
Entry Requirements: *GCE:* 260-280. *SQAH:* AAA-BBBB. *IB:* 24. *BTEC Dip:* DD. *BTEC ExtDip:* DMM. *OCR ND:* D *OCR NED:* M2

C6W6 BA Sport Studies/Film & Television Studies
Duration: 3FT Hon
Entry Requirements: *GCE:* 260-280. *SQAH:* AAA-BBBB. *IB:* 24. *BTEC Dip:* DD. *BTEC ExtDip:* DMM. *OCR ND:* D *OCR NED:* M2

C6W1 BA Sport Studies/Fine Art Painting & Drawing
Duration: 3FT Hon
Entry Requirements: *GCE:* 260-280. *SQAH:* AAA-BBBB. *IB:* 24. *BTEC Dip:* DD. *BTEC ExtDip:* DMM. *OCR ND:* D *OCR NED:* M2

C6R1 BA Sport Studies/French
Duration: 3FT Hon
Entry Requirements: *GCE:* 260-280. *SQAH:* AAA-BBBB. *IB:* 24. *BTEC Dip:* DD. *BTEC ExtDip:* DMM. *OCR ND:* D *OCR NED:* M2

C6L4 BA Sport Studies/Health Studies
Duration: 3FT Hon
Entry Requirements: *GCE:* 260-280. *SQAH:* AAA-BBBB. *IB:* 24. *BTEC Dip:* DD. *BTEC ExtDip:* DMM. *OCR ND:* D *OCR NED:* M2

C6V1 BA Sport Studies/History
Duration: 3FT Hon
Entry Requirements: *GCE:* 260-280. *SQAH:* AAA-BBBB. *IB:* 24. *BTEC Dip:* DD. *BTEC ExtDip:* DMM. *OCR ND:* D *OCR NED:* M2

C6L7 BA Sport Studies/Human Geography
Duration: 3FT Hon
Entry Requirements: *GCE:* 260-280. *SQAH:* AAA-BBBB. *IB:* 24. *BTEC Dip:* DD. *BTEC ExtDip:* DMM. *OCR ND:* D *OCR NED:* M2

C6N6 BA Sport Studies/Human Resource Management
Duration: 3FT Hon
Entry Requirements: *GCE:* 260-280. *SQAH:* AAA-BBBB. *IB:* 24. *BTEC Dip:* DD. *BTEC ExtDip:* DMM. *OCR ND:* D *OCR NED:* M2

C6P5 BA Sport Studies/Journalism
Duration: 3FT Hon
Entry Requirements: *GCE:* 260-280. *SQAH:* AAA-BBBB. *IB:* 24. *BTEC Dip:* DD. *BTEC ExtDip:* DMM. *OCR ND:* D *OCR NED:* M2

C6N2 BA Sport Studies/Management
Duration: 3FT Hon
Entry Requirements: *GCE:* 260-280. *SQAH:* AAA-BBBB. *IB:* 24. *BTEC Dip:* DD. *BTEC ExtDip:* DMM. *OCR ND:* D *OCR NED:* M2

C6L2 BA Sport Studies/Politics
Duration: 3FT Hon
Entry Requirements: *GCE:* 260-280. *SQAH:* AAA-BBBB. *IB:* 24. *BTEC Dip:* DD. *BTEC ExtDip:* DMM. *OCR ND:* D *OCR NED:* M2

C6W3 BA Sport Studies/Popular Music
Duration: 3FT Hon
Entry Requirements: *GCE:* 260-280. *SQAH:* AAA-BBBB. *IB:* 24. *BTEC Dip:* DD. *BTEC ExtDip:* DMM. *OCR ND:* D *OCR NED:* M2

C6C8 BA Sport Studies/Psychology
Duration: 3FT Hon
Entry Requirements: *GCE:* 260-280. *SQAH:* AAA-BBBB. *IB:* 24. *BTEC Dip:* DD. *BTEC ExtDip:* DMM. *OCR ND:* D *OCR NED:* M2

C6L5 BA Sport Studies/Social Care
Duration: 3FT Hon
Entry Requirements: *GCE:* 260-280. *SQAH:* AAA-BBBB. *IB:* 24. *BTEC Dip:* DD. *BTEC ExtDip:* DMM. *OCR ND:* D *OCR NED:* M2

C6L3 BA Sport Studies/Sociology
Duration: 3FT Hon
Entry Requirements: *GCE:* 260-280. *SQAH:* AAA-BBBB. *IB:* 24. *BTEC Dip:* DD. *BTEC ExtDip:* DMM. *OCR ND:* D *OCR NED:* M2

C6G4 BA Sport Studies/Web Design
Duration: 3FT Hon
Entry Requirements: *GCE:* 260-280. *SQAH:* AAA-BBBB. *IB:* 24. *BTEC Dip:* DD. *BTEC ExtDip:* DMM. *OCR ND:* D *OCR NED:* M2

C1C6 BSc Biological Conservation/Sport Studies
Duration: 3FT Hon
Entry Requirements: *GCE:* 260-280. *SQAH:* AAA-BBBB. *IB:* 24.
BTEC Dip: DD. *BTEC ExtDip:* DMM. *OCR ND:* D *OCR NED:* M2

G5C6 BSc Business Computing Systems/Sport Studies
Duration: 3FT Hon
Entry Requirements: *GCE:* 260-280. *SQAH:* AAA-BBBB. *IB:* 24.
BTEC Dip: DD. *BTEC ExtDip:* DMM. *OCR ND:* D *OCR NED:* M2

B1C6 BSc Human Bioscience/Sport Studies
Duration: 3FT Hon
Entry Requirements: *GCE:* 260-280. *SQAH:* AAA-BBBB. *IB:* 24.
BTEC Dip: DD. *BTEC ExtDip:* DMM. *OCR ND:* D *OCR NED:* M2

F8C6 BSc Physical Geography/Sport Studies
Duration: 3FT Hon
Entry Requirements: *GCE:* 260-280. *SQAH:* AAA-BBBB. *IB:* 24.
BTEC Dip: DD. *BTEC ExtDip:* DMM. *OCR ND:* D *OCR NED:* M2

CC86 BSc Sport & Exercise Psychology
Duration: 3FT Hon
Entry Requirements: *GCE:* 280-320. *SQAH:* AABB. *IB:* 26. *BTEC Dip:* DD. *BTEC ExtDip:* DMM. *OCR ND:* D *OCR NED:* M2

C600 BSc Sport & Exercise Science
Duration: 3FT Hon
Entry Requirements: *GCE:* 260-280. *SQAH:* AAA-BBBB. *IB:* 24.
BTEC Dip: DD. *BTEC ExtDip:* DMM. *OCR ND:* D *OCR NED:* M2

C6D4 BSc Sport Studies with Applied Equine Studies
Duration: 3FT Hon
Entry Requirements: *GCE:* 260-280. *SQAH:* AAA-BBBB. *IB:* 24.
BTEC Dip: DD. *BTEC ExtDip:* DMM. *OCR ND:* D *OCR NED:* M2

C6C1 BSc Sport Studies/Biological Conservation
Duration: 3FT Hon
Entry Requirements: *GCE:* 260-280. *SQAH:* AAA-BBBB. *IB:* 24.
BTEC Dip: DD. *BTEC ExtDip:* DMM. *OCR ND:* D *OCR NED:* M2

C6G5 BSc Sport Studies/Business Computing Systems
Duration: 3FT Hon
Entry Requirements: *GCE:* 260-280. *SQAH:* AAA-BBBB. *IB:* 24.
BTEC Dip: DD. *BTEC ExtDip:* DMM. *OCR ND:* D *OCR NED:* M2

C6B1 BSc Sport Studies/Human Bioscience
Duration: 3FT Hon
Entry Requirements: *GCE:* 260-280. *SQAH:* AAA-BBBB. *IB:* 24.
BTEC Dip: DD. *BTEC ExtDip:* DMM. *OCR ND:* D *OCR NED:* M2

C6F8 BSc Sport Studies/Physical Geography
Duration: 3FT Hon
Entry Requirements: *GCE:* 260-280. *SQAH:* AAA-BBBB. *IB:* 24.
BTEC Dip: DD. *BTEC ExtDip:* DMM. *OCR ND:* D *OCR NED:* M2

C6FV BSc Sport Studies/Wastes Management
Duration: 3FT Hon
Entry Requirements: *GCE:* 260-280. *SQAH:* AAA-BBBB. *IB:* 24.
BTEC Dip: DD. *BTEC ExtDip:* DMM. *OCR ND:* D *OCR NED:* M2

CX6C BSc Sports Performance and Coaching (top-up)
Duration: 1FT Hon
Entry Requirements: HND required.

C605 BSc Sports Therapy (top-up)
Duration: 1FT Hon
Entry Requirements: HND required.

F8CP BSc Wastes Management/Sports Studies
Duration: 3FT Hon
Entry Requirements: *GCE:* 260-280. *SQAH:* AAA-BBBB. *IB:* 24.
BTEC Dip: DD. *BTEC ExtDip:* DMM. *OCR ND:* D *OCR NED:* M2

G4C6 BSc Web Design/Sport Studies
Duration: 3FT Hon
Entry Requirements: *GCE:* 260-280. *SQAH:* AAA-BBBB. *IB:* 24.
BTEC Dip: DD. *BTEC ExtDip:* DMM. *OCR ND:* D *OCR NED:* M2

CX61 FdSc Sports Performance and Coaching
Duration: 2FT Fdg
Entry Requirements: *GCE:* 140-160. *SQAH:* BC-CCC. *IB:* 24.
BTEC Dip: MP. *BTEC ExtDip:* MPP. *OCR ND:* P1 *OCR NED:* P2

C601 FdSc Sports Therapy
Duration: 2FT Fdg
Entry Requirements: *GCE:* 140-160. *SQAH:* BC-CCC. *IB:* 24.
BTEC Dip: MP. *BTEC ExtDip:* MPP. *OCR ND:* P1 *OCR NED:* P2

N49 NESCOT, SURREY
REIGATE ROAD
EWELL
EPSOM
SURREY KT17 3DS
t: 020 8394 3038 f: 020 8394 3030
e: info@nescot.ac.uk
// www.nescot.ac.uk

C600 FdSc Sports Therapy
Duration: 2FT Fdg   CRB Check: Required
Entry Requirements: *GCE:* 200.

N64 NORTH LINDSEY COLLEGE
KINGSWAY
SCUNTHORPE
NORTH LINCS DN17 1AJ
t: 01724 294125 f: 01724 295378
e: he@northlindsey.ac.uk
// www.northlindsey.ac.uk

C600 FdSc Sport & Exercise Development
Duration: 2FT Fdg
Entry Requirements: *GCE:* 40.

N77 NORTHUMBRIA UNIVERSITY
TRINITY BUILDING
NORTHUMBERLAND ROAD
NEWCASTLE UPON TYNE NE1 8ST
t: 0191 243 7420 f: 0191 227 4561
e: er.admissions@northumbria.ac.uk
// www.northumbria.ac.uk

C6X1 BA Sport Development with Coaching
Duration: 3FT Hon
Entry Requirements: *GCE:* 300. *SQAH:* BBBBC. *SQAAH:* BBC. *IB:* 26. *BTEC Dip:* DM. *BTEC ExtDip:* DDM. *OCR ND:* M1 *OCR NED:* M1

C6XC BSc Applied Sport Science with Coaching
Duration: 3FT Hon
Entry Requirements: *GCE:* 300. *SQAH:* BBBBC. *SQAAH:* BBC. *IB:* 26. *BTEC Dip:* DM. *BTEC ExtDip:* DDM. *OCR ND:* M1 *OCR NED:* M1

C600 BSc Applied Sport and Exercise Science
Duration: 3FT Hon
Entry Requirements: *GCE:* 320. *SQAH:* BBBBB. *SQAAH:* BBB. *IB:* 27. *OCR ND:* D *OCR NED:* M2

C8C6 BSc Psychology with Sport Science
Duration: 3FT Hon
Entry Requirements: *GCE:* 300. *SQAH:* BBBBC. *SQAAH:* BBC. *IB:* 26. *OCR ND:* D *OCR NED:* M2

CX61 BSc Sport Coaching
Duration: 3FT Hon
Entry Requirements: *GCE:* 300. *SQAH:* BBBBC. *SQAAH:* BBC. *IB:* 26. *BTEC Dip:* DM. *BTEC ExtDip:* DDM. *OCR ND:* M1 *OCR NED:* M1

CN62 BSc Sport Management
Duration: 3FT Hon
Entry Requirements: *GCE:* 300. *SQAH:* BBBBC. *SQAAH:* BBC. *IB:* 26. *BTEC Dip:* DM. *BTEC ExtDip:* DDM. *OCR ND:* M1 *OCR NED:* M1

CB64 BSc Sport, Exercise and Nutrition
Duration: 3FT Hon
Entry Requirements: *GCE:* 300. *SQAH:* BBBBC. *SQAAH:* BBC. *IB:* 26. *BTEC Dip:* DM. *BTEC ExtDip:* DDM. *OCR ND:* M1 *OCR NED:* M1

N79 NORTH WARWICKSHIRE AND HINCKLEY COLLEGE
HINCKLEY ROAD
NUNEATON
WARWICKSHIRE CV11 6BH
t: 024 7624 3395
e: angela.jones@nwhc.ac.uk
// www.nwhc.ac.uk

006C HND Sport & Exercise Sciences
Duration: 2FT HND
Entry Requirements: Contact the institution for details.

N82 NORWICH CITY COLLEGE OF FURTHER AND HIGHER EDUCATION (AN ASSOCIATE COLLEGE OF UEA)
IPSWICH ROAD
NORWICH
NORFOLK NR2 2LJ
t: 01603 773012 f: 01603 773301
e: he_office@ccn.ac.uk
// www.ccn.ac.uk

C601 BSc Applied Sport Health and Exercise Science (Top-Up)
Duration: 1FT Hon
Entry Requirements: Contact the institution for details.

C600 FdA Sport, Health and Exercise
Duration: 2FT Fdg
Entry Requirements: Contact the institution for details.

N91 NOTTINGHAM TRENT UNIVERSITY
DRYDEN BUILDING
BURTON STREET
NOTTINGHAM NG1 4BU
t: +44 (0) 115 848 4200 f: +44 (0) 115 848 8869
e: applications@ntu.ac.uk
// www.ntu.ac.uk

CX63 BA Sport & Leisure and Educational Development
Duration: 3FT Hon   CRB Check: Required
Entry Requirements: *GCE:* 280. *BTEC Dip:* D*D*. *BTEC ExtDip:* DMM. *OCR NED:* M2

CX6H BA Sport & Leisure and Special & Inclusive Education
Duration: 3FT Hon   **CRB Check:** Required
Entry Requirements: *GCE:* 280. *BTEC Dip:* D*D*. *BTEC ExtDip:* DMM. *OCR NED:* M2

CX61 BSc Coaching and Sport Science
Duration: 3FT Hon
Entry Requirements: *GCE:* 300. *BTEC ExtDip:* DDM. *OCR NED:* M1

D422 BSc Equestrian Psychology and Sports Science
Duration: 3FT Hon
Entry Requirements: *GCE:* 240.

DC36 BSc Equine Sports Science
Duration: 3FT Hon
Entry Requirements: *GCE:* 240.

CB64 BSc Exercise, Nutrition and Health
Duration: 3FT Hon
Entry Requirements: *GCE:* 260. *BTEC ExtDip:* DMM. *OCR NED:* M2

CN62 BSc Sport Science and Management
Duration: 3FT Hon
Entry Requirements: *GCE:* 300. *BTEC ExtDip:* DDM. *OCR NED:* M1

CG6C BSc Sport Science and Mathematics
Duration: 3FT Hon
Entry Requirements: *GCE:* 280.

C600 BSc Sport and Exercise Science
Duration: 3FT Hon
Entry Requirements: *GCE:* 340. *BTEC ExtDip:* DDD.

O66 OXFORD BROOKES UNIVERSITY
ADMISSIONS OFFICE
HEADINGTON CAMPUS
GIPSY LANE
OXFORD OX3 0BP
t: 01865 483040 f: 01865 483983
e: admissions@brookes.ac.uk
// www.brookes.ac.uk

CN62 BA/BSc Sport, Coaching and Physical Education/Business Management
Duration: 3FT Hon
Entry Requirements: Contact the institution for details.

C6P9 BA/BSc Sport, Coaching and Physical Education/Communications, Media and Culture
Duration: 3FT Hon
Entry Requirements: Contact the institution for details.

CX63 BA/BSc Sport, Coaching and Physical Education/Education Studies
Duration: 3FT Hon
Entry Requirements: Contact the institution for details.

CQ36 BA/BSc Sport, Coaching and Physical Education/English Language and Communication
Duration: 3FT Hon
Entry Requirements: Contact the institution for details.

CF68 BA/BSc Sport, Coaching and Physical Education/Geography
Duration: 3FT Hon
Entry Requirements: *GCE:* BBC.

CV16 BA/BSc Sport, Coaching and Physical Education/History
Duration: 3FT Hon
Entry Requirements: Contact the institution for details.

CV65 BA/BSc Sport, Coaching and Physical Education/Philosophy
Duration: 3FT Hon
Entry Requirements: Contact the institution for details.

CC86 BA/BSc Sport, Coaching and Physical Education/Psychology
Duration: 3FT Hon
Entry Requirements: Contact the institution for details.

CV66 BA/BSc Sport, Coaching and Physical Education/Religion and Theology
Duration: 3FT Hon
Entry Requirements: Contact the institution for details.

C601 BSc Sport and Exercise Science
Duration: 3FT Hon
Entry Requirements: *GCE:* BBC.

C606 BSc Sport, Coaching and Physical Education
Duration: 3FT Hon
Entry Requirements: Contact the institution for details.

C602 BSc Sports Science
Duration: 3FT Hon
Entry Requirements: *GCE:* BBC.

P35 PEMBROKESHIRE COLLEGE (ACCREDITED COLLEGE OF UNIVERSITY OF GLAMORGAN)
HAVERFORDWEST
PEMBROKESHIRE SA61 1SZ
t: 01437 753000 f: 01437 753001
e: admissions@pembrokeshire.ac.uk
// www.pembrokeshire.ac.uk

C600 FdSc Sport
Duration: 2FT Fdg
Entry Requirements: *GCE:* 80. *IB:* 26.

P51 PETROC
OLD STICKLEPATH HILL
BARNSTAPLE
NORTH DEVON EX31 2BQ
t: 01271 852365 f: 01271 338121
e: he@petroc.ac.uk
// www.petroc.ac.uk

C600 FdSc Sport Coaching, Health and Fitness
Duration: 2FT Fdg
Entry Requirements: Contact the institution for details.

P60 PLYMOUTH UNIVERSITY
DRAKE CIRCUS
PLYMOUTH PL4 8AA
t: 01752 585858 f: 01752 588055
e: admissions@plymouth.ac.uk
// www.plymouth.ac.uk

X1X3 BEd Primary (Physical Education)
Duration: 3FT Hon   CRB Check: Required
Entry Requirements: *GCE:* 240. *IB:* 26. *OCR ND:* D Interview required.

CB64 BSc Exercise, Nutrition and Health
Duration: 3FT Hon
Entry Requirements: *GCE:* 280-320. *IB:* 26.

C606 BSc Health and Fitness
Duration: 1FT Hon
Entry Requirements: Contact the institution for details.

CJ6P BSc Marine Sports Sciences
Duration: 3FT/4SW Hon
Entry Requirements: *GCE:* 280. *IB:* 28.

BC46 BSc Nutrition Exercise and Health
Duration: 3FT/4SW Hon
Entry Requirements: *GCE:* 280. *IB:* 26.

C604 FdSc Sports Therapy
Duration: 2FT Fdg
Entry Requirements: *GCE:* 120-180. *IB:* 24.

C609 FdSc Strength Conditioning and Sports Coaching
Duration: 2FT Fdg
Entry Requirements: *GCE:* 120-180. *IB:* 24.

P63 UCP MARJON - UNIVERSITY COLLEGE PLYMOUTH ST MARK & ST JOHN
DERRIFORD ROAD
PLYMOUTH PL6 8BH
t: 01752 636890 f: 01752 636819
e: admissions@marjon.ac.uk
// www.ucpmarjon.ac.uk

CX6H BA Children's Physical Education
Duration: 3FT Hon   CRB Check: Required
Entry Requirements: *GCE:* 220.

C601 BA Outdoor Studies
Duration: 1FT Hon   CRB Check: Required
Entry Requirements: Contact the institution for details.

C602 BA Sports Development
Duration: 3FT Hon   CRB Check: Required
Entry Requirements: *GCE:* 220.

C606 BA Sports Development and Coaching
Duration: 1FT Hon   CRB Check: Required
Entry Requirements: Contact the institution for details.

CB69 BSC Health Exercise and Physical Activity
Duration: 3FT Hon   CRB Check: Required
Entry Requirements: *GCE:* 240.

CX61 BSc Applied Sports Science & Coaching
Duration: 3FT Hon   CRB Check: Required
Entry Requirements: *GCE:* 240.

CX63 BSc Coaching and Fitness Education
Duration: 1FT Hon   CRB Check: Required
Entry Requirements: Contact the institution for details.

C607 BSc Sports Therapy
Duration: 1FT Hon   CRB Check: Required
Entry Requirements: Interview required.

CX6D BSc Strength and Conditioning
Duration: 1FT Hon   CRB Check: Required
Entry Requirements: Contact the institution for details.

CX6C FdA Sports Development and Coaching
Duration: 2FT Fdg   CRB Check: Required
Entry Requirements: *GCE:* 160.

P80 UNIVERSITY OF PORTSMOUTH
ACADEMIC REGISTRY
UNIVERSITY HOUSE
WINSTON CHURCHILL AVENUE
PORTSMOUTH PO1 2UP
t: 023 9284 8484 f: 023 9284 3082
e: admissions@port.ac.uk
// www.port.ac.uk

C600 BSc Sport and Exercise Science
Duration: 3FT Hon
Entry Requirements: *GCE:* 320. *IB:* 27. *BTEC Dip:* DD. *BTEC ExtDip:* DDM.

CN62 BSc Sports Business Management
Duration: 3FT Hon
Entry Requirements: *GCE:* 280. *IB:* 25. *BTEC Dip:* D*D*. *BTEC ExtDip:* DMM.

R36 ROBERT GORDON UNIVERSITY
ROBERT GORDON UNIVERSITY
SCHOOLHILL
ABERDEEN
SCOTLAND AB10 1FR
t: 01224 26 27 28 f: 01224 26 21 47
e: UGOffice@rgu.ac.uk
// www.rgu.ac.uk

C600 BSc Applied Sports and Exercise Science
Duration: 4FT Hon   CRB Check: Required
Entry Requirements: *GCE:* 240. *SQAH:* BBCC. *IB:* 26. Interview required.

C601 BSc Sports and Exercise Science (Top-Up)
Duration: 2FT Hon
Entry Requirements: Contact the institution for details.

R48 ROEHAMPTON UNIVERSITY
ROEHAMPTON LANE
LONDON SW15 5PU
t: 020 8392 3232 f: 020 8392 3470
e: enquiries@roehampton.ac.uk
// www.roehampton.ac.uk

XCC6 BA Primary Education Foundation Stage & Key Stage 1 (Physical Education)
Duration: 3FT Hon   CRB Check: Required
Entry Requirements: *GCE:* 320. *IB:* 27. *BTEC ExtDip:* DDM. *OCR NED:* D2 Interview required.

XC1P BA Primary Education Key Stage 2 (Physical Education)
Duration: 3FT Hon   CRB Check: Required
Entry Requirements: *GCE:* 320. *IB:* 27. *BTEC ExtDip:* DDM. *OCR NED:* D2 Interview required.

C602 BSc Sport and Exercise Sciences
Duration: 3FT Hon
Entry Requirements: *Foundation:* Distinction. *GCE:* 280. *IB:* 25. *BTEC Dip:* D*D*. *BTEC ExtDip:* DMM. *OCR NED:* M2 Interview required.

XC16 FdA Sports Coaching Practice
Duration: 2FT Fdg
Entry Requirements: *BTEC ExtDip:* DDM. *OCR ND:* D Interview required.

S03 THE UNIVERSITY OF SALFORD
SALFORD M5 4WT
t: 0161 295 4545 f: 0161 295 4646
e: ug-admissions@salford.ac.uk
// www.salford.ac.uk

CB69 BSc Exercise, Physical Activity and Health
Duration: 3FT Hon   CRB Check: Required
Entry Requirements: *GCE:* 280. *IB:* 29. *OCR NED:* M2

BC96 BSc Sport Rehabilitation
Duration: 3FT Hon   CRB Check: Required
Entry Requirements: *GCE:* 300. *SQAH:* AABBB. *SQAAH:* BBB. *IB:* 29.

C610 BSc Sports Science
Duration: 3FT Hon   CRB Check: Required
Entry Requirements: *GCE:* 280. *IB:* 29. *OCR NED:* M2

S21 SHEFFIELD HALLAM UNIVERSITY
CITY CAMPUS
HOWARD STREET
SHEFFIELD S1 1WB
t: 0114 225 5555 f: 0114 225 2167
e: admissions@shu.ac.uk
// www.shu.ac.uk

CL65 BA Sport & Community Development
Duration: 3FT Hon
Entry Requirements: *GCE:* 240.

CL63 BA Sport, Culture and Society
Duration: 3FT Hon
Entry Requirements: *GCE:* 240.

C601 BSc Physical Activity, Health and Exercise Science
Duration: 3FT Hon
Entry Requirements: *GCE:* 320.

C603 BSc Physical Education and Youth Sport
Duration: 3FT Hon
Entry Requirements: *GCE:* 320.

C6N2 BSc Sport Business Management
Duration: 3FT Hon
Entry Requirements: *GCE:* 240.

CX61 BSc Sport Coaching
Duration: 3FT Hon
Entry Requirements: *GCE:* 280.

C6X3 BSc Sport Development with Coaching
Duration: 3FT Hon
Entry Requirements: *GCE:* 280.

C602 BSc Sport Science For Performance Coaching
Duration: 3FT Hon
Entry Requirements: *GCE:* 320.

C6G4 BSc Sport Technology
Duration: 3FT/4SW Hon
Entry Requirements: *GCE:* 280.

C600 BSc Sport and Exercise Science
Duration: 3FT Hon
Entry Requirements: *GCE:* 320.

S22 SHEFFIELD COLLEGE
THE SHEFFIELD COLLEGE
HE UNIT
HILLSBOROUGH COLLEGE AT THE BARRACKS
SHEFFIELD S6 2LR
t: 0114 260 2597
e: heunit@sheffcol.ac.uk
// www.sheffcol.ac.uk

CX61 FdSc Sport and Exercise Coaching
Duration: 2FT Fdg
Entry Requirements: *GCE:* 120.

S26 SOLIHULL COLLEGE
BLOSSOMFIELD ROAD
SOLIHULL
WEST MIDLANDS B91 1SB
t: 0121 678 7006 f: 0121 678 7200
e: enquiries@solihull.ac.uk
// www.solihull.ac.uk

006C HND Sport & Exercise Science
Duration: 2FT HND
Entry Requirements: *GCE:* A-E. *IB:* 24. *BTEC Dip:* DM. *BTEC ExtDip:* MMM. *OCR ND:* M2 *OCR NED:* M3 Interview required. Portfolio required.

S30 SOUTHAMPTON SOLENT UNIVERSITY
EAST PARK TERRACE
SOUTHAMPTON
HAMPSHIRE SO14 0RT
t: +44 (0) 23 8031 9039 f: + 44 (0)23 8022 2259
e: admissions@solent.ac.uk
// www.solent.ac.uk/

NC86 BA Fitness Management and Personal Training
Duration: 3FT Hon
Entry Requirements: *GCE:* 220.

CN68 BA Fitness Management and Personal Training with IFY (Intl only, Sept)
Duration: 4FT Hon
Entry Requirements: Contact the institution for details.

NC8P BA Fitness Management and Personal Training with STFY
Duration: 4FT Hon
Entry Requirements: *GCE:* 80.

CN62 BA Football Studies
Duration: 3FT Hon
Entry Requirements: *GCE:* 220.

C6NC BA Football Studies and Business
Duration: 3FT Hon
Entry Requirements: *GCE:* 220.

C6NB BA Football Studies and Business with STFY
Duration: 4FT Hon
Entry Requirements: *GCE:* 80.

C608 BA Football Studies with IFY (International Only - Jan)
Duration: 4FT Hon
Entry Requirements: Contact the institution for details.

C6Q3 BA Football Studies with IFY (Intl only, Sept)
Duration: 4FT Hon
Entry Requirements: Contact the institution for details.

C606 BA Football Studies with STFY
Duration: 4FT Hon
Entry Requirements: *GCE:* 80.

CX61 BA Sport Coaching and Development
Duration: 3FT Hon
Entry Requirements: *GCE:* 220.

XC16 BA Sport Coaching and Development with STFY
Duration: 4FT Hon
Entry Requirements: *GCE:* 80.

C601 BA Sports Studies
Duration: 3FT Hon
Entry Requirements: *GCE:* 220.

C613 BA Sports Studies and Business with IFY (International Only - Jan)
Duration: 4FT Hon
Entry Requirements: Contact the institution for details.

C6ND BA Sports Studies and Business with International Foundation Year
Duration: 4FT Hon
Entry Requirements: Contact the institution for details.

C6NA BA Sports Studies and Business with STFY
Duration: 4FT Hon
Entry Requirements: *GCE:* 80.

C612 BA Sports Studies with IFY (International Only - Jan)
Duration: 4FT Hon
Entry Requirements: Contact the institution for details.

C6QA BA Sports Studies with International Foundation Year
Duration: 4FT Hon
Entry Requirements: Contact the institution for details.

C603 BA Sports Studies with Sport & Tourism Foundation Year
Duration: 4FT Hon
Entry Requirements: *GCE:* 80.

C602 BSc Applied Sport Science
Duration: 3FT Hon
Entry Requirements: *GCE:* 260.

C610 BSc Fitness and Personal Training
Duration: 3FT Hon
Entry Requirements: *GCE:* 240.

BC96 BSc Health, Exercise and Physical Activity
Duration: 3FT Hon
Entry Requirements: *GCE:* 220.

CX6D BSc Sport Coaching
Duration: 3FT Hon
Entry Requirements: *GCE:* 260.

C609 BSc Sport Coaching with IFY (International Only - Jan)
Duration: 4FT Hon
Entry Requirements: Contact the institution for details.

C6QJ BSc Sport Coaching with International Foundation Year
Duration: 4FT Hon
Entry Requirements: Contact the institution for details.

S32 SOUTH DEVON COLLEGE
LONG ROAD
PAIGNTON
DEVON TQ4 7EJ
t: 08000 213181 f: 01803 540541
e: university@southdevon.ac.uk
// www.southdevon.ac.uk/
welcome-to-university-level

CB69 FdSc Exercise Science and Fitness
Duration: 2FT Fdg
Entry Requirements: Contact the institution for details.

S41 SOUTH CHESHIRE COLLEGE
DANE BANK AVENUE
CREWE CW2 8AB
t: 01270 654654 f: 01270 651515
e: admissions@s-cheshire.ac.uk
// www.s-cheshire.ac.uk

XC1P FdA Coaching and Sports Development
Duration: 2FT Fdg   CRB Check: Required
Entry Requirements: Interview required.

S43 SOUTH ESSEX COLLEGE OF FURTHER & HIGHER EDUCATION
LUKER ROAD
SOUTHEND-ON-SEA
ESSEX SS1 1ND
t: 0845 52 12345 f: 01702 432320
e: Admissions@southessex.ac.uk
// www.southessex.ac.uk

C601 BSc Sports Studies
Duration: 3FT Hon
Entry Requirements: *GCE:* 160. *IB:* 24. Interview required.

C600 CertHE Sports Studies
Duration: 1FT Cer
Entry Requirements: *GCE:* 120. *IB:* 24. Interview required.

C602 DipHE Sports Studies
Duration: 2FT Dip
Entry Requirements: *GCE:* 160. *IB:* 24. Interview required.

C603 FdSc Personal Fitness Training
Duration: 2FT Fdg
Entry Requirements: Contact the institution for details.

S46 SOUTH NOTTINGHAM COLLEGE
WEST BRIDGFORD CENTRE
GREYTHORN DRIVE
WEST BRIDGFORD
NOTTINGHAM NG2 7GA
t: 0115 914 6400 f: 0115 914 6444
e: enquiries@snc.ac.uk
// www.snc.ac.uk

CX69 FdSc Applied Sport Coaching
Duration: 2FT Fdg
Entry Requirements: *GCE:* 160. Interview required.

S51 ST HELENS COLLEGE
WATER STREET
ST HELENS
MERSEYSIDE WA10 1PP
t: 01744 733766 f: 01744 623400
e: enquiries@sthelens.ac.uk
// www.sthelens.ac.uk

C610 FdSc Exercise, Health and Fitness
Duration: 2FT Fdg
Entry Requirements: *GCE:* 40. *IB:* 18.

106C HND Sport (Coaching)
Duration: 2FT HND
Entry Requirements: Contact the institution for details.

S64 ST MARY'S UNIVERSITY COLLEGE, TWICKENHAM
WALDEGRAVE ROAD
STRAWBERRY HILL
MIDDLESEX TW1 4SX
t: 020 8240 4029 f: 020 8240 2361
e: admit@smuc.ac.uk
// www.smuc.ac.uk

X3CP BA Education & Social Science with Physical & Sport Education
Duration: 3FT Hon
Entry Requirements: *GCE:* 240. *SQAH:* BBBC. *IB:* 28. *OCR ND:* D *OCR NED:* M3 Interview required.

CX6H BA Physical and Sport Education
Duration: 3FT Hon
Entry Requirements: *GCE:* 240. *SQAH:* BBBC. *IB:* 28. *OCR ND:* D *OCR NED:* M3 Interview required.

CXP3 BA/BSc Education & Social Science and Sport Science
Duration: 3FT Hon
Entry Requirements: *GCE:* 240. *SQAH:* BBBC. *IB:* 28. *OCR ND:* D *OCR NED:* M3 Interview required.

CN62 BA/BSc Management Studies and Sport Science
Duration: 3FT Hon
Entry Requirements: *GCE:* 240. *SQAH:* BBBC. *IB:* 28. *OCR ND:* D *OCR NED:* M3 Interview required.

CP63 BA/BSc Media Arts and Sport Science
Duration: 3FT Hon
Entry Requirements: *GCE:* 240. *SQAH:* BBBC. *IB:* 28. *OCR ND:* D *OCR NED:* M3 Interview required.

C601 BSc Coaching Science
Duration: 3FT Hon
Entry Requirements: *GCE:* 240. *SQAH:* BBBC. *IB:* 28. *OCR ND:* D *OCR NED:* M3 Interview required.

BCY6 BSc Health, Exercise & Physical Activity and Sport Science
Duration: 3FT Hon
Entry Requirements: *GCE:* 240. *SQAH:* BBBC. *IB:* 28. *OCR ND:* D *OCR NED:* M3 Interview required.

BC4P BSc Nutrition and Sport Science
Duration: 3FT Hon
Entry Requirements: *GCE:* 240. *SQAH:* BBBC. *IB:* 28. *OCR ND:* D *OCR NED:* M3 Interview required.

CX63 BSc Physical & Sport Education and Sport Science
Duration: 3FT Hon
Entry Requirements: *GCE:* 240. *SQAH:* BBBC. *IB:* 28. *OCR ND:* D
OCR NED: M3 Interview required.

CC86 BSc Psychology and Sport Science
Duration: 3FT Hon
Entry Requirements: *GCE:* 240. *SQAH:* BBBC. *IB:* 28. *OCR ND:* D
OCR NED: M3 Interview required.

CL63 BSc Sociology and Sport Science
Duration: 3FT Hon
Entry Requirements: *GCE:* 240. *SQAH:* BBBC. *IB:* 28. *OCR ND:* D
OCR NED: M3 Interview required.

C602 BSc Sport Rehabilitation
Duration: 3FT Hon
Entry Requirements: *GCE:* 240. *SQAH:* BBBC. *IB:* 28. *OCR ND:* D
OCR NED: M3 Interview required.

C600 BSc Sport Science
Duration: 3FT Hon
Entry Requirements: *GCE:* 240. *SQAH:* BBBC. *IB:* 28. *OCR ND:* D
OCR NED: M3 Interview required.

C607 BSc Strength and Conditioning
Duration: 3FT Hon
Entry Requirements: *GCE:* 240. *SQAH:* BBBC. *IB:* 28. *OCR ND:* D
OCR NED: M3 Interview required.

CB6X FdA Sport, Health and Fitness
Duration: 2FT Fdg
Entry Requirements: *GCE:* 120. *SQAH:* BBBC. Interview required.

S72 STAFFORDSHIRE UNIVERSITY
COLLEGE ROAD
STOKE ON TRENT ST4 2DE
t: 01782 292753 f: 01782 292740
e: admissions@staffs.ac.uk
// www.staffs.ac.uk

C603 BA Sports Development and Coaching
Duration: 3FT Hon
Entry Requirements: *GCE:* 180-240. *IB:* 24.

C602 BA Sports Studies
Duration: 3FT Hon
Entry Requirements: *GCE:* 180-240. *IB:* 24.

CX6C BSc PE and Youth Sport Coaching
Duration: 3FT Hon
Entry Requirements: *GCE:* 180-240. *IB:* 24.

C601 BSc Sport and Exercise Science
Duration: 3FT Hon
Entry Requirements: *GCE:* 180-240. *IB:* 24.

C600 BSc Sports Studies
Duration: 3FT Hon
Entry Requirements: *GCE:* 180-240. *IB:* 24.

BC96 BSc Sports Therapy
Duration: 3FT Hon   CRB Check: Required
Entry Requirements: *GCE:* 200-260. *IB:* 24. Interview required.

C606 HND Sports Studies
Duration: 2FT HND
Entry Requirements: Interview required.

S75 THE UNIVERSITY OF STIRLING
STUDENT RECRUITMENT & ADMISSIONS SERVICE
UNIVERSITY OF STIRLING
STIRLING
SCOTLAND FK9 4LA
t: 01786 467044 f: 01786 466800
e: admissions@stir.ac.uk
// www.stir.ac.uk

NC16 BA Business Studies and Sports Studies
Duration: 4FT Hon
Entry Requirements: *GCE:* BBC. *SQAH:* BBBB. *SQAAH:* AAA-CCC.
IB: 32. *BTEC ExtDip:* DMM.

CP63 BA Film & Media and Sports Studies
Duration: 4FT Hon
Entry Requirements: *GCE:* BBC. *SQAH:* BBBB. *SQAAH:* AAA-CCC.
IB: 32. *BTEC ExtDip:* DMM.

VC16 BA History and Sports Studies
Duration: 4FT Hon
Entry Requirements: *GCE:* BBC. *SQAH:* BBBB. *SQAAH:* AAA-CCC.
IB: 32. *BTEC ExtDip:* DMM.

PC56 BA Journalism Studies and Sports Studies
Duration: 4FT Hon
Entry Requirements: *GCE:* BBC. *SQAH:* BBBB. *SQAAH:* AAA-CCC.
IB: 32. *BTEC ExtDip:* DMM.

NC56 BA Marketing and Sports Studies
Duration: 4FT Hon
Entry Requirements: *GCE:* BBC. *SQAH:* BBBB. *SQAAH:* AAA-CCC.
IB: 32. *BTEC ExtDip:* DMM.

CC68 BA Psychology and Sports Studies
Duration: 4FT Hon
Entry Requirements: *GCE:* BBC. *SQAH:* BBBB. *SQAAH:* AAA-CCC.
IB: 32. *BTEC ExtDip:* DMM.

CL63 BA Sociology and Sports Studies
Duration: 4FT Hon
Entry Requirements: *GCE:* BBC. *SQAH:* BBBB. *SQAAH:* AAA-CCC.
IB: 32. *BTEC ExtDip:* DMM.

C600 BA Sports Studies
Duration: 4FT Hon
Entry Requirements: *GCE:* BBC. *SQAH:* BBBB. *SQAAH:* AAA-CCC.
IB: 32. *BTEC ExtDip:* DMM.

NC46 BAcc Accountancy and Sports Studies
Duration: 4FT Hon
Entry Requirements: *GCE:* BBC. *SQAH:* BBBB. *SQAAH:* AAA-CCC.
IB: 32. *BTEC ExtDip:* DMM.

CC61 BSc Sport and Exercise Science
Duration: 4FT Hon
Entry Requirements: *GCE:* BBC. *SQAH:* BBBB. *SQAAH:* AAA-CCC.
IB: 32. *BTEC ExtDip:* DMM.

CX61 BSc Sports Studies, Physical Education and Professional Education
Duration: 4FT Hon   CRB Check: Required
Entry Requirements: *GCE:* BBC. *SQAH:* BBBB. *SQAAH:* AAA-CCC.
IB: 32. *BTEC ExtDip:* DDM.

S78 THE UNIVERSITY OF STRATHCLYDE
GLASGOW G1 1XQ
t: 0141 552 4400 f: 0141 552 0775
// www.strath.ac.uk

CH61 BEng Sports Engineering
Duration: 4FT Hon
Entry Requirements: *GCE:* A*AA-ABB. *SQAH:* AAAA-AAABBB. *IB:* 34. Interview required.

CX63 BSc Sport and Physical Activity
Duration: 4FT Hon   CRB Check: Required
Entry Requirements: *GCE:* BBC. *SQAH:* BBBBC-BBBB. *IB:* 32.

HC16 MEng Sports Engineering
Duration: 5FT Hon
Entry Requirements: *GCE:* A*AA-AAB. *SQAH:* AAAABB-AAAA. *IB:* 36. Interview required.

S82 UNIVERSITY CAMPUS SUFFOLK (UCS)
WATERFRONT BUILDING
NEPTUNE QUAY
IPSWICH
SUFFOLK IP4 1QJ
t: 01473 338833 f: 01473 339900
e: info@ucs.ac.uk
// www.ucs.ac.uk

C600 BSc Sport & Exercise Science
Duration: 3FT Hon
Entry Requirements: *GCE:* 240-280. *IB:* 28. *BTEC ExtDip:* DMM.

C605 BSc Sport and Exercise Science (with Science Foundation Year)
Duration: 4FT Hon
Entry Requirements: *GCE:* 160. *IB:* 28. *BTEC ExtDip:* DMM.

CX61 FdA Football Development & Coaching
Duration: 2FT Fdg
Entry Requirements: *GCE:* 200. *IB:* 28. *BTEC ExtDip:* DMM.

CL65 FdSc Sport, Health & Exercise
Duration: 2FT Fdg
Entry Requirements: *GCE:* 200. *IB:* 28. *BTEC ExtDip:* DMM.

CX6D FdSc Sports Coaching and Development
Duration: 2FT Fdg
Entry Requirements: *GCE:* 200. *IB:* 28. *BTEC ExtDip:* DMM.
Interview required.

S84 UNIVERSITY OF SUNDERLAND
STUDENT HELPLINE
THE STUDENT GATEWAY
CHESTER ROAD
SUNDERLAND SR1 3SD
t: 0191 515 3000 f: 0191 515 3805
e: student.helpline@sunderland.ac.uk
// www.sunderland.ac.uk

N1C6 BA Business Management with Sport
Duration: 3FT Hon
Entry Requirements: *GCE:* 260-360. *OCR ND:* D *OCR NED:* M3

X3C6 BA Childhood Studies with Sport
Duration: 3FT Hon
Entry Requirements: Contact the institution for details.

M9C6 BA Criminology with Sport
Duration: 3FT Hon
Entry Requirements: *GCE:* 260-360. *OCR ND:* D *OCR NED:* M3

W5C6 BA Dance with Sport
Duration: 3FT Hon
Entry Requirements: *GCE:* 260-360. *OCR ND:* D *OCR NED:* M3

W4C6 BA Drama with Sport
Duration: 3FT Hon
Entry Requirements: *GCE:* 260-360. *OCR ND:* D *OCR NED:* M3

Q1C6 BA English Language & Linguistics with Sport
Duration: 3FT Hon
Entry Requirements: *GCE:* 260-360. *OCR ND:* D *OCR NED:* M3

Q3C6 BA English with Sport
Duration: 3FT Hon
Entry Requirements: *GCE:* 260-360. *OCR ND:* D *OCR NED:* M3

V1C6 BA History with Sport
Duration: 3FT Hon
Entry Requirements: *GCE:* 260-360. *OCR ND:* D *OCR NED:* M3

P5C6 BA Journalism with Sport
Duration: 3FT Hon
Entry Requirements: *GCE:* 260-360. *OCR ND:* D *OCR NED:* M3

P3C6 BA Media Studies with Sport
Duration: 3FT Hon
Entry Requirements: *GCE:* 260-360. *OCR ND:* D *OCR NED:* M3

RC16 BA Modern Foreign Languages (French) and Sport
Duration: 3FT Hon
Entry Requirements: *GCE:* 260-360. *IB:* 31. *OCR ND:* D *OCR NED:* M3

CR62 BA Modern Foreign Languages (German) and Sport
Duration: 3FT Hon
Entry Requirements: *GCE:* 260-360. *IB:* 31. *OCR ND:* D *OCR NED:* M3

CR64 BA Modern Foreign Languages (Spanish) and Sport
Duration: 3FT Hon
Entry Requirements: *GCE:* 260-360. *IB:* 31. *OCR ND:* D *OCR NED:* M3

L2C6 BA Politics with Sport
Duration: 3FT Hon
Entry Requirements: *GCE:* 260-360. *OCR ND:* D *OCR NED:* M3

P2C6 BA Public Relations with Sport
Duration: 3FT Hon
Entry Requirements: *GCE:* 260-360. *OCR ND:* D *OCR NED:* M3

C605 BA Sport Studies
Duration: 3FT Hon
Entry Requirements: *GCE:* 260. *IB:* 36. *OCR ND:* D *OCR NED:* M3

CW64 BA Sport and Drama
Duration: 3FT Hon
Entry Requirements: *GCE:* 260-360. *OCR ND:* D *OCR NED:* M3

C6XH BA Sport with Childhood Studies
Duration: 3FT Hon
Entry Requirements: *GCE:* 260-360.

C6L5 BA Sport with Health & Social Care
Duration: 3FT Hon
Entry Requirements: *GCE:* 260-360.

C6V1 BA Sport with History
Duration: 3FT Hon
Entry Requirements: *GCE:* 260-360. *OCR ND:* D *OCR NED:* M3

XCH6 BA/BSc Childhood Studies and Sport
Duration: 3FT Hon
Entry Requirements: *GCE:* 260-360.

LC56 BA/BSc Health & Social Care and Sport
Duration: 3FT Hon
Entry Requirements: *GCE:* 260-360.

L5C6 BA/BSc Health & Social Care with Sport
Duration: 3FT Hon
Entry Requirements: *GCE:* 260-360.

CN61 BA/BSc Sport and Business Management
Duration: 3FT Hon
Entry Requirements: *GCE:* 260-360. *OCR ND:* D *OCR NED:* M3

CM69 BA/BSc Sport and Criminology
Duration: 3FT Hon
Entry Requirements: *GCE:* 260-360. *OCR ND:* D *OCR NED:* M3

CW65 BA/BSc Sport and Dance
Duration: 3FT Hon
Entry Requirements: *GCE:* 260-360. *OCR ND:* D *OCR NED:* M3

CX63 BA/BSc Sport and Education
Duration: 3FT Hon
Entry Requirements: *GCE:* 260-360. *OCR ND:* D *OCR NED:* M3

CQ63 BA/BSc Sport and English
Duration: 3FT Hon
Entry Requirements: *GCE:* 260-360. *OCR ND:* D *OCR NED:* M3

CQ61 BA/BSc Sport and English Language/Linguistics
Duration: 3FT Hon
Entry Requirements: *GCE:* 260-360. *OCR ND:* D *OCR NED:* M3

CP63 BA/BSc Sport and Media Studies
Duration: 3FT Hon
Entry Requirements: *GCE:* 260-360. *OCR ND:* D *OCR NED:* M3

CW66 BA/BSc Sport and Photography
Duration: 3FT Hon
Entry Requirements: *GCE:* 260-360. *OCR ND:* D *OCR NED:* M3

CL62 BA/BSc Sport and Politics
Duration: 3FT Hon
Entry Requirements: *GCE:* 260-360. *OCR ND:* D *OCR NED:* M3

CP62 BA/BSc Sport and Public Relations
Duration: 3FT Hon
Entry Requirements: *GCE:* 260-360. *OCR ND:* D *OCR NED:* M3

CL63 BA/BSc Sport and Sociology
Duration: 3FT Hon
Entry Requirements: *GCE:* 260-360. *OCR ND:* D *OCR NED:* M3

CX61 BA/BSc Sport and TESOL
Duration: 3FT Hon
Entry Requirements: *GCE:* 260-360. *OCR ND:* D *OCR NED:* M3

CN68 BA/BSc Sport and Tourism
Duration: 3FT Hon
Entry Requirements: *GCE:* 260-360. *OCR ND:* D *OCR NED:* M3

C6W4 BA/BSc Sport with Drama
Duration: 3FT Hon
Entry Requirements: *GCE:* 260-360. *OCR ND:* D *OCR NED:* M3

C6R1 BA/BSc Sport with Modern Foreign Languages (French)
Duration: 3FT Hon
Entry Requirements: *GCE:* 260-360. *OCR ND:* D *OCR NED:* M3

C6R2 BA/BSc Sport with Modern Foreign Languages (German)
Duration: 3FT Hon
Entry Requirements: *GCE:* 260-360. *OCR ND:* D *OCR NED:* M3

C8C6 BSc Psychology with Sport
Duration: 3FT Hon
Entry Requirements: *GCE:* 260-360. *OCR ND:* D *OCR NED:* M3

C602 BSc Sport and Exercise Development
Duration: 3FT Hon
Entry Requirements: *GCE:* 260-360. *IB:* 36. *OCR ND:* D *OCR NED:* M3

C601 BSc Sport and Exercise Sciences
Duration: 3FT Hon
Entry Requirements: *GCE:* 260-360. *IB:* 36. *OCR ND:* D *OCR NED:* M3

CV61 BSc Sport and History
Duration: 3FT Hon
Entry Requirements: *GCE:* 220-360. *OCR ND:* D *OCR NED:* M3

CP65 BSc Sport and Journalism
Duration: 3FT Hon
Entry Requirements: *GCE:* 260-360. *OCR ND:* D *OCR NED:* M3

CM61 BSc Sport and Law
Duration: 3FT Hon
Entry Requirements: *GCE:* 260-360. *OCR ND:* D *OCR NED:* M3

C6N1 BSc Sport with Business Management
Duration: 3FT Hon
Entry Requirements: *GCE:* 260-360. *OCR ND:* D *OCR NED:* M3

C6M9 BSc Sport with Criminology
Duration: 3FT Hon
Entry Requirements: *GCE:* 260-360. *OCR ND:* D *OCR NED:* M3

C6W5 BSc Sport with Dance
Duration: 3FT Hon
Entry Requirements: *GCE:* 260-360. *OCR ND:* D *OCR NED:* M3

C6X3 BSc Sport with Education
Duration: 3FT Hon
Entry Requirements: *GCE:* 260-360. *OCR ND:* D *OCR NED:* M3

C6Q3 BSc Sport with English
Duration: 3FT Hon
Entry Requirements: *GCE:* 260-360. *OCR ND:* D *OCR NED:* M3

C6Q1 BSc Sport with English Language/Linguistics
Duration: 3FT Hon
Entry Requirements: *GCE:* 260-360. *OCR ND:* D *OCR NED:* M3

C6P3 BSc Sport with Media Studies
Duration: 3FT Hon
Entry Requirements: *GCE:* 260-360. *OCR ND:* D *OCR NED:* M3

C6W6 BSc Sport with Photography
Duration: 3FT Hon
Entry Requirements: *GCE:* 260-360. *OCR ND:* D *OCR NED:* M3

C6L2 BSc Sport with Politics
Duration: 3FT Hon
Entry Requirements: *GCE:* 260-360. *OCR ND:* D *OCR NED:* M3

C6C8 BSc Sport with Psychology
Duration: 3FT Hon
Entry Requirements: *GCE:* 260-360. *OCR ND:* D *OCR NED:* M3

C6P2 BSc Sport with Public Relations
Duration: 3FT Hon
Entry Requirements: *GCE:* 260-360. *OCR ND:* D *OCR NED:* M3

C6L3 BSc Sport with Sociology
Duration: 3FT Hon
Entry Requirements: *GCE:* 260-360. *OCR ND:* D *OCR NED:* M3

C6X1 BSc Sport with TESOL
Duration: 3FT Hon
Entry Requirements: *GCE:* 260-360. *OCR ND:* D *OCR NED:* M3

C6N8 BSc Sport with Tourism
Duration: 3FT Hon
Entry Requirements: *GCE:* 260-360. *OCR ND:* D *OCR NED:* M3

CX6C BSc Sports Coaching
Duration: 3FT Hon
Entry Requirements: *GCE:* 260. *IB:* 36. *OCR ND:* D *OCR NED:* M3

C606 FdSc Exercise, Health & Fitness
Duration: 2FT Fdg
Entry Requirements: *GCE:* 100-240. *OCR ND:* P2 *OCR NED:* P3

CX6D FdSc Sports Coaching
Duration: 2FT Fdg
Entry Requirements: *GCE:* 100-240. *OCR ND:* P2 *OCR NED:* P3

S93 SWANSEA UNIVERSITY
SINGLETON PARK
SWANSEA SA2 8PP
t: 01792 295111 f: 01792 295110
e: admissions@swansea.ac.uk
// www.swansea.ac.uk

CH61 BEng Sports Science and Engineering
Duration: 3FT Hon
Entry Requirements: *GCE:* BBB. *IB:* 32.

GC16 BSc Mathematics and Sport Science
Duration: 3FT Hon
Entry Requirements: *GCE:* ABB. *IB:* 33.

F3C6 BSc Physics with Sports Science
Duration: 3FT Hon
Entry Requirements: *GCE:* ABB. *IB:* 33.

C600 BSc Sports Science
Duration: 3FT Hon
Entry Requirements: *GCE:* BBB. *IB:* 32.

006C HND Sports Science
Duration: 2FT HND
Entry Requirements: *GCE:* 40-80.

CH6C MEng Sports Science and Engineering
Duration: 4FT Hon
Entry Requirements: *GCE:* AAB. *IB:* 34.

T20 TEESSIDE UNIVERSITY
MIDDLESBROUGH TS1 3BA
t: 01642 218121 f: 01642 384201
e: registry@tees.ac.uk
// www.tees.ac.uk

C600 BSc Sport and Exercise (Applied Exercise Science)
Duration: 3FT Hon
Entry Requirements: *GCE:* 260.

C610 BSc Sport and Exercise (Applied Sport Science)
Duration: 3FT Hon
Entry Requirements: *GCE:* 260.

C611 BSc Sport and Exercise (Coaching Science)
Duration: 3FT Hon   CRB Check: Required
Entry Requirements: *GCE:* 260.

LC36 BSc Sport and Exercise (Sport Studies)
Duration: 3FT Hon
Entry Requirements: *GCE:* 260.

C601 BSc Sports Therapy
Duration: 3FT Hon   CRB Check: Required
Entry Requirements: *GCE:* 260.

CX69 FdA Outdoor Leadership
Duration: 2FT Fdg   CRB Check: Required
Entry Requirements: *GCE:* 120.

C603 FdSc Fitness Instruction and Sports Massage
Duration: 2FT Fdg   CRB Check: Required
Entry Requirements: *GCE:* 120.

C602 FdSc Sport and Exercise (Personal Training)
Duration: 2FT Fdg   CRB Check: Required
Entry Requirements: *GCE:* 120.

T80 UNIVERSITY OF WALES TRINITY SAINT DAVID
COLLEGE ROAD
CARMARTHEN SA31 3EP
t: 01267 676767 f: 01267 676766
e: registry@trinitysaintdavid.ac.uk
// www.tsd.ac.uk

XC96 BA Addysg Gorfforol
Duration: 3FT Hon
Entry Requirements: *GCE:* 180-360. *IB:* 26. Interview required.

BC46 BA Health & Exercise and Sports Studies
Duration: 3FT Hon
Entry Requirements: *GCE:* 180-360. *IB:* 26. Interview required.

CX69 BA Physical Education
Duration: 3FT Hon
Entry Requirements: *GCE:* 180-360. *IB:* 26. Interview required.

BC96 BSc Health & Exercise Referral
Duration: 3FT Hon
Entry Requirements: *GCE:* 180-360. *IB:* 26. Interview required.

T85 TRURO AND PENWITH COLLEGE
TRURO COLLEGE
COLLEGE ROAD
TRURO
CORNWALL TR1 3XX
t: 01872 267122 f: 01872 267526
e: heinfo@trurocollege.ac.uk
// www.truro-penwith.ac.uk

C601 BSc (Hons) Sports Performance and Coaching
Duration: 1FT Deg
Entry Requirements: Interview required.

C604 FdSc Exercise, Health and Fitness
Duration: 2FT Fdg
Entry Requirements: *GCE:* 60-80. *IB:* 24. *BTEC Dip:* MP. *BTEC ExtDip:* PPP. Interview required.

CN62 FdSc Sports Performance Analysis and Management
Duration: 2FT Fdg
Entry Requirements: *GCE:* 60-80. *IB:* 24. *BTEC Dip:* MP. *BTEC ExtDip:* PPP. Interview required.

U20 UNIVERSITY OF ULSTER
COLERAINE
CO. LONDONDERRY
NORTHERN IRELAND BT52 1SA
t: 028 7012 4221 f: 028 7012 4908
e: online@ulster.ac.uk
// www.ulster.ac.uk

C600 BSc Sport and Exercise Sciences
Duration: 3FT Hon   CRB Check: Required
Entry Requirements: *GCE:* AAB. *SQAH:* AAABC. *SQAAH:* ABB. *IB:* 27.

C601 BSc Sports Technology
Duration: 4SW Hon
Entry Requirements: *GCE:* 280. *IB:* 24. Interview required. Admissions Test required.

U40 UNIVERSITY OF THE WEST OF SCOTLAND
PAISLEY
RENFREWSHIRE
SCOTLAND PA1 2BE
t: 0141 848 3727 f: 0141 848 3623
e: admissions@uws.ac.uk
// www.uws.ac.uk

C600 BA Sport Development
Duration: 3FT/4FT Ord/Hon   CRB Check: Required
Entry Requirements: *GCE:* CD. *SQAH:* BBBC.

CX6C BSc Sport Coaching
Duration: 3FT/4FT Ord/Hon   CRB Check: Required
Entry Requirements: *GCE:* CD. *SQAH:* BBCC.

C602 BSc Sport and Exercise Science
Duration: 4FT Hon   CRB Check: Required
Entry Requirements: *GCE:* CC. *SQAH:* BBCC.

CX61 DipHE Sport Coaching
Duration: 2FT Dip   CRB Check: Required
Entry Requirements: *GCE:* D. *SQAH:* CC.

C601 DipHE Sport Development
Duration: 2FT Dip
Entry Requirements: *GCE:* D. *SQAH:* CC.

W08 WAKEFIELD COLLEGE
MARGARET STREET
WAKEFIELD
WEST YORKSHIRE WF1 2DH
t: 01924 789111 f: 01924 789281
e: courseinfo@wakefield.ac.uk
// www.wakefield.ac.uk

C600 BSc Health Related Exercise and Fitness (Top-up)
Duration: 1FT Hon
Entry Requirements: Contact the institution for details.

CB69 FdSc Health Related Exercise and Fitness
Duration: 2FT Fdg
Entry Requirements: *GCE:* 120.

CX61 FdSc Sports Performance Coaching
Duration: 2FT Fdg
Entry Requirements: *GCE:* 120.

W25 WARWICKSHIRE COLLEGE

WARWICK NEW ROAD
LEAMINGTON SPA
WARWICKSHIRE CV32 5JE
t: 01926 884223 f: 01926 318 111
e: kgooch@warkscol.ac.uk
// www.warwickshire.ac.uk

DC36 BSc Equine and Human Sports Science

Duration: 3FT/4SW Hon
Entry Requirements: *GCE:* 220. *IB:* 28. Interview required.

DX41 BSc Equitation Coaching Sports Science

Duration: 3FT/4SW Hon
Entry Requirements: *GCE:* 220. Interview required.

NC86 FdA Sport and Fitness Management

Duration: 2FT Fdg
Entry Requirements: Contact the institution for details.

W36 WEST CHESHIRE COLLEGE

EATON ROAD
HANDBRIDGE
CHESTER
CHESHIRE CH4 7ER
t: 01244 656555 f: 01244 670687
e: info@west-cheshire.ac.uk
// www.west-cheshire.ac.uk

CB69 FdSc Fitness and Health

Duration: 2FT Fdg
Entry Requirements: Contact the institution for details.

W50 UNIVERSITY OF WESTMINSTER

2ND FLOOR, CAVENDISH HOUSE
101 NEW CAVENDISH STREET,
LONDON W1W 6XH
t: 020 7915 5511
e: course-enquiries@westminster.ac.uk
// www.westminster.ac.uk

BC46 BSc Human Nutrition (Nutrition & Exercise Science)

Duration: 3FT Hon
Entry Requirements: *GCE:* CCD. *SQAH:* CCCC. *IB:* 26. Interview required.

BCK6 BSc Human Nutrition (Nutrition and Exercise Science) with Foundation

Duration: 4FT Hon
Entry Requirements: *GCE:* CCD. *SQAH:* CCCC. *IB:* 26. Interview required.

W67 WIGAN AND LEIGH COLLEGE

PO BOX 53
PARSON'S WALK
WIGAN
GREATER MANCHESTER WN1 1RS
t: 01942 761605 f: 01942 761164
e: applications@wigan-leigh.ac.uk
// www.wigan-leigh.ac.uk

BC96 FdSc Health & Personal Training

Duration: 2FT Fdg
Entry Requirements: Interview required.

CX61 FdSc Sports Coaching

Duration: 2FT Fdg
Entry Requirements: *GCE:* D. Interview required.

W75 UNIVERSITY OF WOLVERHAMPTON

ADMISSIONS UNIT
MX207, CAMP STREET
WOLVERHAMPTON
WEST MIDLANDS WV1 1AD
t: 01902 321000 f: 01902 321896
e: admissions@wlv.ac.uk
// www.wlv.ac.uk

C603 BA Physical Education

Duration: 3FT Hon   CRB Check: Required
Entry Requirements: *GCE:* 280. *IB:* 25. *BTEC Dip:* D*D*. *BTEC ExtDip:* DMM. *OCR NED:* M2

C601 BA Sports Studies

Duration: 3FT Hon   CRB Check: Required
Entry Requirements: *GCE:* 240. *IB:* 24. *BTEC Dip:* DD. *BTEC ExtDip:* MMM. *OCR ND:* D *OCR NED:* M3

CB69 BSc Physical Activity, Exercise and Health

Duration: 3FT Hon   CRB Check: Required
Entry Requirements: *GCE:* 200. *IB:* 24. *BTEC Dip:* DM. *BTEC ExtDip:* MMP. *OCR ND:* M1 *OCR NED:* P1

C604 BSc Sport & Exercise Science

Duration: 3FT Hon   CRB Check: Required
Entry Requirements: *GCE:* 240. *IB:* 24. *BTEC Dip:* DD. *BTEC ExtDip:* MMM. *OCR ND:* D *OCR NED:* M3

C605 BSc Sports Coaching

Duration: 3FT Hon   CRB Check: Required
Entry Requirements: *GCE:* 240. *IB:* 24. *BTEC Dip:* DD. *BTEC ExtDip:* MMM. *OCR ND:* D *OCR NED:* M3

C600 FdSc Sport and Exercise Science

Duration: 2FT Fdg
Entry Requirements: *GCE:* 100. *IB:* 24. *BTEC Dip:* MP. *BTEC ExtDip:* PPP. *OCR NED:* P3

W76 UNIVERSITY OF WINCHESTER
WINCHESTER
HANTS SO22 4NR
t: 01962 827234 f: 01962 827288
e: course.enquiries@winchester.ac.uk
// www.winchester.ac.uk

WC86 BA Creative Writing and Sports Studies
Duration: 3FT Hon
Entry Requirements: *Foundation:* Merit. *GCE:* 260-300. *IB:* 24.

NC8P BA Event Management and Sports Studies
Duration: 3FT Hon
Entry Requirements: *Foundation:* Merit. *GCE:* 260-300. *IB:* 24.

PCM6 BA Journalism Studies and Sports Studies
Duration: 3FT Hon
Entry Requirements: *Foundation:* Merit. *GCE:* 260-300. *IB:* 24.

MC16 BA Law and Sports Studies
Duration: 3FT Hon
Entry Requirements: *Foundation:* Merit. *GCE:* 260-300. *IB:* 24.

PC36 BA Media Production and Sports Studies
Duration: 3FT Hon
Entry Requirements: *Foundation:* Merit. *GCE:* 260-300. *IB:* 24.

CP63 BA Media Studies and Sports Studies
Duration: 3FT Hon
Entry Requirements: *Foundation:* Merit. *GCE:* 260-300. *IB:* 25.

XCC6 BA Physical Education: Primary (3 years QTS)
Duration: 3FT Hon
Entry Requirements: *GCE:* 280-300. Interview required.

LC2P BA Politics & Global Studies and Sports Studies
Duration: 3FT Hon
Entry Requirements: *Foundation:* Merit. *GCE:* 260-300. *IB:* 24.

LC36 BA Sociology and Sports Studies
Duration: 3FT Hon
Entry Requirements: *Foundation:* Pass. *GCE:* 260-300. *IB:* 24. *OCR ND:* D

CX61 BA Sports Coaching & Development
Duration: 3FT Hon
Entry Requirements: *Foundation:* Distinction. *GCE:* 260-300. *IB:* 24. *OCR ND:* D *OCR NED:* M2

C600 BA Sports Studies
Duration: 3FT Hon
Entry Requirements: *Foundation:* Pass. *GCE:* 220-260. *IB:* 24. *OCR ND:* D

CW6H BA Sports Studies and Vocal & Choral Studies
Duration: 3FT Hon
Entry Requirements: *Foundation:* Pass. *GCE:* 260-300. *IB:* 24. *OCR ND:* D

C602 BSc Sports Science
Duration: 3FT Hon
Entry Requirements: *Foundation:* Distinction. *GCE:* 260-300. *IB:* 24. *OCR ND:* D *OCR NED:* M2

W80 UNIVERSITY OF WORCESTER
HENWICK GROVE
WORCESTER WR2 6AJ
t: 01905 855111 f: 01905 855377
e: admissions@worc.ac.uk
// www.worcester.ac.uk

CX61 BA Sport Coaching and Development
Duration: 3FT Hon
Entry Requirements: *GCE:* 280. *IB:* 25. *OCR ND:* D *OCR NED:* M3

QC3P BA/BSc English Language Studies and Sports Studies
Duration: 3FT Hon
Entry Requirements: *GCE:* 240-300. *IB:* 24. *OCR ND:* D Interview required. Portfolio required.

QC36 BA/BSc English Literary Studies and Sports Studies
Duration: 3FT Hon
Entry Requirements: *GCE:* 240-300. *IB:* 24. *OCR ND:* D Interview required. Portfolio required.

BCK6 BA/BSc Human Nutrition and Sports Studies
Duration: 3FT Hon
Entry Requirements: Contact the institution for details.

PC5P BA/BSc Journalism and Sports Studies
Duration: 3FT Hon
Entry Requirements: *GCE:* 240-300. *IB:* 24. *OCR ND:* D Interview required. Portfolio required.

CFP8 BA/BSc Physical Education and Physical Geography
Duration: 3FT Hon
Entry Requirements: Contact the institution for details.

LC36 BA/BSc Sociology and Sports Studies
Duration: 3FT Hon
Entry Requirements: *GCE:* 240-300. *IB:* 24. *OCR ND:* D Interview required. Portfolio required.

LC76 BSc Geography and Sports Studies
Duration: 3FT Hon
Entry Requirements: *GCE:* 280-300. *IB:* 25. *OCR ND:* D *OCR NED:* M3

CCD6 BSc Human Biology and Physical Education
Duration: 3FT Hon
Entry Requirements: *GCE:* 280. *IB:* 25. *OCR ND:* D *OCR NED:* M3

CC61 BSc Human Biology and Sports Coaching Science
Duration: 3FT Hon
Entry Requirements: *GCE:* 280. *IB:* 25. *OCR ND:* D *OCR NED:* M3

C690 BSc Physical Education and Sports Coaching Science
Duration: 3FT Hon
Entry Requirements: *GCE:* 280. *IB:* 25. *OCR ND:* D *OCR NED:* M3

C691 BSc Physical Education and Sports Studies
Duration: 3FT Hon
Entry Requirements: *GCE:* 280. *IB:* 25. *OCR ND:* D *OCR NED:* M3

CN62 BSc Sport Business Management
Duration: 3FT Hon
Entry Requirements: *GCE:* 280. *IB:* 25. *OCR ND:* D *OCR NED:* M3

C601 BSc Sports Coaching Science
Duration: 3FT Hon
Entry Requirements: *GCE:* 280. *IB:* 25. *OCR ND:* D *OCR NED:* M3

C6X3 BSc Sports Studies
Duration: 3FT Hon
Entry Requirements: *GCE:* 280. *IB:* 25. *OCR ND:* D *OCR NED:* M3

C603 BSc Sports Therapy
Duration: 3FT Hon
Entry Requirements: *GCE:* 280. *IB:* 25. *OCR ND:* D *OCR NED:* M3

C600 BSc Sports and Exercise Science
Duration: 3FT Hon
Entry Requirements: *GCE:* 280. *IB:* 25. *OCR ND:* D *OCR NED:* M3

26NC HND Sports Coaching
Duration: 2FT HND
Entry Requirements: *GCE:* 120. *IB:* 24. *OCR ND:* M2 *OCR NED:* P2

16XC HND Sports Performance and Coaching
Duration: 2FT HND
Entry Requirements: *GCE:* 140. *IB:* 24. *OCR ND:* M2 *OCR NED:* P2

006C HND Sports Studies
Duration: 2FT HND
Entry Requirements: *GCE:* 140. *IB:* 24. *OCR ND:* M2 *OCR NED:* P2

W81 WORCESTER COLLEGE OF TECHNOLOGY
DEANSWAY
WORCESTER WR1 2JF
t: 01905 725555 f: 01905 28906
// www.wortech.ac.uk

C600 FdSc Fitness Training & Healthy Lifestyle
Duration: 2FT Fdg
Entry Requirements: *GCE:* 120.

W85 WRITTLE COLLEGE
ADMISSIONS
WRITTLE COLLEGE
CHELMSFORD
ESSEX CM1 3RR
t: 01245 424200 f: 01245 420456
e: admissions@writtle.ac.uk
// www.writtle.ac.uk

CD64 BSc Human and Equine Sports Performance
Duration: 3FT Hon
Entry Requirements: *GCE:* 260. *IB:* 24. *BTEC Dip:* D*D*. *BTEC ExtDip:* DMM. *OCR NED:* M2

C600 BSc Sports and Exercise Performance
Duration: 3FT Hon
Entry Requirements: *GCE:* 260. *IB:* 24. *BTEC Dip:* D*D*. *BTEC ExtDip:* DMM. *OCR NED:* M2

Y70 YORK COLLEGE
SIM BALK LANE
YORK YO23 2BB
t: 01904 770448 f: 01904 770499
e: admissions.team@yorkcollege.ac.uk
// www.yorkcollege.ac.uk

C600 FdSc Sports Therapy
Duration: 2FT Fdg   CRB Check: Required
Entry Requirements: *GCE:* CCC. Interview required.

Y75 YORK ST JOHN UNIVERSITY
LORD MAYOR'S WALK
YORK YO31 7EX
t: 01904 876598 f: 01904 876940/876921
e: admissions@yorksj.ac.uk
// w3.yorksj.ac.uk

CL66 BA Sport, Society & Development
Duration: 3FT Hon
Entry Requirements: *GCE:* 220-260. *IB:* 24.

C602 BSc Sport Science for Performance Conditioning
Duration: 3FT Hon
Entry Requirements: *GCE:* 220-260. *IB:* 24.

CB6X BSc Sports Science and Injury Management
Duration: 3FT Hon
Entry Requirements: *GCE:* 220-260. *IB:* 24.

CB69 BSc Sports Science: Exercise Practice
Duration: 3FT Hon
Entry Requirements: *GCE:* 220-260. *IB:* 24.

SPORTS EXERCISE AND HEALTH

A20 THE UNIVERSITY OF ABERDEEN
UNIVERSITY OFFICE
KING'S COLLEGE
ABERDEEN AB24 3FX
t: +44 (0) 1224 273504 f: +44 (0) 1224 272034
e: sras@abdn.ac.uk
// www.abdn.ac.uk/sras

C603 BSc Sports Studies (Exercise and Health)
Duration: 4FT Hon
Entry Requirements: *GCE:* BBB. *SQAH:* BBBB. *SQAAH:* BCC. *IB:* 30.

C601 MSci Sports Studies (Exercise and Health) with Industrial Placement
Duration: 5FT Hon
Entry Requirements: *GCE:* ABB. *SQAH:* AABB. *IB:* 32.

B32 THE UNIVERSITY OF BIRMINGHAM
EDGBASTON
BIRMINGHAM B15 2TT
t: 0121 415 8900 f: 0121 414 7159
e: admissions@bham.ac.uk
// www.birmingham.ac.uk

BC17 BSc Sport and Exercise Sciences
Duration: 3FT Hon
Entry Requirements: *GCE:* AAA-AAB. *SQAH:* AAAAB-AAABB. *SQAAH:* AA. *IB:* 36.

C10 CANTERBURY CHRIST CHURCH UNIVERSITY
NORTH HOLMES ROAD
CANTERBURY
KENT CT1 1QU
t: 01227 782900 f: 01227 782888
e: admissions@canterbury.ac.uk
// www.canterbury.ac.uk

CM89 BA Applied Criminology and Sport & Exercise Psychology
Duration: 3FT Hon
Entry Requirements: *GCE:* 240. *IB:* 24.

GC5V BA Business Computing and Sport & Exercise Psychology
Duration: 3FT Hon
Entry Requirements: *GCE:* 240. *IB:* 24.

G5CV BA Business Computing with Sport & Exercise Psychology
Duration: 3FT Hon
Entry Requirements: *GCE:* 240. *IB:* 24.

GCK8 BA Internet Computing and Sport & Exercise Psychology
Duration: 3FT Hon
Entry Requirements: *GCE:* 240. *IB:* 24.

C8GM BA Sport & Exercise Psychology with Business Computing
Duration: 3FT Hon
Entry Requirements: Contact the institution for details.

C8GA BA Sport & Exercise Psychology with Internet Computing
Duration: 3FT Hon
Entry Requirements: Contact the institution for details.

M9CV BA/BSc Applied Criminology with Sport & Exercise Psychology
Duration: 3FT Hon
Entry Requirements: *GCE:* 240. *IB:* 24.

X3CV BA/BSc Early Childhood Studies with Sport & Exercise Psychology
Duration: 3FT Hon   CRB Check: Required
Entry Requirements: *GCE:* 240. *IB:* 24.

V1CV BA/BSc History with Sport & Exercise Psychology
Duration: 3FT Hon
Entry Requirements: *GCE:* 240. *IB:* 24.

MC28 BA/BSc Legal Studies and Sport & Exercise Psychology
Duration: 3FT Hon
Entry Requirements: *GCE:* 240. *IB:* 24.

M2C8 BA/BSc Legal Studies with Sport & Exercise Psychology
Duration: 3FT Hon
Entry Requirements: *GCE:* 240. *IB:* 24.

C8M9 BA/BSc Sport & Exercise Psychology with Applied Criminology
Duration: 3FT Hon
Entry Requirements: Contact the institution for details.

C8WC BA/BSc Sport & Exercise Psychology with Art
Duration: 3FT Hon
Entry Requirements: Contact the institution for details.

C8XH BA/BSc Sport & Exercise Psychology with Early Childhood Studies
Duration: 3FT Hon
Entry Requirements: Contact the institution for details.

C8VC BA/BSc Sport & Exercise Psychology with History
Duration: 3FT Hon
Entry Requirements: Contact the institution for details.

C8M2 BA/BSc Sport & Exercise Psychology with Legal Studies
Duration: 3FT Hon
Entry Requirements: Contact the institution for details.

GC48 BSc Computing and Sport & Exercise Psychology
Duration: 3FT Hon
Entry Requirements: *GCE:* 240. *IB:* 24.

G4C8 BSc Computing with Sport & Exercise Psychology
Duration: 3FT Hon
Entry Requirements: *GCE:* 240. *IB:* 24.

C813 BSc Psychology (Sport and Exercise)
Duration: 3FT Hon   CRB Check: Required
Entry Requirements: *GCE:* 260. *IB:* 24. Interview required.

C8G4 BSc Sport & Exercise Psychology with Computing
Duration: 3FT Hon
Entry Requirements: Contact the institution for details.

CX83 BSc/BA Sport & Exercise Psychology and Early Childhood Studies
Duration: 3FT Hon   CRB Check: Required
Entry Requirements: *GCE:* 240. *IB:* 24.

VC18 BSc/BA Sport & Exercise Psychology and History
Duration: 3FT Hon
Entry Requirements: *GCE:* 240. *IB:* 24.

C58 UNIVERSITY OF CHICHESTER
BISHOP OTTER CAMPUS
COLLEGE LANE
CHICHESTER
WEST SUSSEX PO19 6PE
t: 01243 816002 f: 01243 816161
e: admissions@chi.ac.uk
// www.chiuni.ac.uk

C841 BSc Sport & Exercise Psychology
Duration: 3FT Hon
Entry Requirements: *GCE:* BCD-CCC. *SQAH:* CCC. *IB:* 30. *BTEC Dip:* DD. *BTEC ExtDip:* DMM.

E42 EDGE HILL UNIVERSITY
ORMSKIRK
LANCASHIRE L39 4QP
t: 01695 657000 f: 01695 584355
e: study@edgehill.ac.uk
// www.edgehill.ac.uk

C813 BSc Sport & Exercise Psychology
Duration: 3FT Hon
Entry Requirements: *GCE:* 280. *IB:* 26. *OCR ND:* D *OCR NED:* M2

G70 UNIVERSITY OF GREENWICH
GREENWICH CAMPUS
OLD ROYAL NAVAL COLLEGE
PARK ROW
LONDON SE10 9LS
t: 020 8331 9000 f: 020 8331 8145
e: courseinfo@gre.ac.uk
// www.gre.ac.uk

CB94 BSc Sport Exercise and Nutrition
Duration: 3FT Hon
Entry Requirements: Contact the institution for details.

K12 KEELE UNIVERSITY
KEELE UNIVERSITY
STAFFORDSHIRE ST5 5BG
t: 01782 734005 f: 01782 632343
e: undergraduate@keele.ac.uk
// www.keele.ac.uk

B1B9 BSc Physiotherapy with Health Foundation Year
Duration: 4FT Hon   CRB Check: Required
Entry Requirements: GCE: BBB. SQAAH: BBB. IB: 28. Interview required.

L24 LEEDS TRINITY UNIVERSITY COLLEGE
BROWNBERRIE LANE
HORSFORTH
LEEDS LS18 5HD
t: 0113 283 7150 f: 0113 283 7222
e: enquiries@leedstrinity.ac.uk
// www.leedstrinity.ac.uk

C600 BSc Sport and Exercise Sciences (Sport Psychology)
Duration: 3FT Hon
Entry Requirements: Contact the institution for details.

L36 LEICESTER COLLEGE
FREEMEN'S PARK CAMPUS
AYLESTONE ROAD
LEICESTER LE2 7LW
t: 0116 224 2240 f: 0116 224 2041
e: info@leicestercollege.ac.uk
// www.leicestercollege.ac.uk

86NC HND Sport (Coaching, Leisure Management and Exercise Sciences)
Duration: 2FT HND
Entry Requirements: Contact the institution for details.

M40 THE MANCHESTER METROPOLITAN UNIVERSITY
ADMISSIONS OFFICE
ALL SAINTS (GMS)
ALL SAINTS
MANCHESTER M15 6BH
t: 0161 247 2000
// www.mmu.ac.uk

B121 BSc Physiology (Physical Activity and Health)
Duration: 3FT/4SW Hon
Entry Requirements: GCE: 280. IB: 27.

B122 BSc Physiology (Physical Activity and Health) (Foundation)
Duration: 4FT/5SW Hon
Entry Requirements: GCE: 160. IB: 24. BTEC Dip: MM. BTEC ExtDip: MPP.

C841 BSc Psychology of Sport and Exercise
Duration: 3FT Hon
Entry Requirements: GCE: 280. IB: 28. BTEC Dip: D*D*. BTEC ExtDip: DMM.

C842 BSc Psychology of Sport and Exercise (Foundation)
Duration: 4FT Hon
Entry Requirements: GCE: 160. IB: 24. BTEC Dip: MM. BTEC ExtDip: MPP.

M80 MIDDLESEX UNIVERSITY
MIDDLESEX UNIVERSITY
THE BURROUGHS
LONDON NW4 4BT
t: 020 8411 5555 f: 020 8411 5649
e: enquiries@mdx.ac.uk
// www.mdx.ac.uk

B120 BSc Healthcare Science (Respiratory and Sleep Science)
Duration: 3FT Hon
Entry Requirements: Contact the institution for details.

P63 UCP MARJON - UNIVERSITY COLLEGE PLYMOUTH ST MARK & ST JOHN
DERRIFORD ROAD
PLYMOUTH PL6 8BH
t: 01752 636890 f: 01752 636819
e: admissions@marjon.ac.uk
// www.ucpmarjon.ac.uk

C608 BSc Rehabilitation in Sport and Exercise
Duration: 1FT Hon   CRB Check: Required
Entry Requirements: Contact the institution for details.

C630 BSc Rehabilitation in Sport and Exercise
Duration: 3FT Hon   CRB Check: Required
Entry Requirements: *GCE:* 240. *OCR ND:* D Interview required.

S27 UNIVERSITY OF SOUTHAMPTON
HIGHFIELD
SOUTHAMPTON SO17 1BJ
t: 023 8059 4732 f: 023 8059 3037
e: admissions@soton.ac.uk
// www.southampton.ac.uk

B120 BSc Healthcare Science
Duration: 3FT Hon   CRB Check: Required
Entry Requirements: Contact the institution for details.

S49 ST GEORGE'S, UNIVERSITY OF LONDON
CRANMER TERRACE
LONDON SW17 0RE
t: +44 (0)20 8725 2333 f: +44 (0)20 8725 0841
e: enquiries@sgul.ac.uk
// www.sgul.ac.uk

B120 BSc (Hons) Healthcare Science (Physiological Sciences)
Duration: 3FT Hon   CRB Check: Required
Entry Requirements: *IB:* 25. Interview required.

S64 ST MARY'S UNIVERSITY COLLEGE, TWICKENHAM
WALDEGRAVE ROAD
STRAWBERRY HILL
MIDDLESEX TW1 4SX
t: 020 8240 4029 f: 020 8240 2361
e: admit@smuc.ac.uk
// www.smuc.ac.uk

BXY3 BA Health Exercise & Physical Activity and Physical & Sport Education
Duration: 3FT Hon
Entry Requirements: *GCE:* 240. *SQAH:* BBBC. *IB:* 28. *OCR ND:* D *OCR NED:* M3 Interview required.

S72 STAFFORDSHIRE UNIVERSITY
COLLEGE ROAD
STOKE ON TRENT ST4 2DE
t: 01782 292753 f: 01782 292740
e: admissions@staffs.ac.uk
// www.staffs.ac.uk

C810 BSc Sport and Exercise Psychology
Duration: 3FT Hon
Entry Requirements: *GCE:* 200-280. *IB:* 24.

W51 CITY OF WESTMINSTER COLLEGE
CITY OF WESTMINSTER COLLEGE
PADDINGTON GREEN CAMPUS
25 PADDINGTON GREEN
LONDON W2 1NB
t: 020 7723 8826
e: customer.services@cwc.ac.uk
// www.cwc.ac.uk

046C HND Sport (Health, Fitness and Exercise)
Duration: 2FT HND
Entry Requirements: Contact the institution for details.

W75 UNIVERSITY OF WOLVERHAMPTON
ADMISSIONS UNIT
MX207, CAMP STREET
WOLVERHAMPTON
WEST MIDLANDS WV1 1AD
t: 01902 321000 f: 01902 321896
e: admissions@wlv.ac.uk
// www.wlv.ac.uk

B120 BSc Healthcare Science (Physiological Sciences)
Duration: 3FT/4SW Hon
Entry Requirements: *GCE:* 220-240. *IB:* 30.

W76 UNIVERSITY OF WINCHESTER
WINCHESTER
HANTS SO22 4NR
t: 01962 827234 f: 01962 827288
e: course.enquiries@winchester.ac.uk
// www.winchester.ac.uk

LN85 BA Health, Community & Social Care Studies and Sports Management
Duration: 3FT Hon
Entry Requirements: Contact the institution for details.

LC65 BA Health, Community & Social Care Studies and Sports Studies
Duration: 3FT Hon
Entry Requirements: Contact the institution for details.

W80 UNIVERSITY OF WORCESTER
HENWICK GROVE
WORCESTER WR2 6AJ
t: 01905 855111 f: 01905 855377
e: admissions@worc.ac.uk
// www.worcester.ac.uk

C813 BSc Sport & Exercise Psychology
Duration: 3FT Hon
Entry Requirements: *GCE:* 280. *IB:* 25. *OCR ND:* D *OCR NED:* M3

SPORTS THERAPY

B16 UNIVERSITY OF BATH
CLAVERTON DOWN
BATH BA2 7AY
t: 01225 383019 f: 01225 386366
e: admissions@bath.ac.uk
// www.bath.ac.uk

CB69 FdSc Sport (Sports Therapy)
Duration: 2FT Fdg   CRB Check: Required
Entry Requirements: *GCE:* 80.

B22 UNIVERSITY OF BEDFORDSHIRE
PARK SQUARE
LUTON
BEDS LU1 3JU
t: 0844 8482234 f: 01582 489323
e: admissions@beds.ac.uk
// www.beds.ac.uk

CB63 BSc Sports Therapy
Duration: 3FT Hon
Entry Requirements: *Foundation:* Pass. *GCE:* 200. *SQAH:* BCC.
SQAAH: BCC. *IB:* 24. *OCR ND:* M1 *OCR NED:* P1

C605 FdSc Sports Therapy
Duration: 2FT Fdg
Entry Requirements: Contact the institution for details.

E28 UNIVERSITY OF EAST LONDON
DOCKLANDS CAMPUS
UNIVERSITY WAY
LONDON E16 2RD
t: 020 8223 3333 f: 020 8223 2978
e: study@uel.ac.uk
// www.uel.ac.uk

C630 BSc Sports Therapy
Duration: 3FT Hon
Entry Requirements: *GCE:* 240. *IB:* 24.

G50 THE UNIVERSITY OF GLOUCESTERSHIRE
PARK CAMPUS
THE PARK
CHELTENHAM GL50 2RH
t: 01242 714501 f: 01242 714869
e: admissions@glos.ac.uk
// www.glos.ac.uk

C610 BSc Sports Strength and Conditioning
Duration: 2FT Hon   CRB Check: Required
Entry Requirements: Contact the institution for details.

P63 UCP MARJON - UNIVERSITY COLLEGE PLYMOUTH ST MARK & ST JOHN
DERRIFORD ROAD
PLYMOUTH PL6 8BH
t: 01752 636890 f: 01752 636819
e: admissions@marjon.ac.uk
// www.ucpmarjon.ac.uk

C631 BSc Sports Therapy
Duration: 3FT Hon   CRB Check: Required
Entry Requirements: *GCE:* 240. *OCR ND:* D Interview required.

C632 BSc Strength and Conditioning
Duration: 3FT Hon   CRB Check: Required
Entry Requirements: Contact the institution for details.

T85 TRURO AND PENWITH COLLEGE
TRURO COLLEGE
COLLEGE ROAD
TRURO
CORNWALL TR1 3XX
t: 01872 267122 f: 01872 267526
e: heinfo@trurocollege.ac.uk
// www.truro-penwith.ac.uk

C630 FdSc Sports Rehabilitation
Duration: 2FT Fdg
Entry Requirements: *GCE:* 60. *IB:* 24. *BTEC Dip:* MP. *BTEC ExtDip:* PPP. Interview required.

W85 WRITTLE COLLEGE
ADMISSIONS
WRITTLE COLLEGE
CHELMSFORD
ESSEX CM1 3RR
t: 01245 424200 f: 01245 420456
e: admissions@writtle.ac.uk
// www.writtle.ac.uk

DD4H BSc Equine Sports Therapy
Duration: 3FT Hon
Entry Requirements: *GCE:* 260. *IB:* 24. *BTEC Dip:* D*D*. *BTEC ExtDip:* DMM. *OCR NED:* M2

SPORTS EDUCATION

A60 ANGLIA RUSKIN UNIVERSITY
BISHOP HALL LANE
CHELMSFORD
ESSEX CM1 1SQ
t: 0845 271 3333 f: 01245 251789
e: answers@anglia.ac.uk
// www.anglia.ac.uk

C602 BSc Sports Coaching and Physical Education
Duration: 3FT Hon
Entry Requirements: *GCE:* 200. *SQAH:* CCCC. *SQAAH:* CC. *IB:* 24. *OCR ND:* M1 *OCR NED:* P1

B72 UNIVERSITY OF BRIGHTON
MITHRAS HOUSE 211
LEWES ROAD
BRIGHTON BN2 4AT
t: 01273 644644 f: 01273 642607
e: admissions@brighton.ac.uk
// www.brighton.ac.uk

XC36 BA (Hons) Physical Education
Duration: 3FT Hon
Entry Requirements: *GCE:* AAB.

C20 CARDIFF METROPOLITAN UNIVERSITY (UWIC)
ADMISSIONS UNIT
LLANDAFF CAMPUS
WESTERN AVENUE
CARDIFF CF5 2YB
t: 029 2041 6070 f: 029 2041 6286
e: admissions@cardiffmet.ac.uk
// www.cardiffmet.ac.uk

XB39 BA Educational Studies and Sport & Physical Activity
Duration: 3FT Hon   CRB Check: Required
Entry Requirements: *GCE:* 260. *IB:* 24. *BTEC ExtDip:* DMM. *OCR NED:* M2

C58 UNIVERSITY OF CHICHESTER
BISHOP OTTER CAMPUS
COLLEGE LANE
CHICHESTER
WEST SUSSEX PO19 6PE
t: 01243 816002 f: 01243 816161
e: admissions@chi.ac.uk
// www.chiuni.ac.uk

CX36 BA Sports Coaching and Physical Education
Duration: 3FT Hon   CRB Check: Required
Entry Requirements: Contact the institution for details.

E28 UNIVERSITY OF EAST LONDON
DOCKLANDS CAMPUS
UNIVERSITY WAY
LONDON E16 2RD
t: 020 8223 3333 f: 020 8223 2978
e: study@uel.ac.uk
// www.uel.ac.uk

XHC6 BA Education Studies with Sports Development
Duration: 3FT Hon
Entry Requirements: *GCE:* 240. *IB:* 24.

BX13 BSc Clinical Science with Education Studies
Duration: 3FT Hon
Entry Requirements: *GCE:* 240. *IB:* 24.

CXP3 BSc Sports Development with Education Studies
Duration: 3FT Hon
Entry Requirements: *GCE:* 240. *IB:* 24.

www.ucas.com

at the heart of connecting people to higher education

E42 EDGE HILL UNIVERSITY
ORMSKIRK
LANCASHIRE L39 4QP
t: 01695 657000 f: 01695 584355
e: study@edgehill.ac.uk
// www.edgehill.ac.uk

X390 BA Physical Education & School Sport
Duration: 3FT Deg   CRB Check: Required
Entry Requirements: *GCE:* 320. *IB:* 26. *OCR ND:* D *OCR NED:* M1

G50 THE UNIVERSITY OF GLOUCESTERSHIRE
PARK CAMPUS
THE PARK
CHELTENHAM GL50 2RH
t: 01242 714501 f: 01242 714869
e: admissions@glos.ac.uk
// www.glos.ac.uk

XX3C BSc Sports Coaching and Sports Education
Duration: 3FT Hon   CRB Check: Required
Entry Requirements: *GCE:* 280-300.

X151 BSc Sports Education
Duration: 3FT Hon   CRB Check: Required
Entry Requirements: *GCE:* 280-300.

X155 BSc Sports Education
Duration: 2FT Hon   CRB Check: Required
Entry Requirements: Contact the institution for details.

G70 UNIVERSITY OF GREENWICH
GREENWICH CAMPUS
OLD ROYAL NAVAL COLLEGE
PARK ROW
LONDON SE10 9LS
t: 020 8331 9000 f: 020 8331 8145
e: courseinfo@gre.ac.uk
// www.gre.ac.uk

X360 BA Physical Education and Sport
Duration: 3FT Hon
Entry Requirements: *GCE:* 300. *IB:* 24.

N36 NEWMAN UNIVERSITY COLLEGE, BIRMINGHAM
GENNERS LANE
BARTLEY GREEN
BIRMINGHAM B32 3NT
t: 0121 476 1181 f: 0121 476 1196
e: Admissions@newman.ac.uk
// www.newman.ac.uk

XX13 BA Sports Studies and Education Studies
Duration: 3FT Hon
Entry Requirements: *Foundation:* Distinction. *GCE:* 260. *IB:* 24.
BTEC ExtDip: DMM. *OCR ND:* M2 *OCR NED:* M2

N38 UNIVERSITY OF NORTHAMPTON
PARK CAMPUS
BOUGHTON GREEN ROAD
NORTHAMPTON NN2 7AL
t: 0800 358 2232 f: 01604 722083
e: admissions@northampton.ac.uk
// www.northampton.ac.uk

XC16 BA Special Educational Needs & Inclusion/Sport Studies
Duration: 3FT Hon
Entry Requirements: *GCE:* 260-280. *SQAH:* AAA-BBBB. *IB:* 24.
BTEC Dip: DD. *BTEC ExtDip:* DMM. *OCR ND:* D *OCR NED:* M2

N91 NOTTINGHAM TRENT UNIVERSITY
DRYDEN BUILDING
BURTON STREET
NOTTINGHAM NG1 4BU
t: +44 (0) 115 848 4200 f: +44 (0) 115 848 8869
e: applications@ntu.ac.uk
// www.ntu.ac.uk

X392 BA Sport and Leisure, Business and Education
Duration: 3FT Hon   CRB Check: Required
Entry Requirements: *GCE:* 280. *BTEC Dip:* D*D*. *BTEC ExtDip:* DMM. *OCR NED:* M2

XC3V BA Sport and Leisure, Psychology and Education
Duration: 3FT Hon   CRB Check: Required
Entry Requirements: *GCE:* 280. *BTEC Dip:* D*D*. *BTEC ExtDip:* DMM. *OCR NED:* M2

P56 UNIVERSITY CENTRE PETERBOROUGH
PARK CRESCENT
PETERBOROUGH PE1 4DZ
t: 0845 1965750 f: 01733 767986
e: UCPenquiries@anglia.ac.uk
// www.anglia.ac.uk/ucp

N870 BSc Sports Coaching and Physical Education
Duration: 3FT Hon
Entry Requirements: Contact the institution for details.

P63 UCP MARJON - UNIVERSITY COLLEGE PLYMOUTH ST MARK & ST JOHN
DERRIFORD ROAD
PLYMOUTH PL6 8BH
t: 01752 636890 f: 01752 636819
e: admissions@marjon.ac.uk
// www.ucpmarjon.ac.uk

X151 BA Coach and Physical Education
Duration: 3FT Hon   CRB Check: Required
Entry Requirements: *GCE:* 280.

XC63 BA Physical Education (accelerated)
Duration: 2FT Hon
Entry Requirements: *GCE:* 300.

S64 ST MARY'S UNIVERSITY COLLEGE, TWICKENHAM
WALDEGRAVE ROAD
STRAWBERRY HILL
MIDDLESEX TW1 4SX
t: 020 8240 4029 f: 020 8240 2361
e: admit@smuc.ac.uk
// www.smuc.ac.uk

FX83 BA Geography and Physical & Sport Education
Duration: 3FT Hon
Entry Requirements: *GCE:* 240. *SQAH:* BBBC. *IB:* 28. *OCR ND:* D *OCR NED:* M3 Interview required.

XW38 BA Physical & Sport Education and Creative & Professional Writing
Duration: 3FT Hon
Entry Requirements: *GCE:* 240. *SQAH:* BBBC. *IB:* 28. *OCR ND:* D *OCR NED:* M3 Interview required.

LX33 BA Physical & Sport Education and Sociology
Duration: 3FT Hon
Entry Requirements: *GCE:* 240. *SQAH:* BBBC. *IB:* 28. *OCR ND:* D *OCR NED:* M3 Interview required.

W76 UNIVERSITY OF WINCHESTER
WINCHESTER
HANTS SO22 4NR
t: 01962 827234 f: 01962 827288
e: course.enquiries@winchester.ac.uk
// www.winchester.ac.uk

XNHW BA Education Studies (Early Childhood) and Sports Management
Duration: 3FT Hon
Entry Requirements: *Foundation:* Distinction. *GCE:* 260-300. *IB:* 24. *OCR ND:* D *OCR NED:* M2

XLH3 BA Education Studies (Early Childhood) and Sports Studies
Duration: 3FT Hon
Entry Requirements: *Foundation:* Merit. *GCE:* 260-300. *IB:* 24.

NX8J BA Education Studies and Sports Management
Duration: 3FT Hon
Entry Requirements: *Foundation:* Pass. *GCE:* 260-300. *IB:* 24. *OCR ND:* D

LXJ3 BA Education Studies and Sports Studies
Duration: 3FT Hon
Entry Requirements: *Foundation:* Merit. *GCE:* 260-300. *IB:* 24.

Y75 YORK ST JOHN UNIVERSITY
LORD MAYOR'S WALK
YORK YO31 7EX
t: 01904 876598 f: 01904 876940/876921
e: admissions@yorksj.ac.uk
// w3.yorksj.ac.uk

XX31 BA Physical Education and Sports Coaching
Duration: 3FT Hon   CRB Check: Required
Entry Requirements: *GCE:* 260. *IB:* 24.

XX32 BA Physical Education and Sports Coaching (International only)
Duration: 4FT Hon
Entry Requirements: *GCE:* 260.

SPORTS COACHING

A44 ACCRINGTON & ROSSENDALE COLLEGE
BROAD OAK ROAD,
ACCRINGTON,
LANCASHIRE, BB5 2AW.
t: 01254 389933 f: 01254 354001
e: info@accross.ac.uk
// www.accrosshighereducation.co.uk/

CX16 FdA Sports Coaching
Duration: 2FT Fdg
Entry Requirements: Interview required.

B16 UNIVERSITY OF BATH
CLAVERTON DOWN
BATH BA2 7AY
t: 01225 383019 f: 01225 386366
e: admissions@bath.ac.uk
// www.bath.ac.uk

CX63 BA Sport and Social Sciences
Duration: 3FT Hon
Entry Requirements: *GCE:* AAB. *SQAAH:* ABB. *IB:* 35.

CX6H BA Sport and Social Sciences
Duration: 4SW Hon
Entry Requirements: *GCE:* AAB. *SQAAH:* ABB. *IB:* 35.

C602 BSc Sports Performance (Work-based Learning)
Duration: 1FT Ord
Entry Requirements: Contact the institution for details.

CX61 FdSc Sport (Coaching)
Duration: 2FT Fdg   CRB Check: Required
Entry Requirements: Contact the institution for details.

C601 FdSc Sport (Sports Performance)
Duration: 2FT Fdg
Entry Requirements: *GCE:* CCC. *OCR ND:* M2 *OCR NED:* M3

B22 UNIVERSITY OF BEDFORDSHIRE
PARK SQUARE
LUTON
BEDS LU1 3JU
t: 0844 8482234 f: 01582 489323
e: admissions@beds.ac.uk
// www.beds.ac.uk

CX6D FdSc Sports Coaching
Duration: 2FT Fdg
Entry Requirements: Contact the institution for details.

XC16 FdSc Sports Coaching
Duration: 2FT Fdg
Entry Requirements: Contact the institution for details.

CX6C FdSc Sports Fitness and Personal Training
Duration: 2FT Fdg
Entry Requirements: Contact the institution for details.

B35 UNIVERSITY COLLEGE BIRMINGHAM
SUMMER ROW
BIRMINGHAM B3 1JB
t: 0121 604 1040 f: 0121 604 1166
e: admissions@ucb.ac.uk
// www.ucb.ac.uk

N1C6 FdA Community Sport and Business Management
Duration: 2FT Fdg
Entry Requirements: Contact the institution for details.

B40 BLACKBURN COLLEGE
FEILDEN STREET
BLACKBURN BB2 1LH
t: 01254 292594 f: 01254 679647
e: he-admissions@blackburn.ac.uk
// www.blackburn.ac.uk

C620 FdA Community Coaching and Sport Development
Duration: 2FT Fdg
Entry Requirements: Contact the institution for details.

B50 BOURNEMOUTH UNIVERSITY
TALBOT CAMPUS
FERN BARROW
POOLE
DORSET BH12 5BB
t: 01202 524111
// www.bournemouth.ac.uk

CX81 BSc Sport Psychology and Coaching Sciences
Duration: 4SW Hon
Entry Requirements: *GCE:* 320. *IB:* 32. *BTEC SubDip:* D. *BTEC Dip:* DD. *BTEC ExtDip:* DDM.

B94 BUCKINGHAMSHIRE NEW UNIVERSITY
QUEEN ALEXANDRA ROAD
HIGH WYCOMBE
BUCKINGHAMSHIRE HP11 2JZ
t: 0800 0565 660 f: 01494 605 023
e: admissions@bucks.ac.uk
// bucks.ac.uk

NX21 BA Sports Management and Coaching Studies
Duration: 3FT Hon
Entry Requirements: *GCE:* 200-240. *IB:* 24. *OCR ND:* M1 *OCR NED:* M3

C22 COLEG SIR GAR / CARMARTHENSHIRE COLLEGE
SANDY ROAD
LLANELLI
CARMARTHENSHIRE SA15 4DN
t: 01554 748000 f: 01554 748170
e: admissions@colegsirgar.ac.uk
// www.colegsirgar.ac.uk

C610 BSc Sports Coaching and Performance
Duration: 3FT Hon   CRB Check: Required
Entry Requirements: Contact the institution for details.

C611 FdSc Sports, Coaching and Performance
Duration: 2FT Fdg   CRB Check: Required
Entry Requirements: Contact the institution for details.

C75 COLCHESTER INSTITUTE
SHEEPEN ROAD
COLCHESTER
ESSEX CO3 3LL
t: 01206 712777 f: 01206 712800
e: info@colchester.ac.uk
// www.colchester.ac.uk

C610 HNC Sport (Coaching and Sports Development)
Duration: 1FT HNC   CRB Check: Required
Entry Requirements: Contact the institution for details.

D55 DUCHY COLLEGE
STOKE CLIMSLAND
CALLINGTON
CORNWALL PL17 8PB
t: 01579 372327 f: 01579 372200
e: uni@duchy.ac.uk
// www.duchy.ac.uk

DX41 FdSc Equine Sports Performance & Coaching
Duration: 2FT Fdg
Entry Requirements: *GCE:* 100-120.

E28 UNIVERSITY OF EAST LONDON
DOCKLANDS CAMPUS
UNIVERSITY WAY
LONDON E16 2RD
t: 020 8223 3333 f: 020 8223 2978
e: study@uel.ac.uk
// www.uel.ac.uk

N8X1 BA Events Management with Sports Coaching
Duration: 3FT Hon
Entry Requirements: *GCE:* 240. *IB:* 24.

GX41 BSc Multimedia Design Technology and Sports Coaching
Duration: 3FT Hon
Entry Requirements: *GCE:* 240.

X1L6 BSc Sports Coaching with Anthropology
Duration: 3FT Hon
Entry Requirements: *GCE:* 240. *IB:* 24.

X1P9 BSc Sports Coaching with Communication Studies
Duration: 3FT Hon
Entry Requirements: *GCE:* 240. *IB:* 24.

X1X3 BSc Sports Coaching with Early Childhood Studies
Duration: 3FT Hon
Entry Requirements: *GCE:* 240. *IB:* 24.

X1L5 BSc Sports Coaching with Youth & Community Work
Duration: 3FT Hon
Entry Requirements: *GCE:* 240. *IB:* 24.

E30 EASTON COLLEGE
EASTON
NORWICH
NORFOLK NR9 5DX
t: 01603 731232 f: 01603 741438
e: info@easton.ac.uk
// www.easton.ac.uk

DC46 BSc Equitation and Coaching
Duration: 3FT Hon
Entry Requirements: Contact the institution for details.

G14 UNIVERSITY OF GLAMORGAN, CARDIFF AND PONTYPRIDD
ENQUIRIES AND ADMISSIONS UNIT
PONTYPRIDD CF37 1DL
t: 08456 434030 f: 01443 654050
e: enquiries@glam.ac.uk
// www.glam.ac.uk

C610 BSc Football Coaching and Performance
Duration: 3FT Hon
Entry Requirements: *GCE:* BBC. *BTEC Dip:* D*D*. *BTEC ExtDip:* DMM.

C611 BSc Rugby Coaching and Performance
Duration: 3FT Hon
Entry Requirements: *GCE:* BBC. *BTEC Dip:* D*D*. *BTEC ExtDip:* DMM.

G50 THE UNIVERSITY OF GLOUCESTERSHIRE
PARK CAMPUS
THE PARK
CHELTENHAM GL50 2RH
t: 01242 714501 f: 01242 714869
e: admissions@glos.ac.uk
// www.glos.ac.uk

X152 BSc Sports Coaching
Duration: 3FT Hon   CRB Check: Required
Entry Requirements: *GCE:* 280-300.

X153 FdSc Sports (Coaching)
Duration: 2FT Fdg   CRB Check: Required
Entry Requirements: *GCE:* 120.

L68 LONDON METROPOLITAN UNIVERSITY
166-220 HOLLOWAY ROAD
LONDON N7 8DB
t: 020 7133 4200
e: admissions@londonmet.ac.uk
// www.londonmet.ac.uk

XC18 BSc Sport Psychology and Coaching
Duration: 3FT Hon
Entry Requirements: *GCE:* 220. *IB:* 28.

N58 NORTH EAST WORCESTERSHIRE COLLEGE
PEAKMAN STREET
REDDITCH
WORCESTERSHIRE B98 8DW
t: 01527 570020 f: 01527 572901
e: admissions@ne-worcs.ac.uk
// www.ne-worcs.ac.uk

106C HND Sport (Coaching and Sports Development) .
Duration: 2FT HND
Entry Requirements: *GCE:* 160. Interview required.

N91 NOTTINGHAM TRENT UNIVERSITY
DRYDEN BUILDING
BURTON STREET
NOTTINGHAM NG1 4BU
t: +44 (0) 115 848 4200 f: +44 (0) 115 848 8869
e: applications@ntu.ac.uk
// www.ntu.ac.uk

D323 FdSc Sport Horse Management and Coaching
Duration: 2FT/3SW Fdg
Entry Requirements: *GCE:* 120. Interview required.

S01 SCOTTISH AGRICULTURAL COLLEGE
SAC EDINBURGH
WEST MAINS ROAD
EDINBURGH EH9 3JG
t: 0800 269453 f: 0131 535 4346
e: recruitment@sac.ac.uk
// www.sac.ac.uk/learning

N872 BA Sports Development and Coaching
Duration: 3FT/4FT Ord/Hon
Entry Requirements: *GCE:* CC. *SQAH:* BCC.

S30 SOUTHAMPTON SOLENT UNIVERSITY
EAST PARK TERRACE
SOUTHAMPTON
HAMPSHIRE SO14 0RT
t: +44 (0) 23 8031 9039 f: + 44 (0)23 8022 2259
e: admissions@solent.ac.uk
// www.solent.ac.uk/

C615 BA Fitness Management and Personal Training wth IFY (Intl Only - Jan)
Duration: 4FT Hon
Entry Requirements: Contact the institution for details.

S72 STAFFORDSHIRE UNIVERSITY
COLLEGE ROAD
STOKE ON TRENT ST4 2DE
t: 01782 292753 f: 01782 292740
e: admissions@staffs.ac.uk
// www.staffs.ac.uk

C605 BA Sports Development and Coaching (with Foundation Year)
Duration: 4FT Hon
Entry Requirements: *GCE:* 80. *BTEC ExtDip:* PPP.

CX6D FdA Sports Development and Coaching
Duration: 2FT Fdg
Entry Requirements: Interview required.

T10 TAMESIDE COLLEGE
ASHTON CENTRE
BEAUFORT ROAD
ASHTON-UNDER-LYNE
LANCS OL6 6NX
t: 0161 908 6789 f: 0161 908 6611
e: info@tameside.ac.uk
// www.tameside.ac.uk

N870 FdA Sport Coaching and Fitness Therapy
Duration: 2FT Fdg
Entry Requirements: Contact the institution for details.

T85 TRURO AND PENWITH COLLEGE
TRURO COLLEGE
COLLEGE ROAD
TRURO
CORNWALL TR1 3XX
t: 01872 267122 f: 01872 267526
e: heinfo@trurocollege.ac.uk
// www.truro-penwith.ac.uk

C610 FdSc Sports Coaching
Duration: 2FT Fdg
Entry Requirements: *GCE:* 60-80. *IB:* 24. *BTEC Dip:* MP. *BTEC ExtDip:* PPP. Interview required.

W80 UNIVERSITY OF WORCESTER
HENWICK GROVE
WORCESTER WR2 6AJ
t: 01905 855111 f: 01905 855377
e: admissions@worc.ac.uk
// www.worcester.ac.uk

PCM6 BA/BSc Journalism and Sports Coaching Science
Duration: 3FT Hon   **CRB Check:** Required
Entry Requirements: Contact the institution for details.

C694 BSc Sports Coaching Science with Disability Sport
Duration: 3FT Hon   **CRB Check:** Required
Entry Requirements: Contact the institution for details.

Y70 YORK COLLEGE
SIM BALK LANE
YORK YO23 2BB
t: 01904 770448 f: 01904 770499
e: admissions.team@yorkcollege.ac.uk
// www.yorkcollege.ac.uk

C612 HND Sport (Coaching and Sports Development)
Duration: 2FT HND   **CRB Check:** Required
Entry Requirements: Contact the institution for details.

SPORTS MANAGEMENT

A30 UNIVERSITY OF ABERTAY DUNDEE
BELL STREET
DUNDEE DD1 1HG
t: 01382 308080 f: 01382 308081
e: sro@abertay.ac.uk
// www.abertay.ac.uk

N870 BA Golf Management (Top-Up)
Duration: 1FT Ord   CRB Check: Required
Entry Requirements: HND required.

XC16 BA Performance Golf (Top-Up)
Duration: 1FT Ord   CRB Check: Required
Entry Requirements: HND required.

B37 BISHOP BURTON COLLEGE
BISHOP BURTON
BEVERLEY
EAST YORKSHIRE HU17 8QG
t: 01964 553000 f: 01964 553101
e: enquiries@bishopburton.ac.uk
// www.bishopburton.ac.uk

N890 BA Sport and Adventure Management
Duration: 1FT Hon
Entry Requirements: Contact the institution for details.

CN62 FdA Sport and Adventure Management
Duration: 2FT Fdg
Entry Requirements: *GCE:* 80.

B44 UNIVERSITY OF BOLTON
DEANE ROAD
BOLTON BL3 5AB
t: 01204 903903 f: 01204 399074
e: enquiries@bolton.ac.uk
// www.bolton.ac.uk

N290 BA Sport & Leisure Management
Duration: 3FT Hon
Entry Requirements: *GCE:* 240. Interview required.

B50 BOURNEMOUTH UNIVERSITY
TALBOT CAMPUS
FERN BARROW
POOLE
DORSET BH12 5BB
t: 01202 524111
// www.bournemouth.ac.uk

N2C6 BSc Sports Management (Golf)
Duration: 4SW Hon
Entry Requirements: *GCE:* 300. *IB:* 31. *BTEC SubDip:* D. *BTEC Dip:* DD. *BTEC ExtDip:* DDM.

B72 UNIVERSITY OF BRIGHTON
MITHRAS HOUSE 211
LEWES ROAD
BRIGHTON BN2 4AT
t: 01273 644644 f: 01273 642607
e: admissions@brighton.ac.uk
// www.brighton.ac.uk

CN62 BA Sport and Leisure Management
Duration: 3FT Hon
Entry Requirements: *GCE:* BBB. *IB:* 28.

B94 BUCKINGHAMSHIRE NEW UNIVERSITY
QUEEN ALEXANDRA ROAD
HIGH WYCOMBE
BUCKINGHAMSHIRE HP11 2JZ
t: 0800 0565 660 f: 01494 605 023
e: admissions@bucks.ac.uk
// bucks.ac.uk

N273 BA Sports Management and Golf Studies
Duration: 3FT Hon
Entry Requirements: *GCE:* 200-240. *IB:* 24. *OCR ND:* M1 *OCR NED:* M3

N292 BA Sports Management and Golf Studies (4 years)
Duration: 4FT Hon
Entry Requirements: *GCE:* 200-240. *IB:* 24. *OCR ND:* M1 *OCR NED:* M3

C10 CANTERBURY CHRIST CHURCH UNIVERSITY
NORTH HOLMES ROAD
CANTERBURY
KENT CT1 1QU
t: 01227 782900 f: 01227 782888
e: admissions@canterbury.ac.uk
// www.canterbury.ac.uk

N222 BSc Sport & Leisure Management
Duration: 3FT Hon
Entry Requirements: *GCE:* 240. *IB:* 24.

E56 THE UNIVERSITY OF EDINBURGH
STUDENT RECRUITMENT & ADMISSIONS
57 GEORGE SQUARE
EDINBURGH EH8 9JU
t: 0131 650 4360 f: 0131 651 1236
e: sra.enquiries@ed.ac.uk
// www.ed.ac.uk/studying/undergraduate/

N230 BSc Sport and Recreation Management
Duration: 4FT Hon
Entry Requirements: *GCE:* BCC. *SQAH:* BBBB. *IB:* 32.

G50 THE UNIVERSITY OF GLOUCESTERSHIRE
PARK CAMPUS
THE PARK
CHELTENHAM GL50 2RH
t: 01242 714501 f: 01242 714869
e: admissions@glos.ac.uk
// www.glos.ac.uk

CN6F BA Sports Management
Duration: 4SW Hon
Entry Requirements: Contact the institution for details.

G90 GUILDFORD COLLEGE
STOKE ROAD
GUILDFORD
SURREY GU1 1EZ
t: 01483 448585 f: 01483 448600
e: info@guildford.ac.uk
// www.guildford.ac.uk

N290 BA Golf Management (Top-up)
Duration: 1FT Hon
Entry Requirements: Interview required.

L77 LOUGHBOROUGH COLLEGE
RADMOOR ROAD
LOUGHBOROUGH LE11 3BT
t: 0845 166 2950 f: 0845 833 2840
e: info@loucoll.ac.uk
// www.loucoll.ac.uk

N880 BA Sport Management (Top-Up)
Duration: 1FT Hon
Entry Requirements: HND required.

222N HND Sports and Leisure Management
Duration: 2FT HND
Entry Requirements: *GCE:* 120-160.

P63 UCP MARJON - UNIVERSITY COLLEGE PLYMOUTH ST MARK & ST JOHN
DERRIFORD ROAD
PLYMOUTH PL6 8BH
t: 01752 636890 f: 01752 636819
e: admissions@marjon.ac.uk
// www.ucpmarjon.ac.uk

N880 BA Sports Management
Duration: 3FT Hon
Entry Requirements: Contact the institution for details.

S01 SCOTTISH AGRICULTURAL COLLEGE
SAC EDINBURGH
WEST MAINS ROAD
EDINBURGH EH9 3JG
t: 0800 269453 f: 0131 535 4346
e: recruitment@sac.ac.uk
// www.sac.ac.uk/learning

N873 BA Sport and Recreation Management
Duration: 3FT/4FT Ord/Hon
Entry Requirements: *GCE:* CC. *SQAH:* BCC.

S03 THE UNIVERSITY OF SALFORD
SALFORD M5 4WT
t: 0161 295 4545 f: 0161 295 4646
e: ug-admissions@salford.ac.uk
// www.salford.ac.uk

NN89 BA Sport and Leisure Management with Professional Experience
Duration: 4SW Hon
Entry Requirements: *GCE:* 300. *IB:* 29. *OCR ND:* D

N2C6 BA Sports and Leisure Management
Duration: 3FT Hon
Entry Requirements: *GCE:* 280. *IB:* 28. *BTEC ExtDip:* DMM. *OCR ND:* D *OCR NED:* M2

S21 SHEFFIELD HALLAM UNIVERSITY
CITY CAMPUS
HOWARD STREET
SHEFFIELD S1 1WB
t: 0114 225 5555 f: 0114 225 2167
e: admissions@shu.ac.uk
// www.shu.ac.uk

N8N1 BSc International Sport Business Management
Duration: 1FT Hon
Entry Requirements: Contact the institution for details.

S30 SOUTHAMPTON SOLENT UNIVERSITY
EAST PARK TERRACE
SOUTHAMPTON
HAMPSHIRE SO14 0RT
t: +44 (0) 23 8031 9039 f: + 44 (0)23 8022 2259
e: admissions@solent.ac.uk
// www.solent.ac.uk/

N897 BA Adventure and Extreme Sports Management
Duration: 3FT Hon
Entry Requirements: Contact the institution for details.

N898 BA Adventure and Extreme Sports Mgmt with IFY (Intl Only, Sept)
Duration: 4FT Hon
Entry Requirements: Contact the institution for details.

N89Y BA Adventure and Extreme Sports Mgmt with Sport & Tourism Foundation Year
Duration: 4FT Hon
Entry Requirements: Contact the institution for details.

N899 BA Outdoor Learning and Watersports Management
Duration: 3FT Hon
Entry Requirements: Contact the institution for details.

N89P BA Outdoor Learning and Watersports Mgmt with Sport & Tourism Foundation Year
Duration: 4FT Hon
Entry Requirements: Contact the institution for details.

SPORTS DEVELOPMENT

C30 UNIVERSITY OF CENTRAL LANCASHIRE
PRESTON
LANCS PR1 2HE
t: 01772 201201 f: 01772 894954
e: uadmissions@uclan.ac.uk
// www.uclan.ac.uk

C62H BSc Sports Business (Management) Top-up
Duration: 1FT Hon
Entry Requirements: Contact the institution for details.

C620 BSc Sports Business Management
Duration: 3FT Hon
Entry Requirements: Contact the institution for details.

E28 UNIVERSITY OF EAST LONDON
DOCKLANDS CAMPUS
UNIVERSITY WAY
LONDON E16 2RD
t: 020 8223 3333 f: 020 8223 2978
e: study@uel.ac.uk
// www.uel.ac.uk

B993 BSc Sports Development
Duration: 3FT Hon
Entry Requirements: *GCE:* 240. *IB:* 24.

G14 UNIVERSITY OF GLAMORGAN, CARDIFF AND PONTYPRIDD
ENQUIRIES AND ADMISSIONS UNIT
PONTYPRIDD CF37 1DL
t: 08456 434030 f: 01443 654050
e: enquiries@glam.ac.uk
// www.glam.ac.uk

N900 BA Sports Development
Duration: 3FT Hon
Entry Requirements: *GCE:* BBC. *IB:* 25. *BTEC SubDip:* M. *BTEC Dip:* D*D*. *BTEC ExtDip:* DMM. *OCR NED:* M2

L27 LEEDS METROPOLITAN UNIVERSITY
COURSE ENQUIRIES OFFICE
CITY CAMPUS
LEEDS LS1 3HE
t: 0113 81 23113 f: 0113 81 23129
// www.leedsmet.ac.uk

C620 BA Sport and Recreation Development
Duration: 3FT Hon
Entry Requirements: *GCE:* 280.

M80 MIDDLESEX UNIVERSITY
MIDDLESEX UNIVERSITY
THE BURROUGHS
LONDON NW4 4BT
t: 020 8411 5555 f: 020 8411 5649
e: enquiries@mdx.ac.uk
// www.mdx.ac.uk

CP00 BA Sports and Community Development (Top-Up)
Duration: 1FT Hon
Entry Requirements: Contact the institution for details.

C606 BSc Sports and Community Development (Top-Up)
Duration: 1FT Hon
Entry Requirements: Contact the institution for details.

N33 NEW COLLEGE STAMFORD
DRIFT ROAD
STAMFORD
LINCOLNSHIRE PE9 1XA
t: 01780 484300 f: 01780 484301
e: enquiries@stamford.ac.uk
// www.stamford.ac.uk

N870 FdSc Sport Development
Duration: 2FT Fdg
Entry Requirements: *GCE:* 120. Interview required.

P80 UNIVERSITY OF PORTSMOUTH
ACADEMIC REGISTRY
UNIVERSITY HOUSE
WINSTON CHURCHILL AVENUE
PORTSMOUTH PO1 2UP
t: 023 9284 8484 f: 023 9284 3082
e: admissions@port.ac.uk
// www.port.ac.uk

N280 BSc Sports Development
Duration: 3FT Hon
Entry Requirements: *GCE:* 320. *IB:* 27. *BTEC Dip:* DD. *BTEC ExtDip:* DDM.

S30 SOUTHAMPTON SOLENT UNIVERSITY
EAST PARK TERRACE
SOUTHAMPTON
HAMPSHIRE SO14 0RT
t: +44 (0) 23 8031 9039 f: + 44 (0)23 8022 2259
e: admissions@solent.ac.uk
// www.solent.ac.uk/

C620 BSc Young People and Physical Activity
Duration: 3FT Hon   CRB Check: Required
Entry Requirements: Contact the institution for details.

C621 BSc Young People and Physical Activity (with Sport & Tourism Fdn Year)
Duration: 4FT Hon   CRB Check: Required
Entry Requirements: Contact the institution for details.

T20 TEESSIDE UNIVERSITY
MIDDLESBROUGH TS1 3BA
t: 01642 218121 f: 01642 384201
e: registry@tees.ac.uk
// www.tees.ac.uk

N870 BSc Sports Development
Duration: 3FT Hon
Entry Requirements: *GCE:* 260.

SPORTS STUDIES

B11 BARKING AND DAGENHAM COLLEGE
DAGENHAM ROAD
ROMFORD
ESSEX RM7 0XU
t: 020 8090 3020 f: 020 8090 3021
e: engagement.services@barkingdagenhamcollege.ac.uk
// www.barkingdagenhamcollege.ac.uk

046C HND Sport
Duration: 2FT HND
Entry Requirements: Contact the institution for details.

B22 UNIVERSITY OF BEDFORDSHIRE
PARK SQUARE
LUTON
BEDS LU1 3JU
t: 0844 8482234 f: 01582 489323
e: admissions@beds.ac.uk
// www.beds.ac.uk

NXF1 BA Football Studies
Duration: 3FT Hon
Entry Requirements: *Foundation:* Pass. *GCE:* 200. *SQAH:* BCC. *SQAAH:* BCC. *IB:* 24. *OCR ND:* M1 *OCR NED:* P1

C612 BA Sports Studies
Duration: 3FT Hon
Entry Requirements: *GCE:* 180-220.

B94 BUCKINGHAMSHIRE NEW UNIVERSITY
QUEEN ALEXANDRA ROAD
HIGH WYCOMBE
BUCKINGHAMSHIRE HP11 2JZ
t: 0800 0565 660 f: 01494 605 023
e: admissions@bucks.ac.uk
// bucks.ac.uk

CN63 BA Football Business and Finance
Duration: 3FT Hon
Entry Requirements: *GCE:* 200-240. *IB:* 24. *OCR ND:* M1 *OCR NED:* M3

CN65 BA Football Business and Marketing
Duration: 3FT Hon
Entry Requirements: *GCE:* 200-240. *IB:* 24. *OCR ND:* M1 *OCR NED:* M3

CP63 BA Football Business and Media
Duration: 3FT Hon
Entry Requirements: *GCE:* 200-240. *IB:* 24. *OCR ND:* M1 *OCR NED:* M3

C58 UNIVERSITY OF CHICHESTER
BISHOP OTTER CAMPUS
COLLEGE LANE
CHICHESTER
WEST SUSSEX PO19 6PE
t: 01243 816002 f: 01243 816161
e: admissions@chi.ac.uk
// www.chiuni.ac.uk

C640 BA Sport Studies
Duration: 3FT Hon
Entry Requirements: *GCE:* 260. *SQAAH:* CCC. *IB:* 30. *BTEC Dip:* DM. *BTEC ExtDip:* DMM.

G50 THE UNIVERSITY OF GLOUCESTERSHIRE
PARK CAMPUS
THE PARK
CHELTENHAM GL50 2RH
t: 01242 714501 f: 01242 714869
e: admissions@glos.ac.uk
// www.glos.ac.uk

NC26 BA Sports Management
Duration: 3SW Hon
Entry Requirements: Contact the institution for details.

L27 LEEDS METROPOLITAN UNIVERSITY
COURSE ENQUIRIES OFFICE
CITY CAMPUS
LEEDS LS1 3HE
t: 0113 81 23113 f: 0113 81 23129
// www.leedsmet.ac.uk

N564 BA Sports Marketing
Duration: 3FT Hon
Entry Requirements: *GCE:* 240. *IB:* 24.

N36 NEWMAN UNIVERSITY COLLEGE, BIRMINGHAM
GENNERS LANE
BARTLEY GREEN
BIRMINGHAM B32 3NT
t: 0121 476 1181 f: 0121 476 1196
e: Admissions@newman.ac.uk
// www.newman.ac.uk

QX33 BA English and Sports Studies
Duration: 3FT Hon
Entry Requirements: *Foundation:* Distinction. *GCE:* 260. *IB:* 24. *BTEC ExtDip:* DMM. *OCR ND:* M2 *OCR NED:* M2

VX63 BA Sports Studies and Theology
Duration: 3FT Hon
Entry Requirements: *Foundation:* Distinction. *GCE:* 260. *IB:* 24. *BTEC ExtDip:* DMM. *OCR ND:* M2 *OCR NED:* M2

N8Q3 BSc Sports Studies with English Language
Duration: 3FT Hon
Entry Requirements: *Foundation:* Distinction. *GCE:* 280. *IB:* 25. *BTEC ExtDip:* DMM. *OCR ND:* M2 *OCR NED:* M2

S30 SOUTHAMPTON SOLENT UNIVERSITY
EAST PARK TERRACE
SOUTHAMPTON
HAMPSHIRE SO14 0RT
t: +44 (0) 23 8031 9039 f: + 44 (0)23 8022 2259
e: admissions@solent.ac.uk
// www.solent.ac.uk/

N2N1 BA Sports Studies and Business
Duration: 3FT Hon
Entry Requirements: *GCE:* 220.

S84 UNIVERSITY OF SUNDERLAND
STUDENT HELPLINE
THE STUDENT GATEWAY
CHESTER ROAD
SUNDERLAND SR1 3SD
t: 0191 515 3000 f: 0191 515 3805
e: student.helpline@sunderland.ac.uk
// www.sunderland.ac.uk

L3CP BA Sociology with Sport
Duration: 3FT Hon
Entry Requirements: *GCE:* 260-360.

X1C6 BA TESOL with Sport
Duration: 3FT Hon
Entry Requirements: *GCE:* 260-360.

N8C6 BA Tourism with Sport
Duration: 3FT Hon
Entry Requirements: Contact the institution for details.

U20 UNIVERSITY OF ULSTER
COLERAINE
CO. LONDONDERRY
NORTHERN IRELAND BT52 1SA
t: 028 7012 4221 f: 028 7012 4908
e: online@ulster.ac.uk
// www.ulster.ac.uk

CNP2 BSc Sport Studies
Duration: 3FT/4SW Hon **CRB Check:** Required
Entry Requirements: *GCE:* AAB. *SQAH:* AAABC. *SQAAH:* ABB. *IB:* 27.

W76 UNIVERSITY OF WINCHESTER
WINCHESTER
HANTS SO22 4NR
t: 01962 827234 f: 01962 827288
e: course.enquiries@winchester.ac.uk
// www.winchester.ac.uk

TL7H BA American Studies and Sports Studies
Duration: 3FT Hon
Entry Requirements: *Foundation:* Merit. *GCE:* 260-300. *IB:* 24.

NLF3 BA Business Management and Sports Studies
Duration: 3FT Hon
Entry Requirements: *Foundation:* Merit. *GCE:* 260-300. *IB:* 24.

LC5Q BA Childhood, Youth & Community Studies and Sports Studies
Duration: 3FT Hon
Entry Requirements: *Foundation:* Pass. *GCE:* 260-300. *IB:* 24. *OCR ND:* D

WL53 BA Choreography & Dance and Sports Studies
Duration: 3FT Hon
Entry Requirements: *Foundation:* Merit. *GCE:* 260-300. *IB:* 24.

QL33 BA English and Sports Studies
Duration: 3FT Hon
Entry Requirements: *Foundation:* Merit. *GCE:* 260-300. *IB:* 24.

VL13 BA History and Sports Studies
Duration: 3FT Hon
Entry Requirements: *Foundation:* Merit. *GCE:* 260-300. *IB:* 24.

WL43 BA Performing Arts (Contemporary Performance) and Sports Studies
Duration: 3FT Hon
Entry Requirements: *Foundation:* Merit. *GCE:* 260-300. *IB:* 24.

CL8H BA Psychology and Sports Studies
Duration: 3FT Hon
Entry Requirements: *Foundation:* Merit. *GCE:* 260-300. *IB:* 24.

VLP3 BA Sports Studies and Theology & Religious Studies
Duration: 3FT Hon
Entry Requirements: *Foundation:* Distinction. *GCE:* 260-300. *IB:* 25. *OCR ND:* D *OCR NED:* M2

PHYSIOTHERAPY

B32 THE UNIVERSITY OF BIRMINGHAM
EDGBASTON
BIRMINGHAM B15 2TT
t: 0121 415 8900 f: 0121 414 7159
e: admissions@bham.ac.uk
// www.birmingham.ac.uk

B160 BSc Physiotherapy
Duration: 3FT Hon **CRB Check:** Required
Entry Requirements: *GCE:* AAB. *SQAH:* AAABB-AABBB. *SQAAH:* AA-AB. *IB:* 36. Interview required.

B50 BOURNEMOUTH UNIVERSITY
TALBOT CAMPUS
FERN BARROW
POOLE
DORSET BH12 5BB
t: 01202 524111
// www.bournemouth.ac.uk

B160 BSc Physiotherapy
Duration: 3FT Hon   CRB Check: Required
Entry Requirements: *GCE:* 360. *IB:* 33. *BTEC Dip:* D*D. *BTEC ExtDip:* DMM. Interview required.

B56 THE UNIVERSITY OF BRADFORD
RICHMOND ROAD
BRADFORD
WEST YORKSHIRE BD7 1DP
t: 0800 073 1225 f: 01274 235585
e: course-enquiries@bradford.ac.uk
// www.bradford.ac.uk

B160 BSc Physiotherapy
Duration: 3FT Hon   CRB Check: Required
Entry Requirements: *GCE:* 300. *IB:* 30. Interview required.

B72 UNIVERSITY OF BRIGHTON
MITHRAS HOUSE 211
LEWES ROAD
BRIGHTON BN2 4AT
t: 01273 644644 f: 01273 642607
e: admissions@brighton.ac.uk
// www.brighton.ac.uk

B160 BSc Physiotherapy
Duration: 3FT Hon
Entry Requirements: *GCE:* ABB. *IB:* 32. Interview required.

B80 UNIVERSITY OF THE WEST OF ENGLAND, BRISTOL
FRENCHAY CAMPUS
COLDHARBOUR LANE
BRISTOL BS16 1QY
t: +44 (0)117 32 83333 f: +44 (0)117 32 82810
e: admissions@uwe.ac.uk
// www.uwe.ac.uk

B160 BSc Physiotherapy
Duration: 3FT Hon   CRB Check: Required
Entry Requirements: *GCE:* 340. Interview required.

B84 BRUNEL UNIVERSITY
UXBRIDGE
MIDDLESEX UB8 3PH
t: 01895 265265 f: 01895 269790
e: admissions@brunel.ac.uk
// www.brunel.ac.uk

B160 BSc Physiotherapy
Duration: 3FT Hon   CRB Check: Required
Entry Requirements: *GCE:* ABB. *SQAAH:* ABB. *IB:* 33. *BTEC Dip:* DD. *BTEC ExtDip:* D*DD. Interview required.

C15 CARDIFF UNIVERSITY
PO BOX 927
30-36 NEWPORT ROAD
CARDIFF CF24 0DE
t: 029 2087 9999 f: 029 2087 6138
e: admissions@cardiff.ac.uk
// www.cardiff.ac.uk

B160 BSc Physiotherapy
Duration: 3FT Hon   CRB Check: Required
Entry Requirements: *GCE:* AAB. *SQAAH:* ABB. *IB:* 28.

C30 UNIVERSITY OF CENTRAL LANCASHIRE
PRESTON
LANCS PR1 2HE
t: 01772 201201 f: 01772 894954
e: uadmissions@uclan.ac.uk
// www.uclan.ac.uk

B160 BSc Physiotherapy
Duration: 3FT Hon   CRB Check: Required
Entry Requirements: *GCE:* ABB. *IB:* 32. *OCR ND:* D *OCR NED:* D2 Interview required.

C85 COVENTRY UNIVERSITY
THE STUDENT CENTRE
COVENTRY UNIVERSITY
1 GULSON RD
COVENTRY CV1 2JH
t: 024 7615 2222 f: 024 7615 2223
e: studentenquiries@coventry.ac.uk
// www.coventry.ac.uk

B160 BSc Physiotherapy
Duration: 3FT Hon   CRB Check: Required
Entry Requirements: *GCE:* ABB. *SQAAH:* ABB. Interview required.

C99 UNIVERSITY OF CUMBRIA
FUSEHILL STREET
CARLISLE
CUMBRIA CA1 2HH
t: 01228 616234 f: 01228 616235
// www.cumbria.ac.uk

B160 BSc Physiotherapy
Duration: 3FT Hon   CRB Check: Required
Entry Requirements: *Foundation:* Pass. *GCE:* 300. *IB:* 32.
Interview required.

E14 UNIVERSITY OF EAST ANGLIA
NORWICH NR4 7TJ
t: 01603 591515 f: 01603 591523
e: admissions@uea.ac.uk
// www.uea.ac.uk

B160 BSc Physiotherapy
Duration: 3FT Hon   CRB Check: Required
Entry Requirements: *GCE:* ABB. *SQAH:* AABBB. *SQAAH:* ABB. *IB:*
32. Interview required.

G42 GLASGOW CALEDONIAN UNIVERSITY
STUDENT RECRUITMENT & ADMISSIONS SERVICE
CITY CAMPUS
COWCADDENS ROAD
GLASGOW G4 0BA
t: 0141 331 3000 f: 0141 331 8676
e: undergraduate@gcu.ac.uk
// www.gcu.ac.uk

B160 BSc Physiotherapy
Duration: 4FT Hon   CRB Check: Required
Entry Requirements: *GCE:* BBB. *SQAH:* BBBBBB-BBBBC. *IB:* 32.
OCR NED: M1

B161 BSc Physiotherapy Studies (International Applicants)
Duration: 1FT Hon   CRB Check: Required
Entry Requirements: Contact the institution for details.

H36 UNIVERSITY OF HERTFORDSHIRE
UNIVERSITY ADMISSIONS SERVICE
COLLEGE LANE
HATFIELD
HERTS AL10 9AB
t: 01707 284800
// www.herts.ac.uk

B160 BSc Physiotherapy
Duration: 3FT Hon   CRB Check: Required
Entry Requirements: *GCE:* BBB. Interview required.

H60 THE UNIVERSITY OF HUDDERSFIELD
QUEENSGATE
HUDDERSFIELD HD1 3DH
t: 01484 473969 f: 01484 472765
e: admissionsandrecords@hud.ac.uk
// www.hud.ac.uk

B160 BSc Physiotherapy
Duration: 3FT Hon   CRB Check: Required
Entry Requirements: *GCE:* 320. Interview required.

K12 KEELE UNIVERSITY
KEELE UNIVERSITY
STAFFORDSHIRE ST5 5BG
t: 01782 734005 f: 01782 632343
e: undergraduate@keele.ac.uk
// www.keele.ac.uk

B160 BSc Physiotherapy
Duration: 3FT Hon   CRB Check: Required
Entry Requirements: *GCE:* ABB. *SQAAH:* BBB. *IB:* 28. Interview
required.

K60 KING'S COLLEGE LONDON (UNIVERSITY OF LONDON)
STRAND
LONDON WC2R 2LS
t: 020 7836 5454 f: 020 7848 7171
e: prospective@kcl.ac.uk
// www.kcl.ac.uk/prospectus

B160 BSc Physiotherapy
Duration: 3FT Hon   CRB Check: Required
Entry Requirements: *GCE:* AABb. *SQAH:* AABBB. *IB:* 34.

L27 LEEDS METROPOLITAN UNIVERSITY
COURSE ENQUIRIES OFFICE
CITY CAMPUS
LEEDS LS1 3HE
t: 0113 81 23113 f: 0113 81 23129
// www.leedsmet.ac.uk

B160 BSc Physiotherapy
Duration: 3FT Hon   CRB Check: Required
Entry Requirements: *GCE:* 280. *IB:* 30.

L41 THE UNIVERSITY OF LIVERPOOL
THE FOUNDATION BUILDING
BROWNLOW HILL
LIVERPOOL L69 7ZX
t: 0151 794 2000 f: 0151 708 6502
e: ugrecruitment@liv.ac.uk
// www.liv.ac.uk

B160 BSc Physiotherapy
Duration: 3FT Hon   CRB Check: Required
Entry Requirements: *GCE:* ABB. *IB:* 30.

M40 THE MANCHESTER METROPOLITAN UNIVERSITY
ADMISSIONS OFFICE
ALL SAINTS (GMS)
ALL SAINTS
MANCHESTER M15 6BH
t: 0161 247 2000
// www.mmu.ac.uk

B160 BSc Physiotherapy
Duration: 3FT Hon   CRB Check: Required
Entry Requirements: *GCE:* ABB. *SQAH:* AABBB. *SQAAH:* B. *IB:* 30.
Interview required.

N77 NORTHUMBRIA UNIVERSITY
TRINITY BUILDING
NORTHUMBERLAND ROAD
NEWCASTLE UPON TYNE NE1 8ST
t: 0191 243 7420 f: 0191 227 4561
e: er.admissions@northumbria.ac.uk
// www.northumbria.ac.uk

B160 BSc Physiotherapy
Duration: 3FT Hon   CRB Check: Required
Entry Requirements: *SQAH:* BBBBB. *SQAAH:* BBB. *IB:* 27. *OCR ND:* D *OCR NED:* D2 Interview required.

N84 THE UNIVERSITY OF NOTTINGHAM
THE ADMISSIONS OFFICE
THE UNIVERSITY OF NOTTINGHAM
UNIVERSITY PARK
NOTTINGHAM NG7 2RD
t: 0115 951 5151 f: 0115 951 4668
// www.nottingham.ac.uk

B160 BSc Physiotherapy
Duration: 3FT Hon   CRB Check: Required
Entry Requirements: *GCE:* ABB. *SQAAH:* BBB. *IB:* 32. Interview required.

O66 OXFORD BROOKES UNIVERSITY
ADMISSIONS OFFICE
HEADINGTON CAMPUS
GIPSY LANE
OXFORD OX3 0BP
t: 01865 483040 f: 01865 483983
e: admissions@brookes.ac.uk
// www.brookes.ac.uk

B160 BSc Physiotherapy
Duration: 3FT Hon   CRB Check: Required
Entry Requirements: *GCE:* AAB. *SQAAH:* BBB. *IB:* 34.

P60 PLYMOUTH UNIVERSITY
DRAKE CIRCUS
PLYMOUTH PL4 8AA
t: 01752 585858 f: 01752 588055
e: admissions@plymouth.ac.uk
// www.plymouth.ac.uk

B160 BSc Physiotherapy
Duration: 3FT Hon   CRB Check: Required
Entry Requirements: *GCE:* 340. *IB:* 33. *OCR ND:* D *OCR NED:* D1

Q25 QUEEN MARGARET UNIVERSITY, EDINBURGH
QUEEN MARGARET UNIVERSITY DRIVE
EDINBURGH EH21 6UU
t: 0131474 0000 f: 0131 474 0001
e: admissions@qmu.ac.uk
// www.qmu.ac.uk

B160 BSc Physiotherapy
Duration: 4FT Hon   CRB Check: Required
Entry Requirements: *GCE:* 340. *IB:* 32.

R36 ROBERT GORDON UNIVERSITY
ROBERT GORDON UNIVERSITY
SCHOOLHILL
ABERDEEN
SCOTLAND AB10 1FR
t: 01224 26 27 28 f: 01224 26 21 47
e: UGOffice@rgu.ac.uk
// www.rgu.ac.uk

B160 BSc Physiotherapy
Duration: 4FT Hon   CRB Check: Required
Entry Requirements: *GCE:* 300. *SQAH:* ABBC-BBBB. *IB:* 32. Interview required.

S03 THE UNIVERSITY OF SALFORD
SALFORD M5 4WT
t: 0161 295 4545 f: 0161 295 4646
e: ug-admissions@salford.ac.uk
// www.salford.ac.uk

B160 BSc Physiotherapy
Duration: 3FT Hon   CRB Check: Required
Entry Requirements: *GCE:* 300. *SQAH:* AABBB. *SQAAH:* BBB. *IB:* 32. Interview required.

S21 SHEFFIELD HALLAM UNIVERSITY
CITY CAMPUS
HOWARD STREET
SHEFFIELD S1 1WB
t: 0114 225 5555 f: 0114 225 2167
e: admissions@shu.ac.uk
// www.shu.ac.uk

B160 BSc Physiotherapy
Duration: 3FT Hon
Entry Requirements: *GCE:* 320.

S27 UNIVERSITY OF SOUTHAMPTON
HIGHFIELD
SOUTHAMPTON SO17 1BJ
t: 023 8059 4732 f: 023 8059 3037
e: admissions@soton.ac.uk
// www.southampton.ac.uk

B160 BSc Physiotherapy
Duration: 3FT Hon   CRB Check: Required
Entry Requirements: *GCE:* ABBb. *IB:* 33.

S49 ST GEORGE'S, UNIVERSITY OF LONDON
CRANMER TERRACE
LONDON SW17 0RE
t: +44 (0)20 8725 2333 f: +44 (0)20 8725 0841
e: enquiries@sgul.ac.uk
// www.sgul.ac.uk

B160 BSc Physiotherapy
Duration: 3FT Hon   CRB Check: Required
Entry Requirements: *GCE:* 320. Interview required.

T20 TEESSIDE UNIVERSITY
MIDDLESBROUGH TS1 3BA
t: 01642 218121 f: 01642 384201
e: registry@tees.ac.uk
// www.tees.ac.uk

B160 BSc Physiotherapy
Duration: 3FT Hon   CRB Check: Required
Entry Requirements: *GCE:* 300. *IB:* 30. *BTEC SubDip:* D*. *BTEC Dip:* DD. *BTEC ExtDip:* DDM. *OCR ND:* M1 *OCR NED:* D1 Interview required.

U20 UNIVERSITY OF ULSTER
COLERAINE
CO. LONDONDERRY
NORTHERN IRELAND BT52 1SA
t: 028 7012 4221 f: 028 7012 4908
e: online@ulster.ac.uk
// www.ulster.ac.uk

B160 BSc Physiotherapy
Duration: 3FT Hon   CRB Check: Required
Entry Requirements: *GCE:* BBB. *SQAH:* AABCC. *SQAAH:* BBB. *IB:* 25. Admissions Test required.

W67 WIGAN AND LEIGH COLLEGE
PO BOX 53
PARSON'S WALK
WIGAN
GREATER MANCHESTER WN1 1RS
t: 01942 761605 f: 01942 761164
e: applications@wigan-leigh.ac.uk
// www.wigan-leigh.ac.uk

B160 FdSc Spa Management
Duration: 2FT Fdg
Entry Requirements: Interview required.

Y75 YORK ST JOHN UNIVERSITY
LORD MAYOR'S WALK
YORK YO31 7EX
t: 01904 876598 f: 01904 876940/876921
e: admissions@yorksj.ac.uk
// w3.yorksj.ac.uk

B160 BSc Physiotherapy
Duration: 3FT Hon   CRB Check: Required
Entry Requirements: *GCE:* 300. *IB:* 30. *OCR ND:* D Interview required.

PODIATRY

B30 BIRMINGHAM METROPOLITAN COLLEGE (FORMERLY MATTHEW BOULTON COLLEGE)
JENNENS ROAD
BIRMINGHAM B4 7PS
t: 0121 446 4545 f: 0121 503 8590
e: HEEnquiries@bmetc.ac.uk
// www.bmetc.ac.uk/

B985 BSc Podiatry
Duration: 3FT Hon   CRB Check: Required
Entry Requirements: *GCE:* 220. Interview required.

B72 UNIVERSITY OF BRIGHTON
MITHRAS HOUSE 211
LEWES ROAD
BRIGHTON BN2 4AT
t: 01273 644644 f: 01273 642607
e: admissions@brighton.ac.uk
// www.brighton.ac.uk

B985 BSc Podiatry
Duration: 3FT Hon
Entry Requirements: *GCE:* BBB. *IB:* 28. Interview required.

C20 CARDIFF METROPOLITAN UNIVERSITY (UWIC)
ADMISSIONS UNIT
LLANDAFF CAMPUS
WESTERN AVENUE
CARDIFF CF5 2YB
t: 029 2041 6070 f: 029 2041 6286
e: admissions@cardiffmet.ac.uk
// www.cardiffmet.ac.uk

B985 BSc Podiatry
Duration: 3FT Hon   CRB Check: Required
Entry Requirements: *GCE:* 280. *IB:* 25. *BTEC ExtDip:* DMM. *OCR NED:* M2

E28 UNIVERSITY OF EAST LONDON
DOCKLANDS CAMPUS
UNIVERSITY WAY
LONDON E16 2RD
t: 020 8223 3333 f: 020 8223 2978
e: study@uel.ac.uk
// www.uel.ac.uk

B330 BSc Podiatric Medicine
Duration: 3FT Hon
Entry Requirements: *GCE:* 280. *IB:* 26.

G42 GLASGOW CALEDONIAN UNIVERSITY
STUDENT RECRUITMENT & ADMISSIONS SERVICE
CITY CAMPUS
COWCADDENS ROAD
GLASGOW G4 0BA
t: 0141 331 3000 f: 0141 331 8676
e: undergraduate@gcu.ac.uk
// www.gcu.ac.uk

B985 BSc Podiatry
Duration: 4FT Hon   CRB Check: Required
Entry Requirements: *GCE:* BBC. *SQAH:* AABB. *IB:* 26.

B170 BSc Podiatry Studies (International Applicants)
Duration: 1FT Hon   CRB Check: Required
Entry Requirements: Contact the institution for details.

H60 THE UNIVERSITY OF HUDDERSFIELD
QUEENSGATE
HUDDERSFIELD HD1 3DH
t: 01484 473969 f: 01484 472765
e: admissionsandrecords@hud.ac.uk
// www.hud.ac.uk

B985 BSc Podiatry
Duration: 3FT Hon   CRB Check: Required
Entry Requirements: *GCE:* 300. Interview required.

N28 NEW COLLEGE DURHAM
FRAMWELLGATE MOOR CAMPUS
DURHAM DH1 5ES
t: 0191 375 4210/4211 f: 0191 375 4222
e: admissions@newdur.ac.uk
// www.newcollegedurham.ac.uk

B985 BSc Hons Podiatry
Duration: 3FT Hon
Entry Requirements: *GCE:* 160. Interview required.

B170 FdSc Assistant Practitioner (Podiatry)
Duration: 2FT Fdg
Entry Requirements: Contact the institution for details.

N38 UNIVERSITY OF NORTHAMPTON
PARK CAMPUS
BOUGHTON GREEN ROAD
NORTHAMPTON NN2 7AL
t: 0800 358 2232 f: 01604 722083
e: admissions@northampton.ac.uk
// www.northampton.ac.uk

B985 BSc Podiatry
Duration: 3FT Hon   CRB Check: Required
Entry Requirements: *GCE:* 260-280. *SQAH:* AAA-BBBB. *IB:* 24.
BTEC Dip: DD. *BTEC ExtDip:* DMM. *OCR ND:* D *OCR NED:* M2
Interview required.

P60 PLYMOUTH UNIVERSITY
DRAKE CIRCUS
PLYMOUTH PL4 8AA
t: 01752 585858 f: 01752 588055
e: admissions@plymouth.ac.uk
// www.plymouth.ac.uk

B985 BSc Podiatry
Duration: 3FT Hon   CRB Check: Required
Entry Requirements: *GCE:* 240-260. *IB:* 27. *OCR ND:* D *OCR NED:* M2

Q25 QUEEN MARGARET UNIVERSITY, EDINBURGH
QUEEN MARGARET UNIVERSITY DRIVE
EDINBURGH EH21 6UU
t: 0131474 0000 f: 0131 474 0001
e: admissions@qmu.ac.uk
// www.qmu.ac.uk

B985 BSc Podiatry
Duration: 4FT Hon   CRB Check: Required
Entry Requirements: *GCE:* 240. *IB:* 28.

S03 THE UNIVERSITY OF SALFORD
SALFORD M5 4WT
t: 0161 295 4545 f: 0161 295 4646
e: ug-admissions@salford.ac.uk
// www.salford.ac.uk

B985 BSc Podiatry
Duration: 3FT Hon   CRB Check: Required
Entry Requirements: *GCE:* 240. *SQAH:* BCCCC. *SQAAH:* CCC. *IB:* 24. Interview required.

U20 UNIVERSITY OF ULSTER
COLERAINE
CO. LONDONDERRY
NORTHERN IRELAND BT52 1SA
t: 028 7012 4221 f: 028 7012 4908
e: online@ulster.ac.uk
// www.ulster.ac.uk

B985 BSc Podiatry
Duration: 3FT Hon   CRB Check: Required
Entry Requirements: *GCE:* BBB. *SQAH:* AABCC. *SQAAH:* BBB. *IB:* 25. Admissions Test required.

ANATOMY, MEDICAL BIOCHEMISTRY AND HUMAN PHYSIOLOGY

A20 THE UNIVERSITY OF ABERDEEN
UNIVERSITY OFFICE
KING'S COLLEGE
ABERDEEN AB24 3FX
t: +44 (0) 1224 273504 f: +44 (0) 1224 272034
e: sras@abdn.ac.uk
// www.abdn.ac.uk/sras

B9BC BSc Biomedical Science (Anatomy)
Duration: 4FT Hon
Entry Requirements: *GCE:* ABB. *SQAH:* AABB. *IB:* 32.

B9B1 BSc Biomedical Science (Physiology)
Duration: 4FT Hon
Entry Requirements: *GCE:* ABB. *SQAH:* AABB. *IB:* 32.

B120 BSc Physiology
Duration: 4FT Hon
Entry Requirements: *GCE:* 240. *SQAH:* BBBB. *SQAAH:* BCC. *IB:* 28.

B9BD MSci Biomedical Science (Anatomy) with Industrial Placement
Duration: 5FT Hon
Entry Requirements: *GCE:* ABB. *SQAH:* AABB. *IB:* 32.

B9BA MSci Biomedical Science (Physiology) with Industrial Placement
Duration: 5FT Hon
Entry Requirements: *GCE:* ABB. *SQAH:* AABB. *IB:* 32.

B121 MSci Physiology with Industrial Placement
Duration: 5FT Hon
Entry Requirements: *GCE:* ABB. *SQAH:* AABB. *IB:* 32.

B78 UNIVERSITY OF BRISTOL
UNDERGRADUATE ADMISSIONS OFFICE
SENATE HOUSE
TYNDALL AVENUE
BRISTOL BS8 1TH
t: 0117 928 9000 f: 0117 331 7391
e: ug-admissions@bristol.ac.uk
// www.bristol.ac.uk

B120 BSc Physiological Science
Duration: 3FT Hon
Entry Requirements: *GCE:* AAB. *SQAH:* AAAAB-AAABB. *SQAAH:* AA. *IB:* 35.

C15 CARDIFF UNIVERSITY
PO BOX 927
30-36 NEWPORT ROAD
CARDIFF CF24 0DE
t: 029 2087 9999 f: 029 2087 6138
e: admissions@cardiff.ac.uk
// www.cardiff.ac.uk

C74C BSc Biochemistry (Biomedical) (including Preliminary Year)
Duration: 4FT Hon
Entry Requirements: *GCE:* AAB-ABB. *SQAAH:* AAB-ABB. *IB:* 34.

CR41 BSc Biochemistry (Biomedical) (with Preliminary Year and Professional Training Year)
Duration: 5SW Hon
Entry Requirements: *GCE:* AAB-ABB. *SQAAH:* AAB-ABB. *IB:* 34.

B111 BSc Biomedical Sciences (Anatomy)
Duration: 3FT Hon
Entry Requirements: *GCE:* AAB-ABB. *SQAH:* AAABB-AABBB. *SQAAH:* AAB-ABB. *IB:* 34. *OCR NED:* D1

BC17 BSc Biomedical Sciences (Anatomy) (including Preliminary Year)
Duration: 4FT Hon
Entry Requirements: *GCE:* AAB-ABB. *SQAAH:* AAB-ABB. *IB:* 34.

B112 BSc Biomedical Sciences (Anatomy) (including Professional Training Year)
Duration: 4SW Hon
Entry Requirements: *GCE:* AAB-ABB. *SQAH:* AAABB-AABBB. *SQAAH:* AAB-ABB. *IB:* 34. *OCR NED:* D1

BCD7 BSc Biomedical Sciences (Anatomy) (with Preliminary and Professional Training Year)
Duration: 5SW Hon
Entry Requirements: *GCE:* AAB-ABB. *SQAAH:* AAB-ABB. *IB:* 34.

B122 BSc Biomedical Sciences (Physiology including Professional Training Year)
Duration: 4SW Hon
Entry Requirements: *GCE:* AAB-ABB. *SQAH:* AAABB-AABBB. *SQAAH:* AAB-ABB. *IB:* 34. *OCR NED:* D1

B121 BSc Biomedical Sciences (Physiology)
Duration: 3FT Hon
Entry Requirements: *GCE:* AAB-ABB. *SQAH:* AAABB-AABBB. *SQAAH:* AAB-ABB. *IB:* 34. *OCR NED:* D1

BCC7 BSc Biomedical Sciences (Physiology) (including Preliminary Year)
Duration: 4FT Hon
Entry Requirements: *GCE:* AAB-ABB. *SQAAH:* AAB-ABB. *IB:* 34.

C30 UNIVERSITY OF CENTRAL LANCASHIRE
PRESTON
LANCS PR1 2HE
t: 01772 201201 f: 01772 894954
e: uadmissions@uclan.ac.uk
// www.uclan.ac.uk

BB12 BSc Physiology and Pharmacology
Duration: 3FT Hon
Entry Requirements: *GCE:* 240-260. *SQAH:* BBBB-BBBC. *SQAAH:* AAA. *IB:* 28. *OCR ND:* D *OCR NED:* M3

D65 UNIVERSITY OF DUNDEE
NETHERGATE
DUNDEE DD1 4HN
t: 01382 383838 f: 01382 388150
e: contactus@dundee.ac.uk
// www.dundee.ac.uk/admissions/undergraduate/

B110 BSc Anatomical Sciences
Duration: 4FT Hon
Entry Requirements: *GCE:* AAB. *SQAH:* ABBB. *IB:* 30.

B120 BSc Anatomical and Physiological Sciences
Duration: 4FT Hon
Entry Requirements: *GCE:* AAB. *SQAH:* ABBB. *IB:* 30.

B100 BSc Physiological Sciences
Duration: 4FT Hon
Entry Requirements: *GCE:* AAB. *SQAH:* ABBB. *IB:* 30.

E28 UNIVERSITY OF EAST LONDON
DOCKLANDS CAMPUS
UNIVERSITY WAY
LONDON E16 2RD
t: 020 8223 3333 f: 020 8223 2978
e: study@uel.ac.uk
// www.uel.ac.uk

B9BC BSc Clinical Science with Medical Physiology
Duration: 3FT Hon
Entry Requirements: *GCE:* 240. *IB:* 24.

B121 BSc Medical Physiology
Duration: 3FT Hon
Entry Requirements: *GCE:* 240. *IB:* 24.

B1C7 BSc Medical Physiology with Biochemistry
Duration: 3FT Hon
Entry Requirements: *GCE:* 240.

B191 BSc Medical Physiology with Clinical Science
Duration: 3FT Hon
Entry Requirements: *GCE:* 240.

B190 BSc Medical Physiology with Human Biology
Duration: 3FT Hon
Entry Requirements: *GCE:* 240.

B1C5 BSc Medical Physiology with Immunology
Duration: 3FT Hon
Entry Requirements: *GCE:* 240.

BFC7 BSc Toxicology with Biochemistry
Duration: 3FT Hon
Entry Requirements: *GCE:* 240. *IB:* 24.

E56 THE UNIVERSITY OF EDINBURGH
STUDENT RECRUITMENT & ADMISSIONS
57 GEORGE SQUARE
EDINBURGH EH8 9JU
t: 0131 650 4360 f: 0131 651 1236
e: sra.enquiries@ed.ac.uk
// www.ed.ac.uk/studying/undergraduate/

B120 BSc Biological Sciences (Physiology)
Duration: 4FT Hon
Entry Requirements: *GCE:* AAA-ABB. *SQAH:* AAAA-ABBB.

G28 UNIVERSITY OF GLASGOW
71 SOUTHPARK AVENUE
UNIVERSITY OF GLASGOW
GLASGOW G12 8QQ
t: 0141 330 6062 f: 0141 330 2961
e: student.recruitment@glasgow.ac.uk
// www.glasgow.ac.uk

B110 BSc Anatomy
Duration: 4FT Hon
Entry Requirements: *GCE:* ABB. *SQAH:* AAAB-BBBB. *IB:* 32.

B111 BSc Anatomy (Faster Route)
Duration: 3FT Hon
Entry Requirements: *GCE:* AAA. *SQAAH:* AAA. *IB:* 38.

GB41 BSc Computing Science/Physiology (Neuroinformatics)
Duration: 4FT Hon
Entry Requirements: *GCE:* ABB. *SQAH:* AAAB-BBBB. *IB:* 32.

B120 BSc Physiology
Duration: 4FT Hon
Entry Requirements: *GCE:* ABB. *SQAH:* AAAB-BBBB. *IB:* 32.

BC18 BSc Physiology/Psychology
Duration: 4FT Hon
Entry Requirements: *GCE:* ABB. *SQAH:* AAAA-AABB. *IB:* 32.

G42 GLASGOW CALEDONIAN UNIVERSITY
STUDENT RECRUITMENT & ADMISSIONS SERVICE
CITY CAMPUS
COWCADDENS ROAD
GLASGOW G4 0BA
t: 0141 331 3000 f: 0141 331 8676
e: undergraduate@gcu.ac.uk
// www.gcu.ac.uk

B120 BSc Human Biosciences
Duration: 4FT Hon
Entry Requirements: *GCE:* BCC. *SQAH:* AAA-BBBC. *IB:* 24.

H36 UNIVERSITY OF HERTFORDSHIRE
UNIVERSITY ADMISSIONS SERVICE
COLLEGE LANE
HATFIELD
HERTS AL10 9AB
t: 01707 284800
// www.herts.ac.uk

C1B1 BSc Physiology
Duration: 3FT/4SW Hon
Entry Requirements: *GCE:* 240.

B101 BSc Physiology with a year in Europe
Duration: 4FT Hon
Entry Requirements: *GCE:* 240.

B102 BSc Physiology with a year in North America
Duration: 4FT Hon
Entry Requirements: *GCE:* 240.

H60 THE UNIVERSITY OF HUDDERSFIELD
QUEENSGATE
HUDDERSFIELD HD1 3DH
t: 01484 473969 f: 01484 472765
e: admissionsandrecords@hud.ac.uk
// www.hud.ac.uk

C741 BSc Medical Biochemistry
Duration: 3FT/4SW Hon
Entry Requirements: *GCE:* 280.

K12 KEELE UNIVERSITY
KEELE UNIVERSITY
STAFFORDSHIRE ST5 5BG
t: 01782 734005 f: 01782 632343
e: undergraduate@keele.ac.uk
// www.keele.ac.uk

FVC5 BSc Medicinal Chemistry and Philosophy
Duration: 3FT Hon
Entry Requirements: *GCE:* BBB.

K60 KING'S COLLEGE LONDON (UNIVERSITY OF LONDON)
STRAND
LONDON WC2R 2LS
t: 020 7836 5454 f: 020 7848 7171
e: prospective@kcl.ac.uk
// www.kcl.ac.uk/prospectus

B120 BSc Physiology
Duration: 3FT Hon
Entry Requirements: *GCE:* AABc. *SQAH:* AAABB. *IB:* 36.

F1C7 MSci Chemistry with Biomedicine
Duration: 4FT Hon
Entry Requirements: Contact the institution for details.

K84 KINGSTON UNIVERSITY
STUDENT INFORMATION & ADVICE CENTRE
COOPER HOUSE
40-46 SURBITON ROAD
KINGSTON UPON THAMES KT1 2HX
t: 0844 8552177 f: 020 8547 7080
e: aps@kingston.ac.uk
// www.kingston.ac.uk

C741 BSc Medical Biochemistry
Duration: 4SW Hon
Entry Requirements: *GCE:* 200-280.

L14 LANCASTER UNIVERSITY
THE UNIVERSITY
LANCASTER
LANCASHIRE LA1 4YW
t: 01524 592029 f: 01524 846243
e: ugadmissions@lancaster.ac.uk
// www.lancs.ac.uk

BC79 BSc Biochemistry with Biomedicine
Duration: 3FT Hon
Entry Requirements: *GCE:* AAB. *SQAH:* ABBBB. *SQAAH:* AAB. *IB:* 35.

C1C7 BSc Cell Biology with Biomedicine
Duration: 3FT Hon
Entry Requirements: *GCE:* ABB. *SQAH:* BBBBB. *SQAAH:* BBB. *IB:* 32.

L23 UNIVERSITY OF LEEDS
THE UNIVERSITY OF LEEDS
WOODHOUSE LANE
LEEDS LS2 9JT
t: 0113 343 3999
e: admissions@leeds.ac.uk
// www.leeds.ac.uk

B120 BSc Human Physiology
Duration: 3FT/4SW Hon
Entry Requirements: *GCE:* AAB. *SQAAH:* AAB. *BTEC ExtDip:* DDD. Interview required.

C741 BSc Medical Biochemistry
Duration: 3FT/4SW Hon
Entry Requirements: *GCE:* AAB. *SQAAH:* AAB. *BTEC ExtDip:* DDD. Interview required.

B129 MBiol Human Physiology
Duration: 4FT Hon
Entry Requirements: Contact the institution for details.

C749 MBiol Medical Biochemistry
Duration: 4FT Hon
Entry Requirements: Contact the institution for details.

L27 LEEDS METROPOLITAN UNIVERSITY
COURSE ENQUIRIES OFFICE
CITY CAMPUS
LEEDS LS1 3HE
t: 0113 81 23113 f: 0113 81 23129
// www.leedsmet.ac.uk

BB12 BSc Biomedical Sciences (Physiology/Pharmacology)
Duration: 3FT Hon
Entry Requirements: *GCE:* 180. *IB:* 24.

L34 UNIVERSITY OF LEICESTER
UNIVERSITY ROAD
LEICESTER LE1 7RH
t: 0116 252 5281 f: 0116 252 2447
e: admissions@le.ac.uk
// www.le.ac.uk

B1B2 BSc Biological Sciences (Physiology with Pharmacology)
Duration: 3FT Hon
Entry Requirements: *GCE:* ABB. *SQAH:* AABBB. *SQAAH:* ABB. *IB:* 32.

B120 BSc Medical Physiology
Duration: 3FT Hon
Entry Requirements: *GCE:* ABB. *SQAH:* AABBB. *SQAAH:* ABB. *IB:* 32.

L41 THE UNIVERSITY OF LIVERPOOL
THE FOUNDATION BUILDING
BROWNLOW HILL
LIVERPOOL L69 7ZX
t: 0151 794 2000 f: 0151 708 6502
e: ugrecruitment@liv.ac.uk
// www.liv.ac.uk

B110 BSc Anatomy and Human Biology
Duration: 3FT Hon
Entry Requirements: *GCE:* AAB. *SQAAH:* AAB. *IB:* 33. Interview required.

B120 BSc Physiology
Duration: 3FT Hon
Entry Requirements: *GCE:* ABB. *SQAAH:* ABB. *IB:* 32. Interview required.

M20 THE UNIVERSITY OF MANCHESTER
RUTHERFORD BUILDING
OXFORD ROAD
MANCHESTER M13 9PL
t: 0161 275 2077 f: 0161 275 2106
e: ug-admissions@manchester.ac.uk
// www.manchester.ac.uk

B110 BSc Anatomical Sciences
Duration: 3FT Hon
Entry Requirements: *GCE:* AAA-ABB. *SQAH:* AAAAA-AAABB. *SQAAH:* AAA-AAB. Interview required.

B111 BSc Anatomical Sciences with Industrial/Professional Experience (4 years)
Duration: 4SW Hon
Entry Requirements: *GCE:* AAA-ABB. *SQAH:* AAAAA-AAABB. *SQAAH:* AAA-AAB. Interview required.

B114 BSc Anatomical Sciences with a Modern Language (4 years)
Duration: 4FT Hon
Entry Requirements: *GCE:* AAA-ABB. *SQAH:* AAAAA-AAABB. *SQAAH:* AAA-ABB. Interview required.

C724 BSc Medical Biochemistry
Duration: 3FT Hon
Entry Requirements: *GCE:* AAA-ABB. *SQAH:* AAAAA-AAABB. *SQAAH:* AAA-ABB. Interview required.

C741 BSc Medical Biochemistry with Industrial/Professional Experience
Duration: 4FT Hon
Entry Requirements: *GCE:* AAA-ABB. *SQAH:* AAAAA-AAABB. *SQAAH:* AAA-ABB. Interview required.

BB12 BSc Pharmacology and Physiology
Duration: 3FT Hon
Entry Requirements: *GCE:* AAA-ABB. *SQAH:* AAAAA-AAABB. *SQAAH:* AAA-AAB. Interview required.

BBC2 BSc Pharmacology and Physiology with Industrial/Professional Experience (4 years)
Duration: 4SW Hon
Entry Requirements: *GCE:* AAA-ABB. *SQAH:* AAAAA-AAABB. *SQAAH:* AAA-AAB. Interview required.

B120 BSc Physiology
Duration: 3FT Hon
Entry Requirements: *GCE:* AAA-ABB. *SQAH:* AAAAA-AAABB. *SQAAH:* AAA-ABB. Interview required.

B121 BSc Physiology with Industrial/Professional Experience (4 years)
Duration: 4SW Hon
Entry Requirements: *GCE:* AAA-ABB. *SQAH:* AAAAA-AAABB. *SQAAH:* AAA-AAB. Interview required.

B122 BSc Physiology with a Modern Language (4 years)
Duration: 4FT Hon
Entry Requirements: *GCE:* AAA-ABB. *SQAH:* AAAAA-AAABB. *SQAAH:* AAA-ABB. Interview required.

BJ82 MEng Biomaterials Science and Tissue Engineering
Duration: 4FT Hon
Entry Requirements: *GCE:* AAA. *SQAAH:* AAA. *IB:* 37. *OCR NED:* D1

N21 NEWCASTLE UNIVERSITY
KING'S GATE
NEWCASTLE UPON TYNE NE1 7RU
t: 01912083333
// www.ncl.ac.uk

B100 BSc Physiological Sciences
Duration: 3FT Hon
Entry Requirements: *GCE:* AAB. *SQAH:* AAABB.

N84 THE UNIVERSITY OF NOTTINGHAM
THE ADMISSIONS OFFICE
THE UNIVERSITY OF NOTTINGHAM
UNIVERSITY PARK
NOTTINGHAM NG7 2RD
t: 0115 951 5151 f: 0115 951 4668
// www.nottingham.ac.uk

C741 BSc Biochemistry and Molecular Medicine
Duration: 3FT Hon
Entry Requirements: *GCE:* AAB-BBB. *SQAAH:* AAB-BBB. *IB:* 32.

P80 UNIVERSITY OF PORTSMOUTH
ACADEMIC REGISTRY
UNIVERSITY HOUSE
WINSTON CHURCHILL AVENUE
PORTSMOUTH PO1 2UP
t: 023 9284 8484 f: 023 9284 3082
e: admissions@port.ac.uk
// www.port.ac.uk

B121 BSc Human Physiology
Duration: 3FT Hon
Entry Requirements: *GCE:* 280. *IB:* 26. *BTEC Dip:* DD. *BTEC ExtDip:* DMM.

R12 THE UNIVERSITY OF READING
THE UNIVERSITY OF READING
PO BOX 217
READING RG6 6AH
t: 0118 378 8619 f: 0118 378 8924
e: student.recruitment@reading.ac.uk
// www.reading.ac.uk

C741 BSc Biomedical Sciences
Duration: 3FT Hon
Entry Requirements: *GCE:* 320. Interview required.

R72 ROYAL HOLLOWAY, UNIVERSITY OF LONDON
ROYAL HOLLOWAY, UNIVERSITY OF LONDON
EGHAM
SURREY TW20 0EX
t: 01784 414944 f: 01784 473662
e: Admissions@rhul.ac.uk
// www.rhul.ac.uk

C741 BSc Medical Biochemistry
Duration: 3FT Hon
Entry Requirements: *GCE:* 300-320. *IB:* 34.

S18 THE UNIVERSITY OF SHEFFIELD
THE UNIVERSITY OF SHEFFIELD
LEVEL 2, ARTS TOWER
WESTERN BANK
SHEFFIELD S10 2TN
t: 0114 222 8030 f: 0114 222 8032
// www.sheffield.ac.uk

C741 BSc Medical Biochemistry (3 years)
Duration: 3FT Hon
Entry Requirements: *GCE:* AAA-AAB. *SQAH:* AAAAB-AAABB. *SQAAH:* AA-AB. *BTEC ExtDip:* DDD.

S27 UNIVERSITY OF SOUTHAMPTON
HIGHFIELD
SOUTHAMPTON SO17 1BJ
t: 023 8059 4732 f: 023 8059 3037
e: admissions@soton.ac.uk
// www.southampton.ac.uk

CB71 BSc Biochemistry/BiomedicalSc/Pharmacology with Foundation year (4 years)
Duration: 4FT Hon
Entry Requirements: *GCE:* BBB. *IB:* 30.

S84 UNIVERSITY OF SUNDERLAND
STUDENT HELPLINE
THE STUDENT GATEWAY
CHESTER ROAD
SUNDERLAND SR1 3SD
t: 0191 515 3000 f: 0191 515 3805
e: student.helpline@sunderland.ac.uk
// www.sunderland.ac.uk

B120 BSc Physiological Sciences
Duration: 3FT Hon
Entry Requirements: *IB:* 24.

S93 SWANSEA UNIVERSITY
SINGLETON PARK
SWANSEA SA2 8PP
t: 01792 295111 f: 01792 295110
e: admissions@swansea.ac.uk
// www.swansea.ac.uk

B1B8 BSc Clinical Physiology with Cardiology
Duration: 4FT Hon   CRB Check: Required
Entry Requirements: *GCE:* BBB. Interview required.

B121 BSc Clinical Physiology with Respiratory Physiology
Duration: 4FT Hon   CRB Check: Required
Entry Requirements: *GCE:* BBB. Interview required.

C741 BSc Medical Biochemistry
Duration: 3FT Hon
Entry Requirements: *GCE:* ABB. *IB:* 33.

U20 UNIVERSITY OF ULSTER
COLERAINE
CO. LONDONDERRY
NORTHERN IRELAND BT52 1SA
t: 028 7012 4221 f: 028 7012 4908
e: online@ulster.ac.uk
// www.ulster.ac.uk

B120 BSc Clinical Physiology (Cardiology)
Duration: 4SW Hon   CRB Check: Required
Entry Requirements: *GCE:* 280-320.

B121 BSc Clinical Physiology (Respiratory)
Duration: 4SW Hon   CRB Check: Required
Entry Requirements: *GCE:* 280-320.

W50 UNIVERSITY OF WESTMINSTER
2ND FLOOR, CAVENDISH HOUSE
101 NEW CAVENDISH STREET,
LONDON W1W 6XH
t: 020 7915 5511
e: course-enquiries@westminster.ac.uk
// www.westminster.ac.uk

BB12 BSc Pharmacology & Physiology
Duration: 3FT Hon
Entry Requirements: *GCE:* CCD. *SQAH:* CCCC. *IB:* 26. Interview required.

BBC2 BSc Pharmacology & Physiology
Duration: 4FT Hon
Entry Requirements: *GCE:* CCD. *SQAH:* CCCC. *IB:* 26. Interview required.

BIOMECHANICS

B32 THE UNIVERSITY OF BIRMINGHAM
EDGBASTON
BIRMINGHAM B15 2TT
t: 0121 415 8900 f: 0121 414 7159
e: admissions@bham.ac.uk
// www.birmingham.ac.uk

BJ95 BMedSc Biomedical Materials Science
Duration: 3FT Hon   CRB Check: Required
Entry Requirements: *GCE:* ABB. *SQAH:* AABBB-ABBBB. *SQAAH:* AB. *IB:* 34.

I50 IMPERIAL COLLEGE LONDON
REGISTRY
SOUTH KENSINGTON CAMPUS
IMPERIAL COLLEGE LONDON
LONDON SW7 2AZ
t: 020 7589 5111 f: 020 7594 8004
// www.imperial.ac.uk

BH81 BEng Biomedical Engineering
Duration: 3FT Hon
Entry Requirements: *GCE:* AAA. *SQAAH:* AAA. *IB:* 38.

BJ95 MEng Biomaterials and Tissue Engineering
Duration: 4FT Hon
Entry Requirements: *GCE:* AAA. *SQAAH:* AAB. *IB:* 36.

S03 THE UNIVERSITY OF SALFORD
SALFORD M5 4WT
t: 0161 295 4545 f: 0161 295 4646
e: ug-admissions@salford.ac.uk
// www.salford.ac.uk

B984 BSc Prosthetics and Orthotics
Duration: 3FT Hon   CRB Check: Required
Entry Requirements: *GCE:* 280. *SQAH:* BBBCC. *SQAAH:* BBC. *IB:* 24. *OCR NED:* M2

S78 THE UNIVERSITY OF STRATHCLYDE
GLASGOW G1 1XQ
t: 0141 552 4400 f: 0141 552 0775
// www.strath.ac.uk

B984 BSc Prosthetics and Orthotics
Duration: 4FT Hon   CRB Check: Required
Entry Requirements: *GCE:* ABB. *SQAH:* AAABB-AAAB. *IB:* 34. Interview required.

SPORTS PSYCHOLOGY

B94 BUCKINGHAMSHIRE NEW UNIVERSITY
QUEEN ALEXANDRA ROAD
HIGH WYCOMBE
BUCKINGHAMSHIRE HP11 2JZ
t: 0800 0565 660 f: 01494 605 023
e: admissions@bucks.ac.uk
// bucks.ac.uk

C813 BSc Sports Psychology
Duration: 3FT Hon
Entry Requirements: *GCE:* 240-280. *IB:* 25. *OCR ND:* D *OCR NED:* M2

C30 UNIVERSITY OF CENTRAL LANCASHIRE
PRESTON
LANCS PR1 2HE
t: 01772 201201 f: 01772 894954
e: uadmissions@uclan.ac.uk
// www.uclan.ac.uk

C8C6 BSc Sport Psychology
Duration: 3FT Hon
Entry Requirements: *Foundation:* Distinction. *GCE:* 260-300. *SQAH:* BBBBC-BBCCC. *IB:* 30. *OCR NED:* M2

C85 COVENTRY UNIVERSITY
THE STUDENT CENTRE
COVENTRY UNIVERSITY
1 GULSON RD
COVENTRY CV1 2JH
t: 024 7615 2222 f: 024 7615 2223
e: studentenquiries@coventry.ac.uk
// www.coventry.ac.uk

C841 BSc Sport Psychology
Duration: 3FT/4SW Hon
Entry Requirements: *GCE:* BBB. *SQAH:* BBBBC. *IB:* 28. *BTEC ExtDip:* DDM. *OCR NED:* M1

G14 UNIVERSITY OF GLAMORGAN, CARDIFF AND PONTYPRIDD
ENQUIRIES AND ADMISSIONS UNIT
PONTYPRIDD CF37 1DL
t: 08456 434030 f: 01443 654050
e: enquiries@glam.ac.uk
// www.glam.ac.uk

C601 BSc Sport Psychology
Duration: 3FT/4SW Hon
Entry Requirements: *GCE:* BBC. *IB:* 25. *BTEC SubDip:* M. *BTEC Dip:* D*D*. *BTEC ExtDip:* DMM.

L46 LIVERPOOL HOPE UNIVERSITY
HOPE PARK
LIVERPOOL L16 9JD
t: 0151 291 3331 f: 0151 291 3434
e: administration@hope.ac.uk
// www.hope.ac.uk

C891 BSc Sport Psychology
Duration: 3FT Hon
Entry Requirements: *GCE:* 300-320. *IB:* 25.

L51 LIVERPOOL JOHN MOORES UNIVERSITY
KINGSWAY HOUSE
HATTON GARDEN
LIVERPOOL L3 2AJ
t: 0151 231 5090 f: 0151 904 6368
e: courses@ljmu.ac.uk
// www.ljmu.ac.uk

C890 BSc Applied Sport Psychology
Duration: 3FT Hon
Entry Requirements: *GCE:* 280-320. *IB:* 25.

R48 ROEHAMPTON UNIVERSITY
ROEHAMPTON LANE
LONDON SW15 5PU
t: 020 8392 3232 f: 020 8392 3470
e: enquiries@roehampton.ac.uk
// www.roehampton.ac.uk

C813 BSc Sport Psychology
Duration: 3FT Hon
Entry Requirements: *Foundation:* Distinction. *GCE:* 280. *IB:* 25.
BTEC Dip: D*D*. *BTEC ExtDip:* DMM. *OCR NED:* M2 Interview required.

W76 UNIVERSITY OF WINCHESTER
WINCHESTER
HANTS SO22 4NR
t: 01962 827234 f: 01962 827288
e: course.enquiries@winchester.ac.uk
// www.winchester.ac.uk

CN8V BA Psychology and Sports Management
Duration: 3FT Hon
Entry Requirements: *Foundation:* Distinction. *GCE:* 260-300. *IB:* 24. *OCR ND:* D

OTHER SPORT

A60 ANGLIA RUSKIN UNIVERSITY
BISHOP HALL LANE
CHELMSFORD
ESSEX CM1 1SQ
t: 0845 271 3333 f: 01245 251789
e: answers@anglia.ac.uk
// www.anglia.ac.uk

P501 FdA Sports Journalism
Duration: 2FT Fdg
Entry Requirements: *GCE:* 80.

A70 ASKHAM BRYAN COLLEGE
ASKHAM BRYAN
YORK YO23 3FR
t: 01904 772211 f: 01904 772217
e: karen.roper@askham-bryan.ac.uk
// www.askham-bryan.ac.uk

D42F FdSc Equine Sports Management
Duration: 2FT/3SW Fdg
Entry Requirements: *GCE:* 80. Interview required. Portfolio required.

K300 FdSc Sports Surface Management
Duration: 2FT Fdg
Entry Requirements: *GCE:* 80. *OCR NED:* P1 Interview required.

B22 UNIVERSITY OF BEDFORDSHIRE
PARK SQUARE
LUTON
BEDS LU1 3JU
t: 0844 8482234 f: 01582 489323
e: admissions@beds.ac.uk
// www.beds.ac.uk

P590 BA Sport Journalism
Duration: 3FT Hon
Entry Requirements: *Foundation:* Pass. *GCE:* 200. *SQAH:* BCC. *SQAAH:* BCC. *IB:* 24. *OCR ND:* M1 *OCR NED:* P1

B35 UNIVERSITY COLLEGE BIRMINGHAM
SUMMER ROW
BIRMINGHAM B3 1JB
t: 0121 604 1040 f: 0121 604 1166
e: admissions@ucb.ac.uk
// www.ucb.ac.uk

N2C6 BA Sports Management
Duration: 3FT Hon
Entry Requirements: *GCE:* 200. *IB:* 24.

N2CQ FdA Sports Management
Duration: 2FT Fdg
Entry Requirements: *GCE:* 120.

B37 BISHOP BURTON COLLEGE
BISHOP BURTON
BEVERLEY
EAST YORKSHIRE HU17 8QG
t: 01964 553000 f: 01964 553101
e: enquiries@bishopburton.ac.uk
// www.bishopburton.ac.uk

N235 BA Sport Leisure Surface Management
Duration: 3FT Hon
Entry Requirements: Contact the institution for details.

N231 FdA Sport Leisure Surface Management
Duration: 2FT Fdg
Entry Requirements: Contact the institution for details.

B50 BOURNEMOUTH UNIVERSITY
TALBOT CAMPUS
FERN BARROW
POOLE
DORSET BH12 5BB
t: 01202 524111
// www.bournemouth.ac.uk

N290 BSc Sports Management
Duration: 4SW Hon
Entry Requirements: *GCE:* 320. *IB:* 32. *BTEC SubDip:* D. *BTEC Dip:* DD. *BTEC ExtDip:* DDM.

B72 UNIVERSITY OF BRIGHTON
MITHRAS HOUSE 211
LEWES ROAD
BRIGHTON BN2 4AT
t: 01273 644644 f: 01273 642607
e: admissions@brighton.ac.uk
// www.brighton.ac.uk

P500 BA Sport Journalism
Duration: 3FT Hon
Entry Requirements: *GCE:* ABB. *IB:* 32.

B94 BUCKINGHAMSHIRE NEW UNIVERSITY
QUEEN ALEXANDRA ROAD
HIGH WYCOMBE
BUCKINGHAMSHIRE HP11 2JZ
t: 0800 0565 660 f: 01494 605 023
e: admissions@bucks.ac.uk
// bucks.ac.uk

NN1V BA Business and Sports Management
Duration: 3FT Hon
Entry Requirements: *GCE:* 200-240. *IB:* 24. *OCR ND:* M1 *OCR NED:* M3

N272 BA Sports Management and Football Studies
Duration: 3FT Hon
Entry Requirements: *GCE:* 200-240. *IB:* 24. *OCR ND:* M1 *OCR NED:* M3

N274 BA Sports Management and Rugby Studies
Duration: 3FT Hon
Entry Requirements: *GCE:* 200-240. *IB:* 24. *OCR ND:* M1 *OCR NED:* M3

C20 CARDIFF METROPOLITAN UNIVERSITY (UWIC)
ADMISSIONS UNIT
LLANDAFF CAMPUS
WESTERN AVENUE
CARDIFF CF5 2YB
t: 029 2041 6070 f: 029 2041 6286
e: admissions@cardiffmet.ac.uk
// www.cardiffmet.ac.uk

N833 BA Sports Tourism Management
Duration: 3FT/4SW Hon
Entry Requirements: *GCE:* 280. *IB:* 25. *BTEC ExtDip:* DMM. *OCR NED:* M2

C30 UNIVERSITY OF CENTRAL LANCASHIRE
PRESTON
LANCS PR1 2HE
t: 01772 201201 f: 01772 894954
e: uadmissions@uclan.ac.uk
// www.uclan.ac.uk

P216 BA Public Relations (Sports)
Duration: 4SW Hon
Entry Requirements: *GCE:* 260-300. *SQAH:* AABB-BBBC. *IB:* 28. *OCR ND:* D

P221 BA Public Relations (Sports)
Duration: 3FT Hon
Entry Requirements: *GCE:* 260-300. *SQAH:* AABB-BBBC. *IB:* 28. *OCR ND:* D

L2PG BA Public Relations (Sports) with International Study
Duration: 4SW Hon
Entry Requirements: *GCE:* 260-300. *SQAH:* AABB-BBBC. *IB:* 28. *OCR ND:* D

P501 BA Sports Journalism
Duration: 3FT Hon
Entry Requirements: *GCE:* ABB. *SQAH:* AAAB. *IB:* 30. *OCR ND:* D *OCR NED:* D2

H331 BEng Motor Sports Engineering
Duration: 3FT/4SW Hon
Entry Requirements: *GCE:* 240-280. *IB:* 24.

H330 BSc Motor Sport
Duration: 3FT/4SW Hon
Entry Requirements: *GCE:* 220. *IB:* 24.

H336 BSc Motor Sports (Foundation entry)
Duration: 4FT Hon
Entry Requirements: *GCE:* 100. *IB:* 24. *OCR ND:* P2 *OCR NED:* P3

H334 MEng Motor Sports Engineering
Duration: 4FT/5SW Hon
Entry Requirements: *GCE:* 280-320. *IB:* 25.

C55 UNIVERSITY OF CHESTER
PARKGATE ROAD
CHESTER CH1 4BJ
t: 01244 511000 f: 01244 511300
e: enquiries@chester.ac.uk
// www.chester.ac.uk

P590 BA Sports Journalism
Duration: 3FT Hon
Entry Requirements: *Foundation:* Pass. *GCE:* 260-300. *SQAH:* BBBB. *IB:* 28.

C75 COLCHESTER INSTITUTE
SHEEPEN ROAD
COLCHESTER
ESSEX CO3 3LL
t: 01206 712777 f: 01206 712800
e: info@colchester.ac.uk
// www.colchester.ac.uk

N222 BA Management of Sport
Duration: 3FT Hon
Entry Requirements: *GCE:* 120. Interview required.

N225 FdA Management of Sport
Duration: 2FT Fdg
Entry Requirements: *GCE:* 60. Interview required.

C85 COVENTRY UNIVERSITY
THE STUDENT CENTRE
COVENTRY UNIVERSITY
1 GULSON RD
COVENTRY CV1 2JH
t: 024 7615 2222 f: 024 7615 2223
e: studentenquiries@coventry.ac.uk
// www.coventry.ac.uk

N285 BA Sport Management
Duration: 3FT/4SW Hon
Entry Requirements: *GCE:* BCC. *SQAH:* BCCCC. *IB:* 28. *BTEC ExtDip:* DMM. *OCR NED:* M2

N501 BA Sport Marketing
Duration: 3FT/4SW Hon
Entry Requirements: *GCE:* BCC. *SQAH:* BCCCC. *IB:* 28. *BTEC ExtDip:* DMM. *OCR NED:* M2

C93 UNIVERSITY FOR THE CREATIVE ARTS
FALKNER ROAD
FARNHAM
SURREY GU9 7DS
t: 01252 892960
e: admissions@ucreative.ac.uk
// www.ucreative.ac.uk

W803 BA Sports Journalism
Duration: 3FT Hon
Entry Requirements: *GCE:* 220. *IB:* 24. *BTEC ExtDip:* PPP.
Interview required. Portfolio required.

E28 UNIVERSITY OF EAST LONDON
DOCKLANDS CAMPUS
UNIVERSITY WAY
LONDON E16 2RD
t: 020 8223 3333 f: 020 8223 2978
e: study@uel.ac.uk
// www.uel.ac.uk

P502 BA Sports Journalism
Duration: 3FT Hon
Entry Requirements: *GCE:* 280. *IB:* 24.

P503 BA Sports Journalism (Extended)
Duration: 4FT Hon
Entry Requirements: *GCE:* 120.

F33 UNIVERSITY COLLEGE FALMOUTH
WOODLANE
FALMOUTH
CORNWALL TR11 4RH
t: 01326213730
e: admissions@falmouth.ac.uk
// www.falmouth.ac.uk

W233 BA(Hons) Performance Sportswear Design
Duration: 3FT Hon
Entry Requirements: *GCE:* 220. *IB:* 24. Interview required.
Portfolio required.

G14 UNIVERSITY OF GLAMORGAN, CARDIFF AND PONTYPRIDD
ENQUIRIES AND ADMISSIONS UNIT
PONTYPRIDD CF37 1DL
t: 08456 434030 f: 01443 654050
e: enquiries@glam.ac.uk
// www.glam.ac.uk

N222 BA Sport Management
Duration: 3FT Hon
Entry Requirements: *GCE:* BBC. *IB:* 25. *BTEC SubDip:* M. *BTEC Dip:* D*D*. *BTEC ExtDip:* DMM. *OCR NED:* M2

G50 THE UNIVERSITY OF GLOUCESTERSHIRE
PARK CAMPUS
THE PARK
CHELTENHAM GL50 2RH
t: 01242 714501 f: 01242 714869
e: admissions@glos.ac.uk
// www.glos.ac.uk

NC2P BA Strategic Sports Management
Duration: 1FT Hon
Entry Requirements: Contact the institution for details.

X154 FdSc Sports (Fitness)
Duration: 2FT Fdg   CRB Check: Required
Entry Requirements: GCE: 120.

H12 HARPER ADAMS UNIVERSITY COLLEGE
NEWPORT
SHROPSHIRE TF10 8NB
t: 01952 820280 f: 01952 813210
e: admissions@harper-adams.ac.uk
// www.harper-adams.ac.uk

N800 FdSc Adventure Sports and Management
Duration: 2FT Fdg
Entry Requirements: Contact the institution for details.

H60 THE UNIVERSITY OF HUDDERSFIELD
QUEENSGATE
HUDDERSFIELD HD1 3DH
t: 01484 473969 f: 01484 472765
e: admissionsandrecords@hud.ac.uk
// www.hud.ac.uk

P503 BA Sports Journalism
Duration: 3FT Hon
Entry Requirements: GCE: 280. Interview required.

N591 BA Sports Promotion and Marketing
Duration: 3FT/4SW Hon
Entry Requirements: GCE: 300. Interview required.

L24 LEEDS TRINITY UNIVERSITY COLLEGE
BROWNBERRIE LANE
HORSFORTH
LEEDS LS18 5HD
t: 0113 283 7150 f: 0113 283 7222
e: enquiries@leedstrinity.ac.uk
// www.leedstrinity.ac.uk

P591 BA Sports Journalism
Duration: 3FT Hon
Entry Requirements: GCE: 280. IB: 25. OCR NED: M2

L27 LEEDS METROPOLITAN UNIVERSITY
COURSE ENQUIRIES OFFICE
CITY CAMPUS
LEEDS LS1 3HE
t: 0113 81 23113 f: 0113 81 23129
// www.leedsmet.ac.uk

N298 BA Sport Business Management
Duration: 3FT Hon
Entry Requirements: GCE: 260. IB: 28.

N822 BSc Sports Event Management
Duration: 3FT Hon
Entry Requirements: GCE: 240. IB: 24.

L42 LINCOLN COLLEGE
MONKS ROAD
LINCOLN LN2 5HQ
t: 01522 876000 f: 01522 876200
e: enquiries@lincolncollege.ac.uk
// www.lincolncollege.ac.uk

CN62 BA Sports Business Management
Duration: 3FT Hon
Entry Requirements: Contact the institution for details.

L68 LONDON METROPOLITAN UNIVERSITY
166-220 HOLLOWAY ROAD
LONDON N7 8DB
t: 020 7133 4200
e: admissions@londonmet.ac.uk
// www.londonmet.ac.uk

N222 BA Sports Business Management
Duration: 3FT Hon
Entry Requirements: GCE: 240. IB: 28.

L79 LOUGHBOROUGH UNIVERSITY
LOUGHBOROUGH
LEICESTERSHIRE LE11 3TU
t: 01509 223522 f: 01509 223905
e: admissions@lboro.ac.uk
// www.lboro.ac.uk

LN78 BSc Geography and Sport Management
Duration: 3FT Hon
Entry Requirements: GCE: AAB-ABB. SQAAH: AB.

N222 BSc Sport Management
Duration: 3FT Hon
Entry Requirements: GCE: AAB-ABB. IB: 32.

N281 BSc Sport Management
Duration: 4SW Hon
Entry Requirements: GCE: AAB-ABB. IB: 32.

M10 THE MANCHESTER COLLEGE
OPENSHAW CAMPUS
ASHTON OLD ROAD
OPENSHAW
MANCHESTER M11 2WH
t: 0800 068 8585 f: 0161 920 4103
e: enquiries@themanchestercollege.ac.uk
// www.themanchestercollege.ac.uk

N290 FdA Sport and Fitness Management
Duration: 2FT Fdg
Entry Requirements: *GCE:* 160. *BTEC ExtDip:* MPP.

M40 THE MANCHESTER METROPOLITAN UNIVERSITY
ADMISSIONS OFFICE
ALL SAINTS (GMS)
ALL SAINTS
MANCHESTER M15 6BH
t: 0161 247 2000
// www.mmu.ac.uk

N871 BA Sports Management
Duration: 3FT Hon
Entry Requirements: *GCE:* 240-280. *IB:* 29.

N870 BA Sports Management (Sandwich)
Duration: 4SW Hon
Entry Requirements: *GCE:* 240-280. *IB:* 29.

N504 BA Sports Marketing Management
Duration: 3FT Hon
Entry Requirements: *GCE:* 240-280. *IB:* 29.

NNN2 BA Sports Marketing Management (Sandwich)
Duration: 4SW Hon
Entry Requirements: *GCE:* 240-280. *IB:* 29.

M99 MYERSCOUGH COLLEGE
MYERSCOUGH HALL
BILSBORROW
PRESTON PR3 0RY
t: 01995 642222 f: 01995 642333
e: enquiries@myerscough.ac.uk
// www.myerscough.ac.uk

D449 FdSc Sportsturf
Duration: 2FT Fdg
Entry Requirements: *GCE:* A-C. *SQAH:* AA-CC. *SQAAH:* A-C. *IB:* 24. Interview required.

N23 NEWCASTLE COLLEGE
STUDENT SERVICES
RYE HILL CAMPUS
SCOTSWOOD ROAD
NEWCASTLE UPON TYNE NE4 7SA
t: 0191 200 4110 f: 0191 200 4349
e: enquiries@ncl-coll.ac.uk
// www.newcastlecollege.co.uk

NC26 BA Applied Sports Management & Development (Top-Up)
Duration: 1FT Hon   CRB Check: Required
Entry Requirements: Contact the institution for details.

N37 UNIVERSITY OF WALES, NEWPORT
ADMISSIONS
LODGE ROAD
CAERLEON
NEWPORT NP18 3QT
t: 01633 432030 f: 01633 432850
e: admissions@newport.ac.uk
// www.newport.ac.uk

L593 BA Youth and Community Work (Sport)
Duration: 3FT Hon   CRB Check: Required
Entry Requirements: *GCE:* 240. *IB:* 24. Interview required.

N38 UNIVERSITY OF NORTHAMPTON
PARK CAMPUS
BOUGHTON GREEN ROAD
NORTHAMPTON NN2 7AL
t: 0800 358 2232 f: 01604 722083
e: admissions@northampton.ac.uk
// www.northampton.ac.uk

N505 BA Sports Marketing
Duration: 3FT Hon
Entry Requirements: *GCE:* 260-280. *SQAH:* AAA-BBBB. *IB:* 24. *BTEC Dip:* DD. *BTEC ExtDip:* DMM. *OCR ND:* D *OCR NED:* M2

P60 PLYMOUTH UNIVERSITY
DRAKE CIRCUS
PLYMOUTH PL4 8AA
t: 01752 585858 f: 01752 588055
e: admissions@plymouth.ac.uk
// www.plymouth.ac.uk

J601 BSc Marine Sports Technology
Duration: 3FT Hon
Entry Requirements: *GCE:* 220. *IB:* 26.

P63 UCP MARJON - UNIVERSITY COLLEGE PLYMOUTH ST MARK & ST JOHN
DERRIFORD ROAD
PLYMOUTH PL6 8BH
t: 01752 636890 f: 01752 636819
e: admissions@marjon.ac.uk
// www.ucpmarjon.ac.uk

P314 BA Sports Media and Journalism
Duration: 3FT Hon   CRB Check: Required
Entry Requirements: *GCE:* 220.

S30 SOUTHAMPTON SOLENT UNIVERSITY
EAST PARK TERRACE
SOUTHAMPTON
HAMPSHIRE SO14 0RT
t: +44 (0) 23 8031 9039 f: + 44 (0)23 8022 2259
e: admissions@solent.ac.uk
// www.solent.ac.uk/

N804 BA Adventure and Extreme Sports Mgmt with IFY (Intl Only - Jan)
Duration: 4FT Hon
Entry Requirements: Contact the institution for details.

N862 BA Cruise Industry Management with Sport & Tourism Foundation Year
Duration: 4FT Hon
Entry Requirements: Contact the institution for details.

N821 BA Event Management with Sport and Tourism Foundation Year
Duration: 4FT Hon
Entry Requirements: Contact the institution for details.

P590 BA Sport Journalism
Duration: 3FT Hon
Entry Requirements: *Foundation:* Distinction. *GCE:* 240. *SQAAH:* AA-CCD. *IB:* 24. *BTEC ExtDip:* MMM. *OCR ND:* D *OCR NED:* M3 Interview required.

P5QH BA Sport Journalism with International Foundation Year
Duration: 4FT Hon
Entry Requirements: *GCE:* 240. Interview required.

S34 SPARSHOLT COLLEGE HAMPSHIRE
SPARSHOLT
WINCHESTER
HAMPSHIRE SO21 2NF
t: 01962 776441 f: 01962 776587
e: courses@sparsholt.ac.uk
// www.sparsholt.ac.uk

D439 FdSc Sport Fisheries & Aquaculture
Duration: 2FT Fdg
Entry Requirements: *GCE:* D. *SQAH:* C. *SQAAH:* D.

S72 STAFFORDSHIRE UNIVERSITY
COLLEGE ROAD
STOKE ON TRENT ST4 2DE
t: 01782 292753 f: 01782 292740
e: admissions@staffs.ac.uk
// www.staffs.ac.uk

P501 BA Sports Journalism
Duration: 3FT Hon
Entry Requirements: *GCE:* 240-300. *IB:* 24.

PP25 BA Sports PR and Journalism
Duration: 3FT Hon
Entry Requirements: *GCE:* 260.

S84 UNIVERSITY OF SUNDERLAND
STUDENT HELPLINE
THE STUDENT GATEWAY
CHESTER ROAD
SUNDERLAND SR1 3SD
t: 0191 515 3000 f: 0191 515 3805
e: student.helpline@sunderland.ac.uk
// www.sunderland.ac.uk

P505 BA Sports Journalism
Duration: 3FT Hon
Entry Requirements: *GCE:* 260-360. *IB:* 30.

N291 BA Sports Management
Duration: 4SW Hon
Entry Requirements: *OCR ND:* D *OCR NED:* M3

S93 SWANSEA UNIVERSITY
SINGLETON PARK
SWANSEA SA2 8PP
t: 01792 295111 f: 01792 295110
e: admissions@swansea.ac.uk
// www.swansea.ac.uk

J400 BEng Sports Materials
Duration: 3FT Hon
Entry Requirements: *GCE:* BBB. *IB:* 32.

S96 SWANSEA METROPOLITAN UNIVERSITY
MOUNT PLEASANT CAMPUS
SWANSEA SA1 6ED
t: 01792 481000 f: 01792 481061
e: gemma.green@smu.ac.uk
// www.smu.ac.uk

N871 BA Sports Management
Duration: 3FT/4SW Hon
Entry Requirements: *GCE:* 160-360. *IB:* 24. Interview required.

178N HND Sports Management
Duration: 2FT HND
Entry Requirements: *GCE:* 80-360. *IB:* 24. Interview required.

U40 UNIVERSITY OF THE WEST OF SCOTLAND
PAISLEY
RENFREWSHIRE
SCOTLAND PA1 2BE
t: 0141 848 3727 f: 0141 848 3623
e: admissions@uws.ac.uk
// www.uws.ac.uk

P501 BA Sports Journalism
Duration: 3FT/4FT Ord/Hon
Entry Requirements: *GCE:* CC. *SQAH:* BBC. Interview required.

U65 UNIVERSITY OF THE ARTS LONDON
272 HIGH HOLBORN
LONDON WC1V 7EY
t: 020 7514 6000x6197 f: 020 7514 6198
e: c.anderson@arts.ac.uk
// www.arts.ac.uk

W232 BA Fashion Sportswear
Duration: 3FT Hon
Entry Requirements: Foundation Course required. Interview required. Portfolio required.

P506 BA Sports Journalism (Top-Up)
Duration: 1FT Hon
Entry Requirements: Contact the institution for details.

W75 UNIVERSITY OF WOLVERHAMPTON
ADMISSIONS UNIT
MX207, CAMP STREET
WOLVERHAMPTON
WEST MIDLANDS WV1 1AD
t: 01902 321000 f: 01902 321896
e: admissions@wlv.ac.uk
// www.wlv.ac.uk

N292 BA Sport Management
Duration: 3FT Hon
Entry Requirements: *GCE:* 200. *IB:* 24. *BTEC Dip:* DM. *BTEC ExtDip:* MMP. *OCR ND:* M1 *OCR NED:* P1

W76 UNIVERSITY OF WINCHESTER
WINCHESTER
HANTS SO22 4NR
t: 01962 827234 f: 01962 827288
e: course.enquiries@winchester.ac.uk
// www.winchester.ac.uk

TNTV BA American Studies and Sports Management
Duration: 3FT Hon
Entry Requirements: *Foundation:* Pass. *GCE:* 260-300. *IB:* 24. *OCR ND:* D

NN2W BA Business Management and Sports Management
Duration: 3FT Hon
Entry Requirements: *Foundation:* Pass. *GCE:* 260-300. *IB:* 24. *OCR ND:* D

LNNV BA Childhood Youth & Community Studies and Sports Management
Duration: 3FT Hon
Entry Requirements: *Foundation:* Pass. *GCE:* 260-300. *IB:* 24. *OCR ND:* D

WNM8 BA Choreography & Dance and Sports Management
Duration: 3FT Hon
Entry Requirements: *GCE:* 260-300. *IB:* 24.

WNW8 BA Creative Writing and Sports Management
Duration: 3FT Hon
Entry Requirements: *GCE:* 260-300. *IB:* 24.

QN3V BA English and Sports Management
Duration: 3FT Hon
Entry Requirements: *GCE:* 260-300. *IB:* 24.

N893 BA Event Management and Sports Management
Duration: 3FT Hon
Entry Requirements: **Foundation:** Pass. **GCE:** 260-300. **IB:** 24.
OCR ND: D

WN6V BA Film & Cinema Technologies and Sports Management
Duration: 3FT Hon
Entry Requirements: **Foundation:** Pass. **GCE:** 260-300. **IB:** 24.
OCR ND: D

VN1V BA History and Sports Management
Duration: 3FT Hon
Entry Requirements: **Foundation:** Pass. **GCE:** 260-300. **IB:** 24.
OCR ND: D

PNM8 BA Journalism Studies and Sports Management
Duration: 3FT Hon
Entry Requirements: **Foundation:** Pass. **GCE:** 260-300. **IB:** 24.
OCR ND: D

MN1V BA Law and Sports Management
Duration: 3FT Hon
Entry Requirements: **GCE:** 260-300. **IB:** 24.

PN3V BA Media Production and Sports Management
Duration: 3FT Hon
Entry Requirements: **Foundation:** Pass. **GCE:** 260-300. **IB:** 24.
OCR ND: D

PNH8 BA Media Studies and Sports Management
Duration: 3FT Hon
Entry Requirements: **Foundation:** Distinction. **GCE:** 260-300. **IB:** 25. **OCR ND:** D

WNKV BA Performing Arts (Contemporary Performance) and Sports Management
Duration: 3FT Hon
Entry Requirements: **Foundation:** Pass. **GCE:** 260-300. **IB:** 24.
OCR ND: D

LN2W BA Politics & Global Studies and Sports Management
Duration: 3FT Hon
Entry Requirements: **Foundation:** Pass. **GCE:** 260-300. **IB:** 24.
OCR ND: D

LN38 BA Sociology and Sports Management
Duration: 3FT Hon
Entry Requirements: **Foundation:** Pass. **GCE:** 260-300. **IB:** 24.
OCR ND: D

N291 BA Sports Management
Duration: 3FT Hon
Entry Requirements: **Foundation:** Distinction. **GCE:** 260-300. **IB:** 24. **OCR ND:** D **OCR NED:** M2

NW83 BA Sports Management and Vocal & Choral Studies
Duration: 3FT Hon
Entry Requirements: **Foundation:** Pass. **GCE:** 260-300. **IB:** 24.
OCR ND: D

VNPV BA Theology & Religious Studies and Sports Management
Duration: 3FT Hon
Entry Requirements: **Foundation:** Distinction. **GCE:** 260-300. **IB:** 25. **OCR ND:** D **OCR NED:** M2

PS

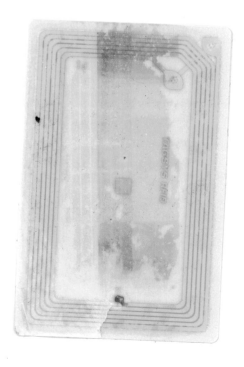